Appraising Management Performance: The Bubble Management Approach

Eugene C. Moncrief
Kevin M. Curran

Industrial Press
New York, New York

Library of Congress Cataloging-in-Publication Data

Moncrief, Eugene C.

asset / Eugene C. Moncrief,

    Kevin Curran.

p. cm.

ISBN 0-8311-3279-5

2006

Industrial Press, Inc.
200 Madison Avenue
New York, NY 10016-4078

First Printing, April, 2006

Sponsoring Editor: John Carleo
Interior Text and Cover Design: Janet Romano
Developmental Editor: Robert Weinstein

Printed in the United States of America

10   9   8   7   6   5   4   3   2   1

*Both authors wish to dedicate this book to
their wives and daughters –
Frankie and Cynthia Moncrief,
and
Cheryl and Courtney Curran –
for their support and patience
throughout the writing process.*

About the Authors

Eugene C. Moncrief has nearly fifty years of experience as a researcher, businessman, and consultant. He spent five years at the Oak Ridge National Laboratory where he performed R&D on the nuclear fuel cycle. He was employed with the Babcock & Wilcox Co. for twenty-three years where he held various positions including VP Manufacturing and most recently, Senior Vice President and Group Executive for B&W's world-wide nuclear and fossil businesses. For the last twenty years he has been Chairman of MerriHill Inc., a consulting firm, and a partner with Inventory Solutions Inc. From 1978-1985 he was a Visiting Professor at the University of Virginia's Darden Graduate Business School. Dr. Moncrief holds a PhD in Chemical Engineering from Virginia Tech. His previous publications include Production Spare Parts – Optimizing the MRO Inventory Asset, Industrial Press (2005).

Kevin M. Curran is currently Executive Vice President of Decision Sciences Corporation where he has been employed for 17 years. He has been instrumental in risk managing decisions as large as $11 billion. He has consulted for public and private sector organizations regarding probabilistic risk management in strategic planning, business expansions, mergers and acquisitions, capital investments, joint ventures, and new product launches. His work in risk management also includes projects in defense weapons development, facility and company closings/shutdowns, information technology, enterprise-wide systems implementation, research and development, project scheduling, and facility relocations. He is a contributing author of Effective Project Management through Applied Cost and Schedule Control and has authored and presented numerous papers for the Association for the Advancement of Cost Engineering (AACE Internation-al), the First (and Second) Congress on Computing in Civil Engineering, the National Association of Purchasing Management, and the Military Engineer. For several years, he was a frequent speaker for the American Management Association (AMA) and the Canadian Management Centre (CMC) on the subject of risk and decision making in seminars covering financial analysis, mergers and acquisitions, advanced strategies for controllers, and company valuations. Mr. Curran is a graduate of Washington University in St. Louis.

Table of Contents

CHAPTER 5: THE BUBBLE MANAGEMENT APPROACH   91

CHAPTER 6: APPLYING THE BUBBLE MANAGEMENT APPROACH TO PRODUCTION COMPANIES   145

Index of Case Studies

Preface

This book is about appraising management performance against goals. Actually it's more than that – it's also about doing something different, namely bringing 21st century concepts into the management appraisal process, namely probability theory.

We call the process for doing this Bubble Management[1]. Bubble Management is about performing these five key management tasks well: 1) setting realistic goals where the probability of achieving them is known, 2) monitoring progress against goals using tactical plans and control charts, 3) evaluating uncertainty and identifying opportunities and risks using Value-Based Risk Management[2], 4) using VBRM[3] bubble charts to improve net opportunities and mitigate net risks, and 5) using Performance Translation Tables to convert goal achievement into a quantitative performance rating for executive compensation and bonuses.

The term *Bubble Management* is derived from the VBRM bubble charts which depict the business plan uncertainties. To control these uncertainties correctly, managers must focus on reducing the size and changing the location of the bubbles in the VBRM bubble charts. In other words, managers must "manage their bubbles."

As a business person, achieving your goals can impact your salary, bonus, next promotion, and even your employment. Businesses set goals to motivate their employees and steer them in the direction chosen by management.

In Chapter 1 we point out some reasons why we believe the goal setting and appraisal process needs a new approach. Our main concern with the traditional goal-setting process is the use of single-value goals. In most cases, the goals are set using the best judgment of management without factoring in the use any modern approaches for predicting expected results.

There are many types of goals, as we will show in Chapter 2. There are *primary* goals, *secondary* goals, and some performance measures we call *management attributes*. There are also *dual-level* goals that distinguish between a commitment level of performance and a higher target level. Also, there are goals for managers at different levels in the corporate hierarchy like the CEO, the business unit executive, the department manager, and the shop foreman. In addition, there are *timing goals* like targets for this quarter, this year, and maybe even for a couple of years. What you don't usually see is really long-range performance goals (five years out, or even longer). That's because, with the rapid turnover and movement of managers in American business today, the focus tends to be on short-term results. Finally, we will introduce the concept of *shared goals*, where more than one manager is rated on the same goal.

A large part of Chapters 2, 5, 6, 7, and 8 are devoted to case studies. The case studies used in this book are based on real financial results, or adaptations thereof, with the case situation simulated. All case studies are named for fictional companies called AJAX, or ALPHA, BETA, and GAMMA. Any resemblance of those names to real companies is purely coincidental.

In Chapters 6, 7, and 8 we will use actual published data from annual reports and 10-K submittals from a select group of *Fortune 500* companies to illustrate how Bubble Management is used to set goals and appraise executives in those companies. Conclusions derived from critiques of those illustrations reflect only the opinion of the authors, and no discussion has been held with any of the real companies whose data are used in the case studies.

To our way of thinking, setting a goal (task 1 of Bubble Management) is only one step in the overall process. Another step involves monitoring results against goal (task 2), whereas another brings into play the appraisal of performance against goal (task 5).

In Chapter 3 we will introduce two ways to track goals: a tactical plan and a control chart. The tactical plan is prepared to ensure that the necessary resources to support the activity are applied in a planned and orderly manner. Tactical plans should be simple, with a single-page format preferred, or two at the most. Because people tend to remember data displayed graphically rather than when just tabulated, we prefer that control charts be graphical. Our choice, among the many ways to display data, is what we call a "clothes line" chart, so named because it resembles clothes pins hanging on a clothes line. Such charts can clearly focus the reader's attention on the deviations against goal.

The main focus of Chapter 3 is a series of case studies that critique each of the goal-setting cases of Chapter 2. For each critique we show an example of a typical tactical plan and control chart that could be used to monitor the goal. If the original goal was determined to be unrealistic or lacked clear definition, we re-defined the goal to meet five goal setting characteristic: 1) was a goal actually set, 2) was it quantitative, 3) was it reasonably obtainable, 4) did it have a time-line, and 5) was ownership for the goal assigned to an individual or organization.

Chapter 4 is an overview of a new technique for appraising management performance. Many years ago a concept known as range estimating was introduced; it used probability theory, Monte Carlo simulation, and some heuristics to calculate the probability of achieving goals (mainly cost goals).

A leader in that field, then and now, is Decision Sciences Corporation of St. Louis, Missouri. Over the last thirty-eight years they have expanded and refined the process, now called Value-Based Risk Management (VBRM), to do an even better job of supporting goal achievement. Instead of focusing on a single-value for a goal, VBRM brings in the concept of managing "uncertainty", which can be a risk, an opportunity, or both (task 3 of Bubble Management). Because a goal has a degree of uncertainty, it therefore has a certain amount of risk and/or opportunity.

We will show how we have merged our original appraisal concept discussed in Chapter 5 with the VBRM process so that goals can be set initially knowing the probability of meeting them. For example, instead of merely setting a single-value goal like "achieve sales of $300 million in 2005," the goal could be set at that level that had, say, a 40% probability of achieving. That might be only $250 million; to get $300 million the probability might be only 20 %, or even less. Thus, management would know in advance what the odds are of making the goal. That also can help quantify the goal rating process.

Also in Chapter 4 we introduce a graphic called a VBRM bubble chart. This bubble chart shows graphically how different elements (the uncertainty drivers) of a goal can impact the likelihood of exceeding the goal, or under running it (task 4 of Bubble Management). It also shows the amount of net risk, and net opportunity and net opportunity the difference between the amount of risk and the amount of opportunity. A case study will help make this clearer.

Chapter 5 focuses on the final task of the Bubble Management process – the appraisal. Here, we will discuss our concept for having an effective performance appraisal. Managers who have conducted performance appraisals know that it can sometimes be a traumatic experience for both them and the subordinate. As we will show, it need not be if both parties to the appraisal know: 1) what results are expected, 2) when, and 3) how performance will be measured. We will also discuss how to agree on goals, how to set a basis for rating performance, and how to calculate a quantitative rating against goal. The whole appraisal process will be illustrated with several case studies including one using statistical forecasting models to set goals for the next year.

The appraisal concept outlined in Chapter 5 goes a long way toward making goal setting an effective and quantitative process. However, our original appraisal concept, when used in the past, had one serious drawback – it relied on using single-value goals. The new approach discussed in Chapter 5 overcomes that problem by applying VBRM, which brings probability into the concept.

Readers should keep in mind that one of the purposes of this book is to demonstrate how VBRM can be applied to appraising management performance using the Bubble Management approach. It is not a how-to book on Value-Based Risk Management because VBRM requires methods and technologies outside the scope of this writing. For that reason, we focus on how we have applied VBRM rather than how VBRM determines the probabilistic forecasts, VBRM bubble charts, etc.

In Chapters 6, 7, and 8 we will cover some suggested performance goals for corporate, business unit, and departmental managers, along with a heavy dose of shared goals as well. Also in these chapters, we will calculate performance ratings for different executives and managers in Fortune 500 companies in the paper, chemical, utility, banking, insurance, and healthcare industries, and also for not-for-profit (NFP) enterprises. Here, we will use known financial results from recent years, and apply the Bubble Management process to set probabilities for goals for 2004 (the last full year of actual results); then we will compare the goals to actual results and rate management performance. Some might call this "Monday morning quarterbacking," but what we are attempting to do is introduce probability into the management performance rating process. We think that will help set more realistic goals in the future. Occasionally, we will comment on how well a company's performance against goals correlates with their share price or other actions taken by the companies or NFPs.

The last chapter of the book will focus on a few organizational concepts that have proven to support a goals orientation in companies. One concept in particular, the Unit President concept, delves into the sensitive issue of defining both a manager's responsibility and authority.

As is customary, the authors wish to thank a number of people who helped bring this book to print by reviewing the content, allowing us to use copyrighted material, or provided help in analyzing selected case studies. They include Thomas Butler, George Clessuras, William Behrens, and Gary Prindiville for reviewing the manuscript; Professor Campbell Harvey of Duke University for the use of his Hypertextual Financial Glossary; and Carl Axelson of Decision Associates Inc. for assisting in the AJAX Manufacturing case study analysis by running data through his statistical forecasting program. No acknowledgement would be complete without thanking the editorial staff at Industrial Press (John Carleo – Editorial Director, Janet Romano – Production Manager/Art Director, and Robert Weinstein – Manuscript Editor) who, through their collective efforts, eliminated all the pain normally associated with working with a publisher.

List of Figures

Notes

Value-Based Risk Management is a service mark of Decision Sciences Corporation, St. Louis, Missouri.

VBRM is a service mark of Decision Sciences Corporation, St. Louis, Missouri.

Bubble Management is a service mark of Decision Sciences Corporation, St. Louis, Missouri.

Provoke-To-Evoke® is a registered service mark of Decision Sciences Corporation, St. Louis, Missouri.

Why Appraising Management Performance Needs a New Approach

This chapter is short by design. We just want to make a few key points here about the process of appraising management performance and then move on to cover the topic in more detail.

Most management teams develop business plans to guide the direction of their company. The planning process can vary widely from a simple statement of a few key goals to a voluminous document containing hundreds of pages. In most cases, the goals are set using the best judgment of management, but without factoring in the uncertainty inherent in the goals. In other words, most of the time we simply set single-value goals that are either exceeded, or not met, but rarely met exactly.

Any single-value goal has a certain amount of uncertainty, which can be a *risk* or an *opportunity*. For example, if we set a goal to achieve earnings-per-share next year of $2.35, there might be a 10% probability we will make $3.00 per share, and a 90% probability we can make at least $1.50 per share. In other words, the actual earnings-per-share will depend on management's ability to capture the opportunities and mitigate risks associated with the goal. How well that's done should be factored into the performance rating of the managers.

The process of managing uncertainty starts with gathering the best information available regarding the factors (or drivers) that can impact the achievement of the goal, including unintentional biases that creep into virtually all forecasts. The results of the gathering process typically include: 1) the probability of achieving the goal, 2) worst-case and best-case scenarios, 3) a ranking of the risk and opportunity elements, and 4) a chart showing each uncertainty driver as a bubble (the *VBRM* Bubble Chart). Figure 1.1 shows a simplified

Chapter 1

VBRM Bubble Chart where the diameter of each bubble represents the amount of net risk or net opportunity associated with the driver, and the position of the bubble on the chart shows each driver's relative contribution to total risk or total opportunity. (We will discuss the *VBRM* Bubble Chart and the definition of these risk and opportunity terms in considerably more detail in Chapter 4).

Figure 1.1 Simplified VBRM Bubble Chart

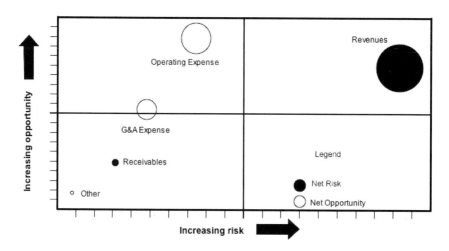

In a way, net risk and net opportunity are analogous to profit and loss on business income statements. If there is more risk than opportunity then there is a net risk (loss); if there is more opportunity than risk then there is a net opportunity (profit). Thus, the *VBRM* Bubble Chart is the primary tool for managing the uncertainty associated with a goal and becomes the mechanism for increasing the probability of achieving the goal.

This element is key to a process we call *Bubble Management.* It is what we mean when we say that the management appraisal process used by most companies needs a new approach to improve the process. That new approach introduces the most critical aspect of management – how well does it manage business uncertainty. The ability to manage uncertainty, or the lack of that ability, regularly determines whether business endeavors are successes or failures.

A New Approach

Bubble management is about performing these five key management tasks well: 1) setting realistic goals where the probability of achieving them is known and reasonably attainable, 2) monitoring progress against goals using tactical plans and control charts, 3) evaluating uncertainty and identifying opportunities and risks using *Value-Based Risk Management (VBRM)*, 4) using *VBRM* Bubble Charts to improve net opportunities and mitigate net risks, and 5) using Performance Translation Tables to convert goal achievement into a quantitative performance rating for executive compensation and bonuses.

Each of the above tasks will be covered in detail in the subsequent chapters of this book. Here we will only highlight a few issues. Let's start with the goal setting process itself. We think each goal should have these characteristics: 1) it should be quantitative, 2) it should be obtainable at an acceptable level of risk, 3) it should have a schedule for completion, and 4) the responsibility for achieving the goal should be clearly assigned. We think the goal-setting process can be improved significantly by adhering to these characteristics.

There's an old saying that people respond to what you inspect, not what you expect. That brings us to the subject of monitoring goals. In Chapter 3 we will introduce two tools for tracking performance against goals: the tactical plan and the control chart. The objective of the tactical plan is to highlight the actions, by whom and by when, needed to achieve the goal successfully and on-time. The control chart is used to graphically display performance against goal so that deviations from goal are quickly recognized.

We think the best way to demonstrate the Bubble Management approach is to illustrate its application in case studies. We start doing that in the next chapter on goal setting and continue all the way through Chapter 8. We will show how Bubble Management can be applied to any business enterprise from manufacturing to not-for-profit organizations, both large and small. We will use real data taken from company financial filings, although we will disguise each company to allow us more latitude to comment on performance when we critique each case study.

Because this book is about appraising management performance, we will introduce a new concept call the Performance Translation Table (PTT). What the PTT does is translate the probability of achieving a goal into a quantitative and discrete performance rating for salary and bonus consideration. By doing so, this step of Bubble Management tends to reduce much of the subjective judgment inherent in rating managers in most performance-rating exercises.

Finally, we want to state upfront that unlike our collective experience with and knowledge of management *appraisal*, neither of the authors is an expert on management *compensation*. Where we have suggested specific levels for salary increases or bonuses, they are for illustrative purposes only.

With this brief introduction, let's move on to discuss each key task of Bubble Management in more detail.

Setting Goals 2

2.1 WHAT THE READER WILL LEARN FROM THIS CHAPTER:

- Why it is necessary to set goals
- The different types of goals
- Why goals should be quantitative
- Case studies on setting goals

2.2 WHY SET GOALS?

Most people have goals in life. Many are achievable, others are not: to own your own company someday (probably achievable); to become a millionaire (also probably achievable); to become President of the United States (unlikely). With personal goals, there's no great penalty if you fail to achieve them, maybe just some disappointment.

Not so in business. Your salary, bonus, and very likely your job depend on meeting your piece of the company goals.

So why do companies set goals? The simple answer is they're expected to by the owners (shareholders). Goals also motivate people, especially if there are rewards for achieving them.

2.3 SETTING GOALS

Let's talk about goals. Like many commercial products, goals come in considerable variety. We have primary, secondary, and management attribute goals; commitment and target-level goals; corporate, business unit, and department goals; short-term, mid-term and long-range goals; and shared goals. We will cover each of these in the following sections. Regardless of the type or level of a goal, having them is what drives an organization toward improved performance.

2.3.1. Primary Goals

Primary goals should concentrate on a key metric that impacts the financial performance of the overall company or a unit of the company. These goals might be in areas such as sales, market share, return-on-investment, inventory, or budget. We think it's best to limit primary goals to one or maybe two goals for each manager in the organization. Often, boards of directors tend to limit the CEO's primary goal to "Earnings per Share" because it's frequently the pinnacle measure of a company's performance and there is no one higher in the organization to pin it on. In Chapters 6, 7, and 8, we'll discuss some corporate measures of performance and suggest which executives in the organizations should carry all or a share of the performance against those goals.

2.3.2   Secondary Goals

Secondary goals can be selected to concentrate on areas where the company needs to improve performance if its primary goals are to be achieved. The secondary goals set for one manager or organization would seldom be appropriate for every other manager or organization. For example, if the engineering organization had recently experienced high personnel attrition, it might need a vigorous new recruitment and training program as a key secondary goal. If shop productivity traditionally slips prior to labor contract negotiations, a special program and goal may be needed by the manufacturing organization to offset or avoid productivity deterioration. Budget goals might be appropriate for all organizations.

2.3.3   Management Attributes

Sometimes we forget that one of the prime responsibilities of a manager is actually to manage. To keep that point in perspective, all managers must be evaluated on some basis against their management skills and ability. In Chapter 6, Figure 6.4, we list management skills that could be considered when rating managers. For now, we will only note that the list considers management skills such as communications, time management, and planning skills. Any evaluation of a manager's performance on management attributes tends to be more subjective than performance measurements of primary and secondary goals.

2.3.4.   Dual Level Goals

Experience has shown that it is useful to set two levels for each goal: a **commitment level** and a **target level**. The commitment level should be set at that level of performance necessary for the department or profit center to meet a level of performance required by higher management to succeed. It has been suggested that the probability of achieving the commitment-level goal should be fairly high, at least 50 percent. If most units meet their commitment level of performance, then the company should be able to meet its obligations to the stockholders and the financial analysts, who have a major impact on the stock price.

The **target level** should be set higher than the commitment level for all goals. Doing so: 1) establishes a stretch for achievement purposes, 2) sets an upper benchmark on the performance evaluation scale, and 3) serves as a basis for setting the following year's commitment level. Target-level goals should be set so that the probability of achieving them is about 30 percent. A higher performance rating should be given if they are achieved.

2.3.5 Organizational Level Goals

Different goals apply to different levels within a company. At the corporate level, the focus should be on top-level goals such as return-on-assets (ROA), turnover, operating profit, net income, and earnings per share.

Figure 2.1 shows how various financial factors affect a company's return-on-assets (ROA) in a financial hierarchy. The chart, from *Colley et al*, will be used extensively in this book, often with adaptations. By considering the impact of each factor over recent years, it is possible to arrive at the probability of making a goal higher up in the hierarchy.

Consider "Operating Profit (before tax + interest)." The amount of operating profit is determined by subtracting "Total Cost of Sales/Expense" from "Sales." The total cost of sales/expense is generally not volatile because its cost elements can be budgeted and controlled tightly. However, sales can be very volatile. In turn, labor or material cost further down in the financial hierarchy could vary widely from budget if, for example, something caused a lot of product rework. Evaluating possible variances from budget is part of accessing the risk for those factors.

Figure 2.1 can also be a good template for setting business unit (BU) goals. If a company had six business units, the top management in each BU could be rated on the top-tier factors just like the Chief Operating Officer. The sum of the performances of the six business units would pretty much determine the overall performance of the

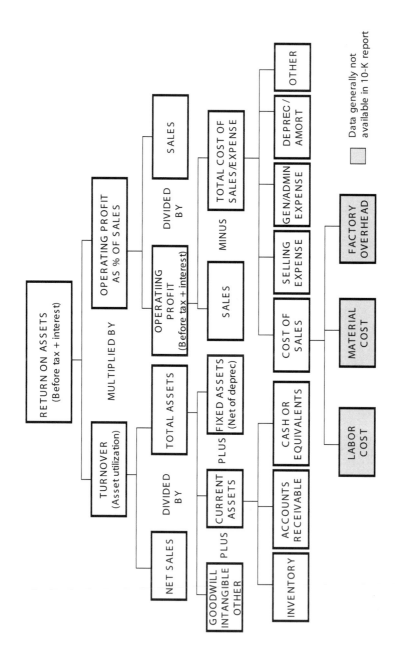

Figure 2.1 Relationship of Factors Affecting Pretax ROA

[ADAPTED FROM COLLEY et al, OPERATIONS PLANNING AND CONTROL]

entire company for the year.

Department-level goals would typically be limited to less encompassing goals like inventory (supply-chain), accounts receivable (controller), and cost of sales (manufacturing). We refer to these as core factors because controlling them is central to the organization's success, or as some might say "where the rubber meets the road."

2.3.6. Timing Level Goals

Anybody who works for an investor-owned business is well aware of the need to issue quarterly financial statements to meet SEC requirements and stock analyst expectations. Meeting quarterly performance targets, therefore, is an example of a short-term goal. Traditionally, the objective here is to beat the performance of the same period last year, or suffer the wrath of the security analysts. We consider goals that are set to meet quarterly performance, or even briefer time periods, to be *short-term* goals.

Medium-term goals typically apply to the annual targets set at the beginning of each calendar or fiscal year by a company's management. The objective here is to beat last year's performance or, better still, to show a significant steady upward performance trend over the last three to five years. Steady, sustained growth is highly welcomed by shareholders and analysts.

Except in areas such as forecasting long-term capital needs, planning new plant construction, or estimating *long-range* cash flow, most U.S. companies do not do much long-range goal setting. (As it is, many have enough trouble achieving their medium-term or annual goals.) Most companies that do set longer-range financial goals, such as a five-year target, typically adjust the goal each year. Then, by year 4, their sights on the 5-year goal have already been revised four times since inception. (Note too that by that point, the goal for year 5 actual becomes their medium-term goal for the coming year, and the long-range goal is set out into even later years.)

Some governments actually do set long-range goals. For years, the Russians were famous for developing 5-year economic plans (although they were seldom met). The Chinese think nothing of setting 50-year plans; their focus may have something to do with the fact that their society has been around for thousands of years. The nature of the U.S. government, in which the chief executive (the President) is only guaranteed a four-year commitment (and a maximum of eight years) and is often checked by members of the opposite party, is such that it is difficult to focus continuously for more than five years. Still, there are often attempts made at long-term planning. The most successful of these was the 1960s' race to the moon where, as a country, we actually stayed successfully focused for ten years on the same goal, driven by the combination of our imaginations and the very real politics of the cold war with the then-Soviet Union.

2.3.7. Shared Goals

Because setting and monitoring goals usually lead to appraising someone's performance against them, we should recognize that no single person has the sole responsibility for achieving most goals. For example, if a goal has been set to cut the internal time to manufacture a product by 20 percent, it's a good bet that engineering, manufacturing, supply-chain, maintenance, administration, quality control, and the shipping department will all play a part in setting and achieving that goal. This sharing does not necessarily mean that each department must be evaluated or rewarded equally, as we will discuss in more detail in Chapter 6.

2.3.8 Goals Should Be Quantitative

On the whole, qualitative goals are not effective. For example, if you set a goal to "improve sales performance," how would you know what result is expected? By when? And how would performance be measured? Certainly many goals can be qualitative such as "winning the game," even though you haven't stated by how many points. But at least in such cases, there is a quantitative basis for knowing who won! The excuse made that "there is no way to measure this" is seldom true.

Admittedly, setting a quantitative value for each primary and secondary goal is not a simple task. Usually, a thorough analysis of past performance is needed, coupled with judgment as to what constitutes a fair and reasonable degree of improvement from current performance. For example, a 20-percent improvement in sales might be a reasonable goal if the market is recovering from a recession. However, that same goal might not be reasonable if you are predicting a recession. As we will discuss shortly, a major flaw in the goal setting process is setting only single-value goals.

Setting Goals

2.4 SOME GOAL SETTING CASE STUDIES

In this section we will present case studies that depict goal setting for some of the core factors that make up the ROA calculation. In all cases, the approach used to reach the goal has been taken from real situations in manufacturing companies. However, the events depicted in the cases, including the names of the companies, are simulated. The cases will focus on goals for improving current assets, fixed assets, cost of sales, selling expenses, and general and administrative (G&A) expenses. In some of the case studies, the goals lacked clarity. In Chapter 3 we will discuss how to improve the goals by rating each against five goal setting characteristics.

CASE STUDY 2-1 AJAX UTILITY*
(Setting an Inappropriate Inventory Goal)

The Situation: AJAX Utility is a large southeastern utility operating both fossil-fired and nuclear generating stations. Over the past few years, the company has expanded into the non-regulated energy market by acquiring several medium-size generating stations in different parts of the country, especially the far west. In a major change compared to past practice, the utility hired and placed at one of their stations a new plant manager who had no previous experience in the utility industry, having in fact come out of a retail organization. Although bright and hard working, the plant manager was somewhat misinformed about how to set goals for station performance improvement.

One new goal in particular gave concern to the plant operations manager, who observed: "Shortly after the new station manager arrived, he started asking us for monthly turnover data on all our operating inventories so that he could set a goal for improvement. Although the numbers seemed to please him for the active and commodity stuff, he kept after us to 'get the spare parts turnover up.' To my way of thinking that was wrong, and I told him so, but he kept insisting that, where he came from, higher turnover was always good. Finally, in desperation I asked an inventory consultant who was working with us to give me some ammunition to refute his argument. This is what the consultant came up with."

*This case study is drawn from *Production Spare Parts,* E. C. Moncrief et al, Industrial Press (2005), with permission.

Chapter 2

Figure 2.2 Comparing AJAX Utility Results Over Time

(Comparison of 2002 initial review and 2004 update)

Item	Initial 2002 review	2004 update
Items reviewed	3,563	3,563
Recommended inventory ($)	13,758,500	12,830,600
Actual inventory ($)	19,351,700	16,166,600
Planned inventory ($)	16,596,100	10,666,100
AVR (a)	0.62	0.31
Percent of items within +/- 1 unit of optimum reorder point	59.6	85.8
Turnover	0.22	0.24

Over the two years the station was able to reduce actual inventory by over $3 million by not replenishing excess inventory and disposing of obsolete items

(a) AVR measures the amount of over and under stocking compared to the optimum amount of total inventory.

The Proposed Solution: After discussing the situation with the operations manager, the consultant suggested they compare the last several years of plant performance using both turnover and a calculation called "AVR" (see Figure 2.2 for a definition) to measure inventory change. The consultant was certain that using the two different metrics would show vastly different conclusions.

The Numbers: Figure 2.2 compares the results after performing a review in 2002 and monitoring progress again in 2004. A total of 3,563 key items of rarely-used spare parts were reviewed in detail. This 16 percent of the total station items represented $19.3 million of actual inventory in 2002, approximately 81 percent of station inventory value. Optimum station inventory for these key items was determined to be $13.7 million in 2002 when applying the desired availability level for each item. The recommended inventory level assumed that all over-stocks were eliminated and all understocks were increased to the optimum level regardless of part criticality.

Setting Goals

Using the station's current reorder points and reorder quantities for each key item, the station was planning to work down inventory to about $16.6 million. However, the inventory was rarely used; therefore, many years would be required to reach the planned inventory level.

Two indicators were calculated to determine performance in 2002. The AVR of 0.62 was better than average for most utility stations reviewed. The percent of key items with reorder point within one unit, plus or minus, of the optimum reorder point was determined to be about 60 percent (also about normal for utility stations). The turnover ratio for 2002 was 0.22.

Using data from 2004, these same items were reviewed again. By this time, over $3 million of excess inventory had been reduced by not replenishing overstocks and disposing of some obsolete spares. Most important, the AVR had decreased to 0.31 and the +/-1 percentage (see Figure 2.5 for definition) increased to 85.8 percent.

A further look at Figure 2.2 reveals an interesting point about adjusting understocks. Notice that the planned inventory in 2004 was $10.6 million, or about $2 million below the suggested optimum. In other words, the station management did not plan to increase all understocks to the recommended level for two reasons: 1) they were willing to accept the risk of not doing so, and 2) they were sure they could acquire extra spares, if necessary, from another AJAX station.

Now compare the turnover values. Even though actual inventory had decreased by 16 percent, and a risk-based plan implemented to reduce inventory by another 34 percent, the turnover ratio only showed a minor change from 0.22 to 0.24.

The Conclusion: Presented with these results, the station manager agreed to drop the use of turnover and start using the AVR for measuring performance for slow-moving spare parts, much to the delight of the operations staff.

Critique of Case Study 2-1: The new station manager was correct in deciding to collect some recent history on inventory before trying to set a meaningful goal. The mistake in this case was basing the goal on a metric (turnover) that was inappropriate for tracking the movement of slow-moving spare parts that were primarily safety/insurance stock.

Chapter 2

CASE STUDY 2-2: AJAX WORLD UTILITY*
(Setting an All-Inclusive Inventory Goal)

The Situation: AJAX World Utility is the eleventh-largest generating utility in the world. All of its generation plants are fueled by coal or natural gas, having decided years ago to forego any investment in nuclear power. The VP for Power Generation, who was a stickler for setting and monitoring performance against pre-set goals, had the usual goals for plant utilization, cost per kilowatt generated, and safety lost-time accidents. He recognized early on that he needed goals to manage the total assets assigned to the Generating Division, and two years ago set goals for the first time. He put it this way, "I've talked to a lot of managers in the same job I'm in at other plants and they tell me they limit what they monitor to just a couple categories of inventory like active items and new spares. I don't think that's enough if you're really going to control the entire inventory asset. So two years ago I asked my staff to put together an all-inclusive set of goals to monitor. I like what they came up with."

The Proposed Solution: The staff recognized that inventory could be broken down into two distinct categories: dependent demand and independent demand. Dependent demand included items that could be scheduled and procured accordingly, such as scheduled overhaul spares and strategic spares

* This case study is drawn from *Production Spare Parts,* E. C. Moncrief et al, Industrial Press (2005), with permission.

Figure 2.3 Setting and Monitoring Stock Targets for AJAX World Utility

(AJAX World Utility used this approach to monitor inventory dollars)

Component of inventory	Value on Jan 1 ($000)	Target on Dec 31 ($000)	Actual on Dec 31 ($000)
[A] Rarely used spares:	63,855	60,900	56,962
All rarely used	63,885	60,000	56,109
To improve availability	-	900	853
[B] Active spares	12,257	9,800	11,210
[C] Inflation projection	-	3,500	2,462
[D] Anticipated new spares	-	800	1,055
Scheduled overhaul items	5,285	7,500	7,690
Reserved items	1,790	2,600	2,425
Strategic spares	9,880	10,500	10,106
Total inventory	93,067	95,600	91,910

Target goal for year not met

14

Setting Goals

(their name for capital spares). Independent demand was driven by generating commitments; it included both active and rarely-used spares. Values for the various categories were developed and a set of targets for year-end were set during meetings between the VP and the individual plant managers. Figure 2.3 shows the goal chart for the entire Generating Division. Each plant also had its own goal chart.

Figure 2.4 Monitoring AVR at AJAX World Utility

(The target AVR for all AJAX World Utility Stations was 0.40).

Station	Qtr 1 AVR	Qtr 2 AVR	Qtr 3 AVR	Qtr 4 AVR	Target met?
A	0.83	0.62	0.46	0.34	Yes
B	0.92	0.71	0.58	0.42	No
C	0.79	0.82	0.71	0.55	No
D	0.74	0.49	0.49	0.37	Yes
E	0.80	0.49	0.39	0.29	Yes
F	0.69	0.41	0.42	0.31	Yes
G	0.55	0.40	0.41	0.38	Yes
H	0.62	0.50	0.41	0.33	Yes
I	0.72	0.60	0.42	0.37	Yes

AVR measures the amount of over and under stocking compared to the optimum amount of total inventory.

Figure 2.5 Monitoring the +/- 1 Percentage at AJAX World Utility

(The target +/-1 percentage for all AJAX World Utility Stations was 90.0).

Station	Qtr 1 %	Qtr 2 %	Qtr 3 %	Qtr 4 %	Target met?
A	78.2	90.3	91.2	91.7	Yes
B	65.3	77.0	84.5	90.9	Yes
C	72.4	86.9	84.7	88.2	No
D	57.5	76.2	78.9	92.3	Yes
E	72.4	81.1	90.6	93.1	Yes
F	84.2	93.2	93.9	92.7	Yes
G	80.1	89.5	91.6	93.9	Yes
H	81.1	91.3	92.2	92.6	Yes
I	57.0	80.4	89.6	91.8	Yes

The = +/-1 percentage measures the number of spares that have their reorder point within one unit of the optimum reorder point.

Chapter 2

The Numbers: As Figure 2.3 shows, goals for all categories were met for the year except for active items, new spares, and scheduled overhauls. The reasons for failing to meet goals for these categories were discussed extensively by the VP and the responsible plant managers at their regularly scheduled monthly meetings. Along with the financial goals, the VP also monitored the AVR and +/-1 percentage to track inventory balance. These metrics are shown in Figure 2.4 and 2.5 respectively. As expected, the +/-1 percentage correlated closely with the AVR; the lower the AVR, the higher the +/-1 percentage. Notice in some cases the AVR did not improve between quarters.

The Conclusion: The VP was satisfied that the goal charts used to monitor inventory had made a major contribution to the $6 million net improvement in rarely-used inventory during the year. He also recognized that more than one person had to share in being accountable for the inventory goals. Therefore, he made inventory improvement a shared goal among the plant manager, the maintenance manager, and the plant supply-chain manager, who also con-trolled purchases. They all got judged accordingly, and collectively.

Critique of Case Study 2-2: The station management did a good job of including all elements of inventory in their control chart. They also recognized that they had to account for inflation as well. They set quantitative goals for AVR and +/-1 Percentage and monitored performance against goals on a quarterly schedule. This schedule allowed the VP to discuss corrective actions through-out the year with his management team. (See Chapter 6 for more discussion about appraising managers against shared goals.)

CASE STUDY 2-3: AJAX DIESEL
(Improving Accounts Receivable)

The Situation: AJAX Diesel is a manufacturer of medium- and heavy-weight diesel engines for the light and heavy truck market. The company's only plant, which is in Indiana, serves both the domestic and international markets. Two years ago the company implemented a series of cost-cutting initiatives includ-ing one to decrease client outstanding past-due balances on accounts receiv-able; these balances had grown to 28 % of receivables recently and extended the average collection period to 41 days. As part of the program, it was decid-ed to track accounts receivable (A/R) using a four-quarter moving average beginning in 2003 (year-end 2002 data were used as the benchmark). A goal

Setting Goals

Figure 2.6 Tracking Past-Due Accounts Receivable Balances at AJAX Diesel

Accounts receivable after 30 days ($ 1000)

Industry breakdown	Benchmark (Dec 31 2002)	Actuals				Goal	
		1Q03	2Q03	3Q03	4Q03	Dec 31	Met?
Domestic light trucking	300.3	290.6	280.2	270.6	260.1	240.2	No
Domestic heavy trucking	280.6	280.0	270.3	250.1	222.0	224.5	Yes
Foreign light trucking	140.1	130.8	130.1	120.9	120.3	112.1	No
Foreign heavy trucking	120.6	120.9	120.5	110.7	110.2	96.5	No

was set to decrease the outstanding A/R balance by 20 percent by the end of 2003 and by another 10 percent in 2004.

The Proposed Solution: Various approaches were used to stimulate collections: 1) where possible, a financing charge on client balances over 30 days was included in all new contracts, 2) foreign sales agents were given incentives to pressure clients to pay on time, 3) discounts were offered to customers to pay by direct withdrawals from their bank at 30 days, and 4) credits against future spares purchases were given for payment made before 15 days.

The Numbers: Figure 2.6 shows the results from the program at the end of 2003, broken down into domestic and foreign receivables and by the light and heavy trucking markets. Only the goal of 20 percent reduction for the domestic heavy trucking market was met (20.9%). The other segments ranged from 9 to 14 percent improvement.

The Conclusion: Although the program was working for all segments, analysis showed that several factors accounted for the short-fall in three of the four segments: 1) currency release rules were delaying payments from some foreign countries, 2) light trucking clients generally carried lower credit ratings and were traditionally slower to pay, 3) the automotive/trucking industry has been more difficult to deal with on commercial terms than most industries, and 4) applying a finance charge on late payments wasn't working in the down-market of 2003. Incentives did seem to be working and would be the focus of the program in 2004. The plan was to attach credit vouchers for specified amounts,

17

good toward future purchases, to all invoices to encourage payment within 15 days. The original goal for 2004 was not changed.

Critique of Case Study 2-3: It is noteworthy that the management did not change the original goal for 2004, but did change the emphasis of the program in 2004 to use what was working in 2003. Managements are often too fast to revise longer-term goals as soon as early results don't meet expectations. At the end of 2004, three out of four segments had met their goals.

CASE STUDY 2-4: AJAX DISTRIBUTORS
(Setting a Cash Management Goal)

The Situation: AJAX's business is to distribute pipe and tubing for use in construction projects, as well as replacement spares to industrial facilities such as chemical plants, refineries, and power stations. They offer a wide variety of pipe and tube materials (copper, stainless steel, aluminum, etc.) in a large choice of sizes (diameter and wall thickness). They purchase all of their stock from pipe and tube mills on the open market, including off-shore, which they stock in three warehouses in Ohio, Georgia, and Texas. Fast delivery from existing stock is their forte, allowing AJAX to command premium prices over what pipe and tube mills can command on contract runs. Lately, a slowdown in collecting receivables was creating a cash crunch for the company, forcing the finance director to seek short-term loans from lending institutions to cover operating expenses (average days receivable was now 43 days). The president called the senior staff together to discuss the problem, and told them: "We need some good ideas on how to improve our cash flow situation. Everybody seems to agree that market conditions alone aren't going to solve our problem, so we need ideas."

The Proposed Solution: Many ideas were presented including: 1) speeding up invoicing, 2) decreasing inventories, 3) slowing down paying the mills, 4) seeking better loan terms, 5) raising prices, 6) refinancing long-term debt, 7) improving warehouse efficiency, and 8) cutting out a shift. Each idea was discussed at length and most were considered worthy of pursuing except number 8 (cutting out a shift) because it was thought to impact severely on their competitive advantage of fast delivery. One wrinkle for decreasing inventory was presented – taking pipe and tubing from the mills on consignment, whereby AJAX would not have to carry the material or pay for it until sold. The mills would surely want some incentive from AJAX to offset their higher costs from not being able to invoice on shipment. A sub-committee was formed to evaluate the alternatives and recommend a goal to the president.

Setting Goals

Figure 2.7 Statement of Cash Flow for AJAX Distributors

	($ 1,000)	
[1] Cash flows from operating activities:	<u>2004</u>	<u>2003</u>
Net income	2,315	2,351
Depreciation	1,009	984
Change in receivables	(2,064)	(1,550)
Change in inventories	(842)	(890)
Change in accounts payable	(91)	62
Other, Net	106	192
Total cash provided by operations	433	1,149
[2] Cash flows from financial activities:		
Repayment of long-term debt	(460)	(512)
Payments toward short-term loans	(812)	(219)
Total cash used for financial activities	(1,272)	(731)
[3] Increase (decrease) in cash	(839)	418
[4] Cash balance beginning of year	892	474
[5] Cash balance end of year	53	892

The Numbers: Figure 2.7 shows a Statement of Cash Flows for AJAX for 2004 compared to 2003. Cash provided from operations was $443,000, whereas cash used for financial activities was $1,272,000, resulting in the year-end cash balance of only $53,000 compared to $892,000 at the beginning of the year. Clearly, the biggest factors affecting this change were the growth in receivables in 2004 for nearly the same sales as last year, and the nearly $600,000 increase in payments toward short-term borrowing.

Conclusion: A task force with representatives from finance, purchasing, and sales was formed to interface with clients to speed up receivables. A goal was set to cut the days receivable from 46 to 35 days by the end of the first quarter of 2005. Credit vouchers were offered to customers, good toward future purchases, for payment within 15 days rather than the customary 30 days. This concept worked and brought the average days outstanding down to 37 during the first quarter, nearly to goal. The consignment concept was discussed with three of AJAX's biggest pipe and tube suppliers. A total of 262 fast-moving varieties of pipe and tubing were ultimately placed in the consignment program. Because AJAX was not required to pay for the pipe and tubing until sold, $333,000 of short-term borrowing at 9% interest was avoided in the first six months of 2005. It was agreed that AJAX would share a percentage of the savings with the mills, calculated on a sliding-scale based on the average turnover of the material each calendar quarter.

Critique of Case Study 2-4: Incentives can work for awhile, but like in the auto industry, customers soon learn to expect them without giving much back in return. Consignment is gaining wide acceptance in many situations because it can provide a competitive advance to both parties – the suppliers get their material in the buyer's plant, and the buyer gets to have the material available for use or sale without owning it.

CASE STUDY 2-5: AJAX ENERGY
(Lowering Fixed Assets)

The Situation: AJAX Energy designs, manufactures, and erects steam generation boilers for municipal and industrial clients. Their main office is in Pennsylvania where their engineering and project management groups reside, as well as a near-by manufacturing facility dedicated to the water-tube package boiler market (smaller boilers shipped in one piece, or "packaged"). AJAX also had two other manufacturing facilities in Georgia and Arkansas where components for their large power boilers and paper market recovery boilers are made. For the last three years, the market for steam generation equipment had been soft, leaving AJAX holding significant excess manufacturing capacity. The CEO and CFO were discussing the situation recently: "We need to seriously consider closing the package boiler facility and moving the product line to either Georgia or Arkansas," stated the CFO. "I agree" said the CEO. "Let's put a task force together to plan how to do it. We just can't continue to operate three separate manufacturing facilities in what looks like a sustained declining market."

The Proposed Solution: The task force consisted of two senior shop superintendents familiar with building package boilers, a finance representative, and two members of the corporate planning department. It was understood that even the fact that they were meeting was to be kept confidential so as not to start rumors at the factory (all meetings were held in the corporate office). Although closing the factory and selling the property would cut fixed assets and boost the ROA, a serious negative impact on profits could result if the move of the package boiler product line to another state resulted in a long-term decline in E/A. (E stood for "Earned Hours," typically a certain number of standard hours needed to complete a task in the manufacture of a package boiler; A stood for the "Actual Hours" needed to complete the task. Thus, an E/A of 100.0 meant the task was completed precisely in the number of standard hours expected. As A varied, E/A could be more or less than 100.0).

It didn't take the task force long to decide that the Arkansas plant was the best location to move the package boiler line for three reasons: 1) most of the

Setting Goals

Figure 2.8 Estimated E/A Performance After Package Boiler Move

Manufacturing task	Benchmark E/A at Pennsylvania plant	Estimated E/A by month after restart					
		1	2	3	4	5	6
Steam drum fabrication	107.1	100	101	102	104	106	108
Burner assembly	103.1	95	97	99	100	101	102
Base frame assembly	104.6	98	100	102	104	105	106
Controls assembly	102.7	97	99	101	102	103	103
Economizer installation	112.3	100	102	104	106	108	110
Air heater installation	106.2	100	101	102	103	104	105
Auxiliary equipment	104.0	95	97	99	101	103	104
Membrane wall welding	102.1	95	98	100	102	103	104
Refractory installation	104.3	96	98	100	101	103	104

Improvement in E/A for tasks highlighted in month 6 was due to move of skilled craftsman with product line and purchase of more modern welding machines.

welding and assembly skills needed were already available there, 2) the average hourly labor rate was lower than at the Georgia plant, and 3) the pool of new available labor was better in Arkansas.

After a week of day and night deliberations, the plan came together as follows: 1) the entire production line including jigs, fixtures, and equipment would be moved and re-assembled over a 60-day period; 2) prior to the move, selected sizes of package boilers would be built for inventory so that sales could continue during the transfer period; 3) nineteen individuals consisting of skilled craftsman, supervisors, maintenance experts, quality control specialists, and production schedulers were designated to move with the product line to Arkansas; 4) hiring and training of additional staff would occur concurrently at the Arkansas plant; and 5) incentives would be given to hourly workers at the Pennsylvania plant prior to the move in order to maintain productivity. The task force also recommended that, to offset local hiring, the company cover direct moving expenses, but not home sale costs, of any terminated workers at the Pennsylvania plant.

The Numbers: The team also estimated the impact of the move on E/A for the first six months after the line was re-assembled in Arkansas (Figure 2.8) The impact on product cost was estimated to be $260,000. Money was provided in the plan to purchase some new modern welding equipment; this equipment was expected to bring the E/A for certain tasks up to or above the benchmark E/A at the Pennsylvania plant within the first six months after the move. With the help of others from the financial department, an estimate of the impact of the

Figure 2.9 Estimated Cash Flow Impact of Package Boiler Move

(For twelve month period after move of line)

[1] Positive cash flow impact:	
Net gain on projected sale of property (after taxes and commissions)	2,163,100
Employment cost savings (after severance) including pension/medical	4,012,500
Total positive	6,175,600
[2] Negative cash flow impact:	
Incentive pay to shop workers to sustain productivity	112,600
Full moving expenses for 19 transfers and 15 volunteers	303,000
Severance pay for 107 terminated employees	1,337,500
Additional hires at Arkansas	2,225,000
Higher product cost from productivity loss	260,000
Move of product line equipment and fixtures	265,000
Purchase of new welding equipment	317,000
Total negative	4,820,100
[3] Project net positive gain in cash flow from product line move:	1,355,500

move on cash flow for the first twelve months after the move was also made (Figure 2.9).

The Conclusion: Figure 2.9 showed that the CFO was projecting about a $1.4 million positive cash flow impact for the year following the move of the product line to Arkansas. He also estimated that product turnover would improve from 1.9 to 2.1 due to the lower asset base, and the ROA before interest and tax would increase from 11 to 14 percent. All things considered, the project was very successful.

Critique of Case Study 2-5: The closing of a manufacturing facility is always a traumatic event for the people and the locality affected. As was customary, incentives to keep the factory in Pennsylvania were suggested by state officials, but were withdrawn when Arkansas agreed to match any inducement. For the most part, the E/A goals were met within six months largely due to the decision to transfer the key supervisors and lead craftsman from Pennsylvania, plus the investment in the new welding equipment. In somewhat of a surprise, fifteen additional hourly workers requested transfer even though they received only direct moving expenses for making the move. In retrospect, the move of the product line proved timely, as the market for steam generating equipment remained soft for nearly four years after the move. Capacity at the two remain-

Setting Goals

ing factories remains above needs, and future moves of product lines, including offshore, continues to be a possibility. As they say, "There's no rest for the weary."

CASE STUDY 2-6: AJAX HYDROTECH
(Lowering the Cost of Sales)

The Situation: AJAX Hydrotech designs and constructs water treatment facilities for municipals and industries. The company does not manufacture any of the equipment included in their designs; instead, they purchase it on the world-wide market to meet the design specifications issued by the buyer (usually prepared by an architect-engineer). Because this is the practice also used by most of their competitors, markups on purchased equipment are generally low. Therefore, AJAX makes the majority of its profit on turnkey projects by bringing the job in under budget, including the field construction phase. Most municipals also require each bidder to break down their bid into specific line-item categories. One recent award of a project by a Midwest municipal to a competitor angered AJAX's president. "We really worked hard to get that job and we got beat out by less than $60,000. We cut our purchased equipment margins to the bone, so our construction estimates must have been too high."

Because the job was a municipal one, the bids from vendors were open to the public for review. On reviewing the bid from the winning company, AJAX's procurement manager noticed that the competitor's cost line was substantially lower than AJAX's for exactly the same brand pumps bid by AJAX.

Figure 2.10 Analysis of Price Premiums to Meet AJAX Specifications

(Price differences are compared to XYZ Water, who was the winning bidder).

Reason for pricing premium	Amount of premium ($)
AJAX specified non-standard capacity pumps in 14 instances requiring vendor to bid next higher capacity	31,864
Material of construction differences versus XYZ Water for 16 centrifugal pumps	20,455
Premium to provide double-acting reciprocating pumps versus single-acting for XYZ Water	16,410
Additional base frame welding costs to meet AJAX weld depth specification	9,045
Total premium	$ 77,774

Chapter 2

The Proposed Solution: A team consisting of engineering and purchasing personnel arranged a meeting with the pump vendor to review the differences between their bid and that of XYZ Water, who was the winning bidder on the project.

The Numbers: At the meeting with the pump vendor, the AJAX team was presented with an analysis of why their price for pumps was higher than XYZ Water's (Figure 2.10). The pump vendor's vice president put it this way: "Your engineers must not have enough to do because it seemed to us they were trying to tell us how to make our pumps instead of just buying what we offer. For example, your weld specification for the base frames would have required our shop to make a second weld pass to meet your minimum weld depth spec. That requirement penalized you by over $9,000. Look at the other differences on the list. I'm sure that you were designing to the same client spec as XYZ Water, but you asked us to bid a higher grade of stainless in 16 instances, and double-acting reciprocal pumps in 8 other cases; XYZ didn't, and maybe that's why they won the job. Somebody needs to reign in your engineers and tell them to quit overspecifying everything".

The Conclusion: AJAX's president, who was livid when hearing the feedback from the meeting, convened a meeting with the engineering department managers and put out this directive: "We can't continue to write purchase specifications that penalize us against the competition. We lost that job on the pump pricing penalties alone. Specify standard off-the-shelf components.

Figure 2.11 Analysis of New "Cash for Unused Sick Leave" Policy

---

[1] Average days sick leave used in 2003 by 176 hourly workers = 8.6

[2] Average hourly wage in 2003 = $16.20/hr

[2] Time-and-one-half pay in 2003 to cover for sick call-ins = $294,244

[3] Projected days sick leave per year after new policy = 5.0

[4] Projected time-and-one-half pay in 2004 @ $17.02/hr* = $179,731

[5] Net pay saving in 2004 versus 2003 = $114,513

[6] Projected payout for sick leave not used in 2004@ $17.02/hr = $119,820

[7] Projected average check per worker = $680

---

* Projected new average hourly wage in 2004 under new contract

---

Setting Goals

That's what our competition does. If we win the job, we can always try to convince the customer to buy better quality equipment. Our goal from now on is to not lose a job because of our purchased equipment prices."

Critique of Case Study 2-6: Engineers have a natural tendency to want to overdesign things. The problem comes when the buyer won't pay for the extra quality or features. For years, many companies prided themselves on providing a better quality product than the competition, and were able to charge for the extra quality (companies like Mercedes-Benz, Maytag, and Caterpillar come to mind). With the advent of the world-market, U.S. suppliers now must find ways to overcome the labor cost advantage available to off-shore competitors. If you can't be competitive on price, you had better be in a niche market or, in some other way, differentiate your product from the competition.

CASE STUDY 2-7: AJAX MANUFACTURING
(Labor Cost Control)

The Situation: AJAX is a midwestern U.S. company engaged in manufacturing medium- and heavy-duty air compressors for industrial duty. Although their labor contract was due to expire in three weeks, the company and union were still far apart on some aspects of the new contract, mainly wages and work-rule changes. The human resources manager was discussing the stalemate with the president: "I think we can work out the differences on the work-rule changes we want, as long as the union doesn't perceive the changes as causing layoffs. I also think we can come out okay on the wage increase if we can 'sweeten the pot a little'. I've got an idea I'd like to try out; see what you think."

The Proposed Solution: The HR manager continued: "You know that many of our employees abuse the sick leave policy that gives them ten paid sick days per year. We all know it's no coincidence that call-ins for sickness increase significantly around hunting season. Here's what I have in mind – offer to pay cash at the worker's hourly wage for sick leave days not used. Make the payout on December 15 so that the check is available for the holidays. In order to sell this, we've got to publicize it so the spouses hear about it well in advance of the union vote on the contract. Any days the workers don't use and we have to pay them for it is a good deal for the company since we have to pay time-and-one-half to cover for them when they call in sick".

The Numbers: The HR manager presented his analysis (Figure 2.11). Even though the projected cash payment for sick days not used was slightly higher than the projected pay savings for 2004 ($119,820 versus $114,513), the work-

Figure 2.12 Estimated Cost to Have Staff Work from Home

Cost item	Estimated annual cost ($)
[1] Separate high speed internet and phone lines	7,900
[2] New all-purpose printer-copier-fax-scanners	3,500
[3] Stipend to cover employee additional electric costs	8,400
[4] Weekly lunch meeting costs	4,000
[5] Web conference fees	1,400
[6] Contingency allowance @ 20%	5,000
Projected total	30,200

ers' average check was projected to be $680. All of this was in addition to a projected 82 cent per hour pay raise in the first year of the contract.

The Conclusion: The company made their final offer to the union negotiating committee and followed it up by sending the offer to each worker's home. In addition to the offer of cash for unused sick leave, wage increases of 5, 4, and 4 percent were offered for the next three years, respectively. No other financial concessions were made. The final union vote was 121 in favor, and 50 against (5 voting members were absent). Several months later, an hourly employee confessed to his supervisor, "I had planned to call in sick today to go hunting, but the ole lady told me to get my hairy hide into work. She wanted the extra money come Christmas."

Critique of Case Study 2-7: The company's original goal was to hold total labor cost increases during the life of the contract to 5 percent per year. An unpriced side benefit from the cash for unused sick policy was the savings by supervisors of time previously devoted to calling in replacements.

CASE STUDY 2-8: AJAX SALES AND SERVICE
(Cutting Overhead, General, and Administrative Costs)

The Situation: AJAX S&S acts as sales representative and service provider for a number of major manufacturers of industrial controls, pumps, valves, and

Setting Goals

fans. They maintain a warehouse in Houston which they own, and rent an office near Hobby airport from which their sales and service people operate. Their sales and service area covered the chemical and petrochemical market from Lake Charles, Louisiana to Point Comfort, Texas, including Beaumont, Baytown, and Houston. Lately, the recession had caused profits to decline and the general manager, who was looking for ways to cut overhead costs, believed "We need to cut overhead by at least 25 percent." The general manager had a radical idea to achieve the goal.

The Proposed Solution: The general manager's idea was to close the Houston office where the lease was going to expire in four months. The logic was as follows: 1) the three sales representatives and two service people only averaged about three hours per week in the office, much of that for the weekly Monday morning meeting, 2) the general manager's time was mostly spend on the telephone talking to suppliers or customers, and could just as well be handled from home, 3) the weekly meeting could be conducted over lunch at a local restaurant that would provide a private room, 4) almost all of their correspondence with suppliers and customers was by e-mail via the Internet, and 5) rarely, if ever, did a customer need to visit their office. Payroll was currently outsourced and secretarial duties usually consisted of answering the telephone, preparing invoices, maintaining records, and other functions that could be handled from home.

The Numbers: The GM compiled the office expenses for the last year. Rent, utilities, phone/fax, copy and postal meter rental, supplies and other services were running about $61,000 per year. The rent was due to increase by $3,500 if the lease was renewed. Salaries and fringe benefits would not be affected whether the office closed or not. The GM next estimated the costs of having everybody operate out of their home (Figure 2.12). Based on the estimate, a net saving of about $34,000 was projected. Not considered in the estimate was the value of some intangible benefits of working out of the homes: 1) avoiding commuting time of at least one hour per day, 2) fuel cost savings by not commuting, and 3) the lower stress by working out of the home. One thing was lost, however – the Monday morning sports discussions around the coffee pot.

The Conclusion: The entire staff embraced the concept and the lease was not renewed. Cost savings after the first six months tracked closely with estimates, resulting in a major improvement against the overhead cost-cutting goal of 25%.

Critique of Case Study 2-8: Many executives are learning to think "outside the box," as shown by the above case study. Slowly, but surely, the Internet

Chapter 2

is making it possible for companies to move to the paper-less society we have all been promised. Examples like downloading financial statements, paying bills on-line, banking on-line, e-mailing versus posting letters are all becoming more common. The virtual office concept may soon join the list of cost-saving practices enjoyed by many companies.

CASE STUDY 2-9 AJAX TECHNOLOGIES
(Reducing Product Cost)

The Situation: "AJAX TECH," as they are known, designs and manufactures controls and equipment for the gas processing industry. They have three principal product lines: 1) process controllers for monitoring temperature, pressure and liquid level, 2) fluid measuring devices, and 3) gas compressors. All products are manufactured and assembled at their Oklahoma City facility, although a large amount of individual parts and sub-assemblies are purchased from suppliers on the open market. About 85 percent of shipments are to the U.S. market, with the balance sold overseas, mainly to the Asian market. Over the last year, product rework costs had doubled from 1.4 to 2.9 percent of sales due to quality defects. The current Quality Assurance (QA) manager seemed at a loss on how to improve the situation, so the president decided to hire a new QA manager with extensive experience in the chemical and nuclear industries. The new manager was asked to present an improvement plan within two weeks of arriving on the job.

The Proposed Solution: The QA manager's plan for improving overall product quality focused on the following key elements: 1) tailoring the level of quality overview to the complexity of the product, 2) monitoring defects at all stages (engineering, manufacturing and field installation), 3) monitoring vendor quality performance, and 4) tracking actual quality performance using control charts.

The Numbers: As a start, the QA manager had a chart prepared showing first quarter 2003 quality corrective costs by product line (Figure 2.13). The data showed that the Process Controls product line, which was the most complex, was causing over 50 percent of the total rework cost. It also accounted for almost half of the corrective orders issued. The data began to suggest some ideas on where to apply needed corrective action.

Next, the QA manager took a look at vendor performance (Figure 2.14), rating AJAX's top six vendors on both defect rate and delivery performance using a 1 to 5 scale. An overall rating was arrived at by weighting the defect and delivery rating, as shown in Figure 2.14. In most cases vendors who had a poor

Setting Goals

Figure 2.13 Product Line Quality Cost Performance for 1Q2003

(Comparison with total company costs).

Type of corrective order	Total company		Process controls			Fluid metering			Gas compressors		
	Issued	$1000	Issued	$1000	%	Issued	$1000	%	Issued	$1000	%
Engineering	61	198	28	107	54.0	22	52	26.3	11	39	19.7
Manufacturing	342	294	170	164	55.8	126	95	32.3	46	35	11.9
Field	38	127	12	62	48.9	18	38	29.9	8	27	21.2
Guarantee	9	82	2	30	36.6	3	32	39.0	4	20	24.4
Other	12	16	6	7	43.7	3	8	50.0	3	1	6.3
Total	462	717	218	370	51.6	172	225	31.4	72	122	17.0

Figure 2.14 Vendor Defect and Delivery Rating for 1Q2003

Vendor	Lots received	Defect rate (%)	Defect rating (1 to 5 scale)	Avg delivery days late	Delivery rating (1 to 5 scale)	Overall rating (a)
A	120	0.3	4	3	4	4.0
B	82	0.7	3	4	3	3.0
C	90	1.1	2	6	2	2.0
D	62	0.1	5	On-time	5	5.0
E	112	0.3	4	On-time	5	4.3
F	104	0.2	5	1	4	4.7

(a) Overall rating based on 70% against defect rating; 30 % against delivery as follows:

Defect rating		Delivery rating	
0.2 or less	5	On-time	5
0.3 ...0.5	4	1-3 days late	4
0.6 ...0.9	3	4-5 days late	3
1.0 ...1.5	2	6-7 days late	2
over 1.5	1	More than 7	1

(low) rating on defects also had a poor rating on delivery performance. That seemed logical because if a company was having trouble making something, you would expect them to be late shipping it.

One final task for the QA manager was to develop a "Quality Cost Control Matrix" which sorted quality control activities into three categories (prevention, appraisal, and failure) and assigned responsibilities for control of each to engineering, purchasing, and manufacturing (Figure 2.15). With this information compiled, and after discussion with the other senior managers, the QA manag-

Figure 2.15 The Quality Cost Control Matrix

Department	Prevention actions	Appraisal actions	Failure actions
Engineering	Design reviews Design checking Code certification Specification review	Prototype inspection Drawing checking Procedure preparation and review	Product redesign Product specification changes
Purchasing	Vendor capability reviews Purchase order review Vendor inspection and testing review	Vendor surveillance Incoming inspection Vendor qualification review	Recover rework costs form vendors Disposition of defective parts and components
Manufacturing	Preventive maintenance Process inspection Tool inspection/control Worker training and certification	Product inspection QA control measurements Equipment calibration Inspector training	Rework defective product Review design with engineering Modify procedures Retrain workers

Prevention: Front-end actions to prevent design errors, manufacturing rework, and vendor product defects.

Appraisal: Actions incurred to evaluate product and certify it meets desired quality level.

Failure: Actions incurred to repair, replace or rework product to meet quality standards and customer specifications.

Figure 2.16 The QA Manager's Summary Plan of Action

(Program goal was to cut product defect cost to <u>less than 1.0% of sales within 6 months</u> of approval)

Detailed preventive actions	Detailed appraisal actions
1. Design codes to be recertified every 6 months [E] 2. Customer specifications to be reviewed before start of initial design [E, M, and QA] 3. Peer review of design drawings before release [E] 4. Vendors B and C placed on probation. Stepped up on-site and receipt inspection [P, QA] 5. All production workers to get free eye exam annually [M] 6. More inspection resource to be allocated to Controls PL [QA] 7. QA instruments to be reviewed for upgrade [QA] 8. Workers with high defect rates to be retrained or released if improvement unsatisfactory [M] 9. Quality control charts to be updated weekly [QA] 10. Customer feedback on product quality to be solicited bi-weekly [QA] 11. Shop defects to be publicized to employees [M] 12. Defect-free award program to be initiated [M]	1. Independent checking of drawing before release [E,QA] 2. All prototypes to be inspected and critiqued before design release [E,M,QA] 3. Department Heads must sign off on any design or manufacturing procedure changes 4. Vendors B and C to get 100% inspection [QA] 5. QA instruments to be recalibrated weekly [QA] 6. Defect product to get expedited analysis [QA] 7. Worker suggestions to avoid defects to be solicited at weekly team meetings [M,QA] 8. Joint engineering-manufacturing committee to meet monthly [E,M] Legend E Engineering department QA Quallity Assurance department P Purchasing department M Manufacturing (first department listed takes lead on action)

Setting Goals

er outlined plans to management highlighting these key issues (see Figure 2.16):

• Experience in other industries shows that for a complex product, inspection hours can be as much as 20% of production hours; for a simple product, inspection may only need to be about 1% of production hours. Our products are not too complex and we should expect to need a factor of about 3%. That's not out of line with what we're currently doing in the shop, so hiring more inspectors was not part of the plan.

• The key to improving in-house quality was to catch errors and defects early in the design or manufacturing process. This meant more design reviews, computer code certification, drawing checking, focused shop inspections, and more frequent procedure reviews.

• To improve vendor performance, vendors with overall ratings below 4.0 would be placed on probation, subject to higher incoming inspection that AJAX planned to bill the vendor for the added cost. Failure to agree would disqualify the vendor from selling to AJAX.

The Conclusion: The QA manager's plan was approved and implemented on July 1, 2003. Tracking of product defect cost by month for the balance of the year showed the following results:

Month	Defect cost (% of monthly sales)
July	2.4
August	1.7
September	1.4
October	0.9
November	0.7
December	0.8

The president commented on the program at the first management meeting in January, "We should all be pleased with meeting the goal for last year on defect cost. I'm not surprised that it went up a little in December, since productivity tends to fall at that time of the year. Maybe correcting that should be a goal for 2004."

Critiques of Case Study 2-9: Bringing in a new manager is often a great way to jump start a new initiative. In this case, the management team quickly recognized the extensive experience of the new QA manager, whose suggestions for improving quality they were quick to accept. Probably the QA manager's biggest achievement was convincing the engineering and manufacturing managers that the earlier an error or defect was detected in the design-manufacturing process, the lower would be the ultimate rework cost. Therefore, to improve the return-on-inspection, it is necessary to place inspection points at the sequences in the design and fabrication process where the highest probability of error exists.

2.5 SOME FINAL POINTS ABOUT GOALS

In the case studies above, we have focused more on setting goals and less on monitoring the results against goal. In the next chapter, we will look more closely at some techniques for tracking progress against a goal and some novel ways to report results.

In Figure 2.1, we limited the ROA calculation to return before interest and taxes. Our reasoning was that those cost elements in the hierarchy below the ROA were pretty much within the control of operating management. We could go higher in the financial hierarchy by calculating Net Income, factoring in taxes, interest, and any accounting changes (more on this below). Or, we could go even higher by determining ROE (return-on-equity) by factoring in debt and equity. For our purposes of evaluating line-management performance in this chapter, we didn't think these higher levels were necessary (we will look at case studies on ROE and earnings-per-share in later chapters).

A couple of final points. Taxes are set by government at the federal, state, county and local level. Although it is possible for a company to legally avoid or defer certain taxes, the tax rate they ultimately pay is outside their control. The same is true with interest rates. The Federal Reserve, the market, economic conditions, and the company's credit rating usually determine what a company has to pay to borrow. The stockholders also have some say in that because they can sell their stock if they feel the return on their investment would be better somewhere else. As for accounting changes, guidelines such as Sarbanes-Oxley and Generally Accepted Accounting Practices (GAAP) usually determine what accounting treatment has to be used, not management. For example, the decision to expense the impact of stock options may not be entirely within the control of corporate management, at least not for long.

For all of the above reasons, we will typically limit the case studies

Setting Goals

later in this book to evaluating various managers on their performance in obtaining a return-on-assets before interest payment, taxes *and accounting changes*. There will be, however, a number of cases where we will focus on Net Income, Earnings per Share (EPS), Return on Equity (ROE), and Operating Gain, when those metrics are more appropriate to the company and industry used in the case study.

Monitoring Goals 3

3.1 WHAT THE READER WILL LEARN FROM THIS CHAPTER

- How to develop a tactical plan
- How to develop a control chart
- Case studies for monitoring goals

3.2 INTRODUCTION

In Chapter 2, we discussed setting goals. We also touched on monitoring goals, but not in depth. In this chapter, we will talk about two issues related to goals: 1) tactical plans for defining specific tasks needed to accomplish goals, and 2) ways to monitor goals by using a control chart that's a little different from most control charts. (We call ours a "clothes line chart" because it resembles clothes pins hanging on a clothes line). For each case study presented in Chapter 2, we will show an example of a tactical plan and control chart. This approach should increase your awareness of these tools for monitoring goals. But first, let's discuss tactical plans and control charts in more detail.

3.3 TACTICAL PLANS

Most cost control programs cross over functional departmental lines of authority and tend to contain a significant number of interrelated events. Therefore, some device is needed to ensure that key actions are implemented in a timely manner. That's where tactical plans come into play.

Each tactical plan is prepared to ensure that the resources necessary to support the activity are applied in a planned and orderly manner toward achieving the goal. The secret to success for using tactical plans is to keep them simple. A single-page format is preferred; two pages is an absolute maximum. A typical tactical plan has these features: 1) the cost control goal of the tactical plan supports some profit center or corporate goal, 2) responsibilities of individuals or departments are clearly defined, 3) the basis for measuring performance against goal is spelled out, and 4) the key milestones are listed along with the responsible individual (or department) and planned completion dates.

As an added feature, the actual completion date for each event on the plan should be recorded. This information helps management measure performance; it also serves as documented evidence for use in subsequent performance appraisals of the responsible personnel.

We recommend that tactical plans be implemented down in the organization to the level of management responsible for cost or profit control activities. This level might be the foreman or superintendent level. The plans can include action items or events by any employee.

A convenient way to control how managers progress with their tactical plans is to computerize the specific events so that the planned and actual completion dates for each event can be easily monitored. Then, some individual (or department) in the organization can monitor the completion dates and report exceptions against plan to the appropriate managers.

3.4 CONTROL CHARTS

There are a variety of ways to display data to form a control chart, including bar charts, data tables, 3-dimentional charts, pie charts, and line charts, just to name a few. Except the data table, all provide some form of graphical representation of the data, which we prefer over merely tabulating numbers. People tend to remember data displayed graphically better than when it is just tabulated.

Regardless of how the data are displayed, the control chart should have these features: 1) it should contain a timeline over which the progress against goal is being tracked, 2) the point where the goal is achieved should be indicated on the chart, 3) the amount of deviation from goals, plus or minus, should be displayed when appropriate, and 4) other appropriate information such as the absolute value of the goal should be included as long as it doesn't overly clutter up the chart.

Figure 3.1 shows a control chart that meets all of the above criteria. It shows how monthly shipments track against goal throughout a program that is now completed; a look at the chart during the program

Monitoring Goals

Figure 3.1 Typical Clothes Line Chart for Monitoring Performance Against Goal

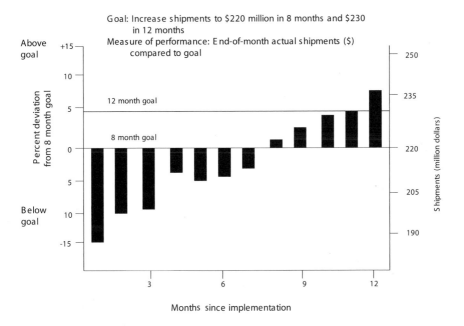

would have shown future shipments as "planned" or "forecasted." Here you can see why we call it a clothes line chart.

This chart happens to show two goals, which is a bit unusual, but allowable nevertheless. The deviation (in percent plus or minus) and the absolute value of the goal (shipments dollars in this example) are shown on different axes. Notice that the goal and the basis for measuring performance against goal are clearly identified. Throughout this chapter we will show many variations of this basic chart to track progress of the goals set in the Chapter 2 case studies.

3.5 MONITORING THE CHAPTER 2 CASE STUDY GOALS

In this section, we will use both a tactical plan and a control chart to critique the goals set in each case study of Chapter 2. We will evaluate each goal to determine:

1) Was a goal actually set?
2) Is the goal quantitative?
3) Is the goal reasonably obtainable?

Chapter 3

4) Does the goal have a timeline?

5) Has responsibility for achieving the goals been assigned?

Throughout the remainder of this book, we will frequently use the abbreviation **TP** to stand for Tactical Plan and **CC** to stand for Control Chart. When a goal is deficient on any of the five characteristics listed above, we will re-define that goal before developing the TP or CC. Before getting started, let's summarize the issue covered by each case, for the benefit of readers who may prefer to jump directly to a particular case study.

Table 3.1 Summary of Case Study Issues

Case number	Company	Issue covered
2-1	AJAX Utility	Inappropriate goals
2-2	AJAX World Utility	All-inclusive goals
2-3	AJAX Diesel	Improving receivables
2-4	AJAX Distributors	Cash management
2-5	AJAX Energy	Lowering fixed assets
2-6	AJAX Hydrotech	Lowering cost of sales
2-7	AJAX Manufacturing	Labor cost control
2-8	AJAX Sales/Service	Cutting G&A expense
2-9	AJAX Technologies	Reducing product cost

CRITIQUE OF CASE STUDY 2-1 (AJAX Utility)
The Goal: [No Defined Goal]

The new station manager not only failed to set a goal, he failed to meet any of the other goal characteristics shown in the chart for Case 2-1. It also turns out that he was applying an inappropriate goal, turnover, to measure production spares parts where **less usage is actually better!** Had he thought it out more thoroughly, he could have set a quantitative goal for the slow-moving spares (e.g., AVR) that would have quantified over- or under-stocking.

Monitoring Goals

Goal characteristic	Was characteristic met?
Actually set	No
Quantitative	No
Obtainable	Uncertain
Timeline	No
Responsibility set	No

Production spares are used to support production, generally replacing parts that are worn out or defective. In this case, turnover is not an appropriate measure of performance. Why? Because turnover is normally a financial measure applied to retail inventory (e.g., clothing sales, grocery sales). Higher turnover of retail inventory means the asset is being replaced (purchased) more often during the accounting period. Thus, higher turnover would mean higher revenues. However, if it is applied to production inventory, higher turnover means higher expenses.

Redefining the Goal: Let's redefine the goal the station manager should have set. Refer back to Figure 2.2, which shows inventory data over a two-year period. Notice that the AVR decreased by a factor of 2, whereas turnover barely changed. Even the two-fold decrease in AVR to 0.31 is nothing to brag about because a value of less than 0.1 is reasonably obtainable over a two-year period. Therefore, we will redefine the goal to read:

- achieve an AVR of 0.1 by March 31, 2004

Now we're met four of the five goal characteristics, all except assigning responsibility. Optimizing the amount of production spare parts inventory is mainly controlled by several organizations: 1) supply-chain, 2) maintenance, and 3) purchasing. Therefore, the goal should be a shared one. We will assign primary responsibility for making it happen to the supply-chain manager. Now we're ready to develop the **TP** and **CC**.

The Tactical Plan: Figure 3.2 shows the suggested TP for achieving the AVR goal of 0.1. (eleven events are shown). Event 1 calculates some "what if" scenarios to determine the value of the AVR if certain actions

Chapter 3

Figure 3.2 Tactical Plan for Achieving AVR Goal for AJAX Utility

Title: TP 2-1 Optimize station slow-moving inventory
Date Issued: Jan 12, 2003
Purpose: Obtain an AVR of 0.1 by March 31, 2004
Performance Measure: Calculated AVR at the end of each quarter for
                    3563 key items

Key Milestones

Event	Responsibility	Planned Completion	Actual
1. Calculate "What if" scenarios	Supply chain	Jan 20	Jan 19
2. Set criticalities/ set size for items	Maintenance	Mar 1	Mar 3
3. Determine MIN/MAXs for items	Supply chain	Mar 10	Mar11
4. Review MIN/MAXs	Maintenance	Apr 30	Apr 30
5. Make changes in material system	Supply chain	May 15	May17
6. Select items for vendor LT review	Supply chain	Jun 1	Jun 1
7. Solicit lower lead times from vendors	Purchasing	Jul 1	Jul 9
8. Purchase understocked inventory	Purchasing	Aug1	Aug 7
9. Enter lower vendor MINs in system	Supply chain	Aug 30	Aug 30
10. Evaluate AVR	Supply chain	Sept 5	Sept 4
11. Update AVR quarterly	Supply chain	Sept 10	Sept 30
		Dec 30	Dec 30
		Mar 31	Mar 30

are taken to adjust the MIN/MAX levels for the key items. Setting critical-
ities for the items and determining the number to purchase if the item
is used as a "set" is solely a maintenance responsibility. Processing the
data through stocking codes (event 3) is the responsibility of supply
chain, as are most of the other events. The purchasing department's role
is to deal with vendors when soliciting shorter lead times (event 7) and
purchasing additional inventory for understocked items (event 8).

The Control Chart: Figure 3.3 show the CC for tracking the AVR from
the September 4, 2003 benchmark value to the end of March 2004.
Notice that, for this chart, the timeline moves from right to left. Recall
that the AVR adds the amount of overstocked inventory to the amount
of understocked inventory (the total imbalance) and divides the total
imbalance by the optimum amount of needed inventory. Thus, the
length of the bar above the base line reflects the amount of imbalance
due to overstocking, whereas the length of the bar below the base line
relates to the amount of understocking.

Because the AVR is based on planned inventory (the amount determined by the MIN/MAXs in the material system), a new AVR can be
determined once changes are made to the MIN/MAXs; we don't have

Monitoring Goals

Figure 3.3 Control Chart for Tracking AVR

⬅ Time line

Mar 31, 2004   Dec 30. 2003   Sept 30, 2003   Sept 4 Benchmark

Percent deviation

Over

80
60
40

Final AVR = 0.09

20

Base line

20

40

60

Under

80

The height of the bar above the base line relates to overstocks
The height of the bar below the base line relates to understocks

0   0.1   0.2   0.3   0.4   0.5   0.6

AVR

to wait for the excess to work off or for the understocks to be replenished.

Notice that by September 30, the length of the bar both above and below the base line is smaller, indicating that reductions in both planned overstocks and understocks were made. Some additional understocked items had their MIN/MAXs adjusted a bit more by December 30, but no further adjustments were made in the first quarter of 2004. Adjustments to overstocked items continued to be made during the entire timeline. By March 31, 2004, the MIN/MAXs for the 3,563 key items had sufficient adjustments made to yield an AVR of 0.09, slightly better than goal. Because the amount of optimum inventory changes as demand for the spares changes or lead times change, it is prudent to adjust stock MIN/MAXs and recalculate the AVR regularly.

CRITIQUE OF CASE STUDY 2-2 (AJAX World Utility)
The Goal: [Total Inventory <$95.6 Million by Year- End]

The VP of Power Generation did an excellent job of setting the all-inclusive goal; it met all five of the goal characteristics.

Chapter 3

Case 2-2 AJAX World Utility

Goal characteristic	Was characteristic met?
Actually set	Yes
Quantitative	Yes
Obtainable	Yes
Timeline	Yes
Responsibility set	Yes

Better still, he asked his staff to come up with the recommended sub-goals, which gave them a sense that it was *their* goals and not something imposed on them by the VP. Because this was the first time the all-inclusive goal was set, the results shown in Figure 2.3 are very commendable. In our judgment there is no need to restate the goal; it met the five characteristics and achieved the total inventory objective for the year.

The Tactical Plan: Because each of the components of inventory being monitored (e.g., active spares, new spares) required a different set of

Figure 3.4 Tactical Plan for Achieving Overhaul Inventory Goal for AJAX World Utility

Title:	TP 2-2 Meet target overhaul inventory goal
Date Issued:	Dec 15, 2003
Purpose:	Hold overhaul inventory for 2004 to $7.5 million
Performance Measure:	Overall inventory status at end of each month and at year-end

Key Milestones

Event	Responsibility	Planned Completion	Actual
1. Determine spares for May outage	Maintenance	Jan 15	Jan 19
2. Place orders for purchased material	Purchasing	Jan 31	Jan 27
3. Stage material by outage tasks	Supply chain	Apr 15	Apr 15
4. Complete May overhaul	Maintenance	May 3	May 30
5. Return unused spares to vendors	Supply chain	Jun 15	Jun 17
6. Complete mid-year cycle count	Supply chain	Jul 30	Aug 6
7. Determine spares for Nov outage	Maintenance	Aug 1	Aug 9
8. Place orders for purchased material	Purchasing	Aug 15	Aug 17
9. Stage material by outage tasks	Supply chain	Oct 15	Oct 15
10. Complete Nov overhaul	Maintenance	Dec 10	Dec 12
11. Return unused spares to vendors	Supply chain	Dec 30	Dec 30
12. Tabulate 2004 overhaul usage	Supply chain	Dec 30	Dec 30

Monitoring Goals

activities to achieve the goal, each inventory type needed to have a tactical plan. Figure 3.4 shows a suggested TP for activities to control the scheduled overhaul items. A key to coming within 2.5% of goal for the year was the timely return of unused outage spares to vendors after each overhaul. Wisely, AJAX had negotiated the right to return unused spares when they contracted for outage spares each year.

The mid-year cycle count was also important because many of the overhaul spares were withdrawn from the station storeroom. Major errors in the computerized inventory balances versus the actual storeroom count could have had two adverse impacts: 1) not having a spare for the outage, even though the spare was shown to be in stock, and 2) causing a spare to be bought when it was in fact in stock.

The Control Chart: Figure 3.5 shows the control chart for monitoring overhaul inventory throughout 2004. The CC shows the status of overhaul inventory against goal for each month of the year. Starting from about $2 million below goal in January, the plan was to increase outage spares prior to each overhaul, and then work the inventory balance back down below goal. As stated earlier, returning spares to vendors was vital to this strategy, and it was successful after the May outage.

However, the plan was too optimistic in December. The excess was not able to be returned completely that month, leaving the station

Figure 3.5 Control Chart for Monitoring Outage Spares in 2004

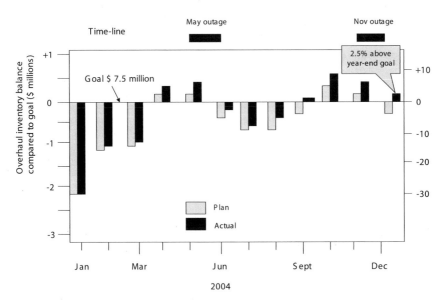

about 2.5% above the year-end goal. In reviewing the results in January, the VP commented, "I think we were all too optimistic when we set the goal for December. Everybody knows you can't get much done the week before New Year's."

CRITIQUE OF CASE STUDY 2-3 (AJAX Diesel)
The Goal: [Decrease A/R by 20% in 2003; 10 % More in 2004]

The goal to decrease accounts receivable met three and possibly four of the goal characteristics, as shown in the chart nearby. The fact that only one of the four AJAX Diesel industry segments met goal (see Figure 2.6) may be a result of underestimating the bureaucracy of foreign customer accounts payable departments, host country currency control restrictions, and the traditional slow-paying practice of domestic auto and truck manufacturers. Setting a single-value goal always has a high risk of never being right, suggesting the need to look at the probability of meeting goals, as we will cover in Chapters 5, 6, 7, and 8.

Case 2-3 AJAX Diesel

Goal characteristic	Was characteristic met?
Actually set	Yes
Quantitative	Yes
Obtainable	Probably
Timeline	Yes
Responsibility set	No

The Tactical Plan: Figure 3.6 shows a TP for meeting the accounts receivable goal. The plan to add a financing fee to new contract orders was initiated, but was unsuccessful most of the time. Sales and Finance worked together to devise new incentive programs for getting customers to pay earlier, such as offering credits toward future spares purchases for paying before 15 days. The TP also included two critiques of results, one after the first quarter and another after the second quarter, to determine if fine-tuning of the incentive programs was necessary. Event 13 of the plan required quarterly reporting of results for the balance of 2003 and 2004.

Monitoring Goals

Figure 3.6 Tactical Plan for Achieving Accounts Receivable Goal for AJAX Diesel

Title:	TP 2-3 Meet target accounts receivable goal
Date Issued:	January 12, 2003
Purpose:	Reduce accounts receivable balance by 20% in 2003 and 10% more in 2004
Performance Measure:	Calculate actuals using December 31, 2002 benchmark

Key Milestones

Event	Responsibility	Planned Completion	Actual
1. Negotiate financing fee on new orders	Purchasing	Continuing	Continuing
2. Design customer incentive program	Sales/Finance	Jan 31	Jan 27
3. Explain incentives to agents	Sales	Feb 15	Feb 10
4. Devise discount program for direct pay	Sales/Finance	Feb 20	Feb 22
5. Devise credit plan for early pay	Sales/Finance	Feb 28	Mar 2
6. Compute results for 1Q 2003	Finance	Apr 15	Apr 14
7. Critique 1Q results	Senior staff	Apr 20	Apr 20
8. Modify program as necessary	Sales/Finance	May 1	May 2
9. Explain changes to agents	Sales	May 15	May 12
10. Compute results for 2Q 2003	Finance	Jul 15	Jul 13
11. Critique 2Q results	Senior staff	Jul 20	Jul 20
12. Make additional adjustments	Sales/Finance	Aug 1	Jul 28
13. Compute/present results quarterly	Finance	Quarterly	Quarterly

Figure 3.7 Control Chart for Monitoring Accounts Receivable Program

(Results for Domestic and Foreign Light and Heavy Trucking)

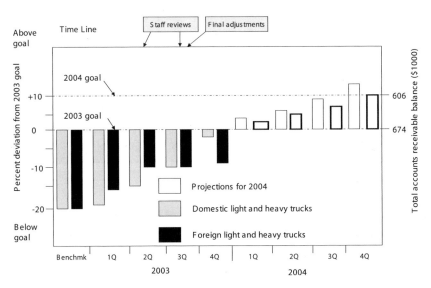

Chapter 3

The Control Chart: Figure 3.7 shows the CC for the program after the fourth quarter 2003 results were in (see also Figure 2.6 for quarterly details). Results against goal are plotted for both the domestic and foreign truck product lines. Combined results for domestic truck receivables came within 3 percent of goal for 2003, with heavy truck receivables meeting goal and light trucks failing to meet goal. Neither the light or heavy truck foreign receivables met goal. Projections are shown for 2004 where both receivable groups are projected to meet the combined goal of $606,000.

CRITIQUE OF CASE STUDY 2-4 (AJAX Distributors)
The Goal: [Cut Days Receivable from 43 to 35 Days]

The goal to cut days receivables from 43 to 35 days, although quantitative, fails to identify the dollar benefit from achieving the goal. Likewise, the pursuit of consignment was undertaken without a target dollar amount being set. Most of the actions proposed would have an impact on both the amount of outstanding receivables and on the need for short-term borrowing. We believe each of these areas of improvement would benefit from redefining the goal as shown below.

Case 2-4 AJAX Distributors

Goal characteristic	Was characteristic met?
Actually set	Partial
Quantitative	Partial
Obtainable	Yes
Timeline	Yes
Responsibility set	Yes

Redefining the Goal: We think it would be useful to redefine the original goal for AJAX into two goals, one for cutting outstanding receivables and one for cutting short-term borrowing.

The outstanding receivables balance would improve by: 1) quicker invoicing, and 2) getting the customers to pay sooner by following up more closely after invoicing, and (3) offering incentives to pay before

Monitoring Goals

the customary 30-day grace period. The need for short-term borrowing could be reduced by: 1) working down inventories, 2) delaying payments to suppliers, 3) seeking better loan terms, 4) raising prices, and 5) cutting overhead costs. Let's redefine the goals as follows:

- Reduce outstanding receivables — *reduce outstanding receivables by $500,000 by June 30, 2005*

- Days receivables — *improve cash flow by $300,000 by reducing days receivable from 43 to 35 days by August 31, 2005*

In the following sections, a TP and CC will be developed for each goal.

The Tactical Plan: Figure 3.8 shows the TP for reducing receivable balances. Events 1 and 2 focus on issuing invoices sooner (3 days compared to past practice of about 10 days) and having the sales force follow up with customers to see that they got the invoice and had no issues standing in the way of paying. Events 3, 4, and 5 focus on incentives to encourage customers to pay sooner, preferably by allowing AJAX to draw down the amount due directly from the customer's bank

Figure 3.8 Tactical Plan for Achieving Accounts Receivable Goal for AJAX Distributors

Title: TP 2-4A Meet target accounts receivable goal
Date Issued: January 5, 2005
Purpose: Reduce outstanding receivable by $500,000 by June 30, 2005
Measure of Performance: Outstanding receivables balance on June 30 versus December 31, 2004 balance

Key milestones

	Event	Responsibility	Planned completion	Actual
1.	Invoice within 3 days of shipment	Accounting	Continuing	Continuing
2.	Follow up invoices within 10 days	Sales/Accounting	Jan 31	Jan 27
3.	Develop incentive program	Sales/Finance	Feb 15	Feb 10
4.	Devise discount program for direct pay	Sales/Finance	Feb 20	Feb 22
5.	Devise credits plan for early pay	Sales/Finance	Feb 28	Mar 2
6.	Develop consignment program	Finance	Mar 1	Mar 1
7.	Monitor A/R status weekly	Finance	Continuing	Continuing
8.	Review program benefits	Senior staff	Monthly	Monthly

Figure 3.9 Tactical Plan for Reducing Days Receivables at AJAX Distributors.

Title: TP 2-4B   Meet days receivable goal
Date Issued: January 4, 2005
Purpose: Reduce days receivables from 43 to 35 by August 31, 2005 and
   Improve cash flow by $300,000
Measure of Performance: Days receivables balance and cash flow improvement

Key milestones

	Event	Responsibility	Planned completion	Actual
1.	Cut inventory purchases by 5%	Supply chain	Continuing	Continuing
2.	Defer supplier payments by 10 days	Accounting	Jan 6	Continuing
3.	Seek better short-term loan terms	Finance	Feb 1	Feb 10
4.	Increase prices on selected items	Sales/Finance	Feb 20	Feb 22
5.	Cut overhead expenses by 5%	All Departments	Continuing	Continuing

---

account. Because of the short time span of the program, results are reviewed monthly at the senior staff meeting.

The TP for reducing days receivables is shown in Figure 3.9. Two of the tasks (Events 1 and 5) are pure expense cuts that should contribute to improved cash flow by the August deadline. Event 2 (deferring payments to suppliers by 10 days) carries risk that some suppliers may retaliate in some way such as delaying shipments or going to a "payment upon delivery" philosophy. Raising prices on selected items should always be on the table for consideration.

The Control Chart: Two CCs are shown, one for each goal. The good news is that both goals were exceeded, reducing outstanding receivables by an extra $100,000 and cash flow by $68,000. Also impressive, days receivables reached 31 days during August, 4 days better than the goal. Clearly, invoicing quicker and following up with the customers both helped. Faster improvement also occurred after the incentive program was initiated, as shown by the $250,000 improvement from March to April (Figure 3.10). The impact of the positive effect of the consignment program can be seen in Figure 3.11 by the steady improvement in cash flow as short-term borrowing interest was avoided. This case study clearly shows the benefits of keeping a close eye on receivables and justifies aggressive programs to accelerate receivables.

Monitoring Goals

Figure 3.10 Control Chart for Reducing Outstanding Receivables

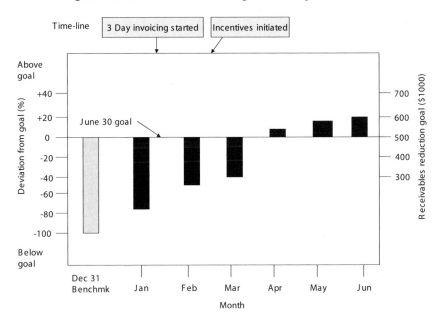

Figure 3.11 Control Chart for Days Receivables and Cash Flow Improvement

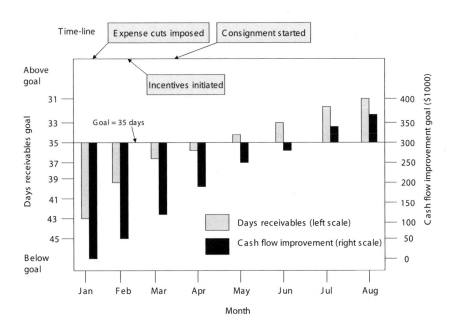

Chapter 3

CRITIQUE OF CASE STUDY 2-5 (AJAX Energy)
The Goal: [Lower Fixed Assets]

It's debatable that any specific goals were set by management, although four estimates were made (E/A impact, and improvements in cash flow, turnover, and ROA). Therefore, some restatement of goals is needed.

Case 2-5 AJAX Energy

Goal characteristic	Was characteristic met?
Actually set	Estimated
Quantitative	Yes
Obtainable	Probably
Timeline	Yes
Responsibility set	No

Redefining the Goal: We will redefine the goal for E/A to state:

- Match the E/A benchmarks for the Pennsylvania plant within six months of startup in Arkansas

We will simply change the estimates for cash flow, turnover, and ROA to read:

Within one year of moving the Package Boiler Product:

- Achieve a $1.4 million positive cash flow
- Improve product turnover to 2.0
- Improve ROA to 14 percent

The Tactical Plan: The TP for achieving the E/A goal is shown in Figure 3.12. The key to keeping the cost of moving the package boiler line within budget was the pre-fabrication of selected package boilers for inventory in February and March, in time to allow the transfer of the remaining jigs and fixtures to the Arkansas plant. Paying incentives to maintain productivity at the Pennsylvania plant also proved effective. The target to complete the sale of the plant was not met by November 1. Final sale of the plant was completed in January, 2005, resulting in a recordable profit from the sale of $2,416,000 after commissions and closing out state and local tax liabilities.

No tactical plans are shown for the other financial goals. Several control charts are discussed below.

Monitoring Goals

Figure 3.12 Tactical Plan for Achieving E/A Goals After Package Boiler Move

Title:	TP 2-5 Meet Pennsylvania manufacturing task E/As within six months
Date Issued:	February 4, 2004
Purpose:	Achieve Pennsylvania plant E/A goals for nine tasks
Performance Measure:	Compare Arkansas plant E/As versus PA plant

Key Milestones

Event	Responsibility	Planned Completion	Actual
1. Buildup package boiler inventory	Manufacturing	Apr 10	Apr 15
2. Hiring and training at Arkansas	Manufacturing	Apr 15	Apr 20
3. Move jigs and fixtures	Manufacturing	Apr 10	Apr 14
4. Purchase new welding equipment	Purchasing	Feb 25	Mar 1
5. Arrange accommodation for transfers	Human Resource	Apr 15	Apr 12
6. Implement incentives at PA plant	Human Resource	Feb 15	Feb 15
7. Select realtor to sell PA plant	Finance	Mar 1	Feb 27
8. Move remainder of equipment	Manufacturing	Apr 12	Apr 16
9. Install new welding equipment	Manufacturing	Apr 10	Apr 13
10. Shutdown PA plant	Manufacturing	May 1	May 7
11. Complete sale of PA plant	Finance	Nov 1	Continuing

Figure 3.13 Control Chart for Tracking Selected Tasks Against E/A Goal

(Chart for drum fabrication ,economizer installation and membrane welding only)

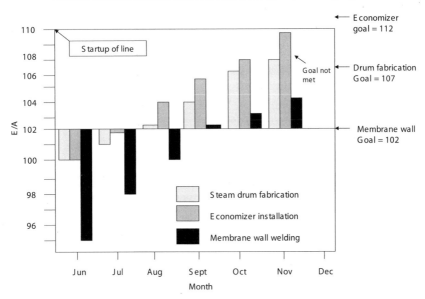

Chapter 3

The Control Chart: Figure 3.13 shows a CC for tracking E/A for three of the nine tasks (drum fabrication, economizer installation, and membrane wall welding). The goal for economizer installation (E/A = 112) was the only goal not met within the six-month target.

Figure 3.14 shows a statement of cash flow status during the three phases of the package boiler product line move: 1) Phase I – the 60-day period covering the move to Arkansas, 2) Phase II – the six-month ramp up period, and 3) Phase III – the first six months of steady state production. Net cash flow was negative during Phase I due to the costs of moving the product line, adding additional employees at the Arkansas plant, and covering severance costs at the Pennsylvania plant. Positive cash flow began in Phase II ($529,000) and peaked in Phase III with the gain on the sale of the Pennsylvania property. The final tally after all phases showed a $170,000 net positive cash flow improvement over the original estimate.

Figure 3.15 shows a CC of the net cash flow change over the three phases. Figure 3.16 shows a CC tracking the turnover and ROA goals for the fourteen months after announcing the package boiler move. As

Figure 3.14 Cash Flow Status from Move of Package Boiler Line

(for twelve month period after move of line)

	Dollars ($1000)				
[1] Positive Cash Flow Impact:	Original estimate	Phase I	Phase II	Phase III	Final tally
Net gain on sale of property	2,163	-	-	2,416	2,416
Employment cost savings	4,012	-	1,950	1,925	3,875
Total positive	6,175	-	1,950	4,341	6,291
[2] Negative Cash Flow Impact:					
Incentive pay	113	132	-	-	132
Moving expenses	303	284	45	-	329
Severance pay	1,338	980	350	-	1,330
Additional hiring cost	2,225	1,250	616	225	2,091
Impact of productivity loss	260	-	325	-	325
Move of equipment	265	155	85	-	240
Purchase new equipment	317	319	-	-	319
Total negative	4,820	3,120	1,421	225	4,766
[3] Net positive gain in cash flow	1,355	(3,120)	529	4,116	1,525

Monitoring Goals

Figure 3.15 Control Chart for Net Cash Flow During Program Phases

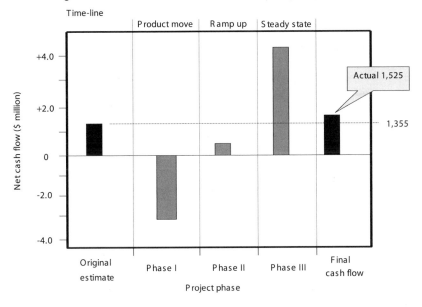

Figure 3.16 Control Chart for Turnover and ROA after Product Move

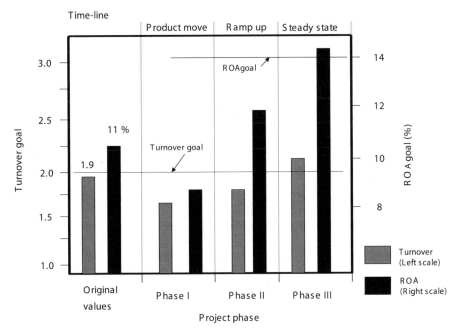

Chapter 3

expected, both turnover and ROA decreased in Phase I due to: 1) the build up in inventory, 2) the use of cash to cover product move expenses, including severance pay, and 3) additional factory labor and overhead costs incurred during the 60-day move. Improvement in turnover was relatively minor during Phase II, but the ROA showed a 3-percent gain, mainly from higher operating profit due to factory cost improvements and lower G&A expenses. The benefit of selling the Pennsylvania facility kicked in during Phase III, raising both turnover and ROA above goal.

CRITIQUE OF CASE STUDY 2-6 (AJAX Hydrotech)
The Goal: [Not Lose a Contract Due to Purchased Component Prices]

The directive set by the President failed to meet any of the goal character-istics shown on the chart for Case 2-6. His statement "not to lose another job due to purchased equipment prices" did not provide the company any useful information upon which to take corrective action. A better approach would have been to convene a review of recent public bids to determine the extent to which AJAX's purchased component prices were out-of-line. From that information, a goal could have been set for fixing the problem. Clearly, the goal for AJAX needs to be redefined.

Case 2-6 AJAX Hydrotech

Goal characteristic	Was characteristic met?
Actually set	Directive only
Quantitative	No
Obtainable	Uncertain
Timeline	No
Responsibility set	No

Redefining the Goal: A team was assembled; it reviewed the last three pub-lic bids to determine where AJAX's purchased equipment prices were out of line with XYZ Water, their prime competitor. The results of the review are sum-marized below:

Monitoring Goals

Equipment Category	Price Deviation	Main Reason
Pumps	8 % high	More expensive materials
Fans	6 % high	Purchased higher capacity
Controls	11 % high	More expensive models
Transformers	No deviation	Purchased stock models

Because the first three categories above accounted for about 85% of AJAX's price deviation, the goals for improvement focused on these items only. The redefined goals agreed upon are summarized below:

- achieve parity with XYZ Water on pump prices on bids after 45 days
- achieve parity with XYZ Water on fan prices on bids after 45 days
- achieve parity with XYZ Water on controls prices on bids after 60 days

More time was allowed to set new standards for purchasing controls because there were more technical tradeoffs to consider than for pumps and fans. Also, it was not considered appropriate to set quantitative price improvement goals for the items because customer specifications required some re-engineering on nearly all projects (seeking "parity" was considered acceptable). Responsibility for preparing the bid specifications was assigned to the engineering department, whereas price and terms negotiation was assigned to purchasing.

The Tactical Plan: Figure 3.17 shows the TP for achieving price parity. The focus of the plan was to redraft purchase specifications to allow vendors to bid standard equipment as much as possible. Initial vendor feedback on the new specifications (event 3) was important to insure the purchased components were consistent with existing vendor products. Notice that performance was an item for review at the senior staff meeting once per month.

The Control Chart: A CC was designed to show the results of the latest four available public bids to compare prices between AJAX and XYZ Water (Figure 3.18). Progress was made to hold down purchased component prices, but the first two bids still went to XYZ Water. With some fine-tuning of the specifications, and some keener negotiating of

Chapter 3

Figure 3.17 Tactical Plan for Achieving Price Parity with XYZ Water

Title: TP 2-6 <u>Meet XYZ Waters purchased prices on selected components</u>
Date Issued: June <u>4, 2004</u>
Purpose: <u>Achieve price parity with XYZ Water on pumps, fans and
controls within 45 to 60 days.</u>
Measure of Performance: Public bid prices for bids after 45 days.

Key milestones

	Event	Responsibility	Planned completion	Actual
1.	Draft new pump and fan spec	Mechanical group	June 15	Jun 16
2.	Draft new controls spec	Controls group	Jul 1	Jul 1
3.	Review new specs with vendors	Engr/purchasing	Jul 8	Jul 10
4.	Modify specs as necessary	Engineering	Jul 15	Jul 15
5.	Issue new specs on pumps/fans	Purchasing	Jul 15	Continuing
6.	Issue new specs on controls	Purchasing	Jul 30	Continuing
7.	Obtain public bid prices by XYZ Water	Purchasing	Continuing	Continuing
8.	Analyze bid prices	Engineering	Continuing	Continuing
9.	Review performance	Senior staff	Monthly	Continuing

Figure 3.18 Control Chart Comparing Purchased Component Pricing

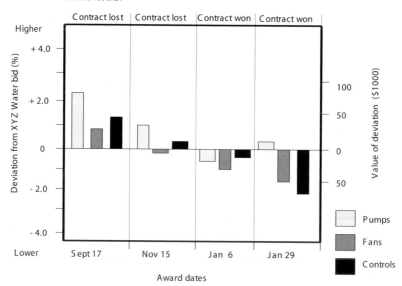

56

Monitoring Goals

Figure 3.19 Tactical Plan for Labor Contract Negotiation

Title: TP 2-7 Labor contract negotiation
Date Issued: March 1, 2004
Purpose: Reach agreement on 3-year labor contract by July 15 and hold wage increases to 5%/year maximum.
Measure of Performance: Contract wage increase 5% or Less

Key milestones

	Event	Responsibility	Planned completion	Actual
1.	Select management negotiation team	AJAX President	Mar 15	Mar 12
2.	Evaluate financial offer	Negotiating team/HR	Mar 20	Mar 21
3.	Determine work rules issues	Negotiating team /HR	Mar 30	Mar 30
4.	Draft contract offer to Union	Negotiating team/HR	Apr 15	Apr 15
5.	First meeting with union	Human Resources *	May 1	May 3
6.	Second meeting with union	Human Resources	May 14	May 14
7.	Third meeting with union	Human Resources	June 1	June 3
8.	Fourth meeting with union	Human Resources	June 14	June 14
9.	Fifth meeting with union	Human Resources	June 28	Jun 28
10.	Final offer made to union	Negotiating team	Jul 5	Jul 7
11.	Expected union vote on offer	-	Jul 10	Jul 13

contract terms by purchasing, success was achieved on the third bid, and continued to the fourth bid even though AJAX's pump prices were above XYZ Water's pump prices.

At the first staff meeting in February the President remarked, "I'm pleased with our progress over the last six months. But we can't just continue to depend on cutting purchased component prices to win bids. We need to sharpen our pencils on some of our design concepts. I hear XYZ Water is looking at modular designs with more shop assembly and less field erection. We better jump on that also."

CRITIQUE OF CASE STUDY 2-7 (AJAX Manufacturing)
The Goal: [Hold Labor Cost Increases to < 5 % Per Year]

No timeline was set for the labor contract because of the open-ended nature of labor negotiations. Although no responsibility was set, it was implicit that the Human Resources manager was the one ultimately responsible for achieving a successful negotiation.

Chapter 3

Case 2-7 AJAX Manufacturing

Goal characteristic	Was characteristic met?
Actually set	Yes
Quantitative	Yes
Obtainable	Yes
Timeline	No
Responsibility set	No

Figure 3.20 Control Chart for Labor Contract Wage Negotiation

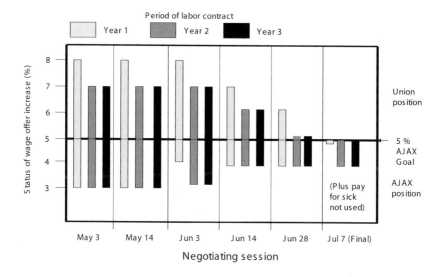

The Tactical Plan: Figure 3.19 shows the TP drawn up by the Human Resources manager three months prior to starting the labor contract negotiation with the union. History showed that it took about five preliminary meetings with the union before a final offer could be made. It also indicated that it was wishful thinking to expect the union committee to submit the contract to the membership for a vote until a day or two prior to contract expiration. Three years before, the union committee pooled the members ten days before contract expiration and the offer was overwhelmingly voted down – the membership attitude being "go back and get more, the contract doesn't expire for ten days."

Monitoring Goals

The Control Chart: The AJAX president wanted to be kept abreast of the movement of wage negotiations during the run up to the vote by the union members. Figure 3.20 shows what the Human Resources manager presented after each negotiation session. No movement was made by either party until the June 3 session, when the company raised the first year offer from 3 to 4 percent. In session 4, the union countered by dropping their demands for each year by one percent; AJAX held firm. On June 28, the union agreed to drop their demands another one percent for each year; again AJAX held firm. As its final offer, AJAX raised the first year wage increase to 5 percent, and added the pay-for-unused-sick-leave proposal as a sweetener. The final company offer passed by a 70 percent favorable vote.

CRITIQUE OF CAST STUDY 2-8 (AJAX Sales and Service)
The Goal: [Cut Overhead 25 %]

The reduction goal of 25 percent overhead met most of the goal characteristics. A timeline was needed as was naming the person responsible. We've corrected the problem by redefining the goal below.

Case 2-8 AJAX Sales and Service

Goal characteristic	Was characteristic met?
Actually set	Yes
Quantitative	Yes
Obtainable	Yes
Timeline	No
Responsibility set	No

Redefining the Goal: The timeline and responsibility characteristics were redefined below:

- Achieve the goal of 25 % reduction between now (March 10) and December 31.
- Responsibility – General Manager

The Tactical Plan: The General Manager drew up a TP for tracking the costs of closing the office (Figure 3.21). The plan was to have all

Chapter 3

Figure 3.21 Tactical Plan for Overhead Cost Reduction

Title: TP 2-8 Overhead cost reduction
Date Issued: March 10, 2004
Purpose: Cut office overhead 25 % by December 31, 2004
Measure of Performance: December monthly costs versus march

Key milestones

	Event	Responsibility	Planned completion	Actual
1.	Install new communications	Bob Mitchell	May 15	May 13
2.	Purchase new printers	General Mgr	Apr 30	Apr 29
3.	Arrange luncheon venue	General Mgr	May 20	May 20
4.	Arrange web conference option	General Mgr	May 15	May 18
5.	Notify rental agent	General Mgr	May 1	May 1
6.	Track overhead expenses	General Mgr	Continuing	Continuing

Figure 3.22 Control Chart for Tracking Monthly Overhead Costs

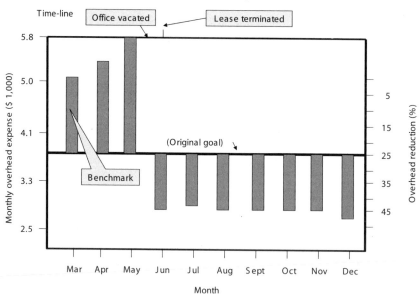

(Excludes salaries and fringe benefit costs)

arrangements in place by the end of April, notify the landlord by May 1 (30-day notice required under the lease), and vacate the office during May.

The Control Chart: Figure 3.22 shows the CC for tracking actual monthly overhead expenses. Average monthly expenses were nearly one-half those when the office was used. Clearly the original goal of a 25-percent reduction in overhead was understated. The increase in April and May overhead was due to the purchase of the all-purpose printers-copiers-scanners for the staff, as well as fees and prepayment of certain costs associated with installing high-speed internet service and separate telephone lines. Web conferencing was used more extensively in subsequent months and overran the original estimate by a factor of 2 during the year. Most of the $5,000 contingency allowance was not used.

CRITIQUE OF CASE STUDY 2-9 (AJAX Technologies)
The Goal: [Cut Defect Cost to < 1 % of Sales in 6 Months]

The experience of the new QA manager was obvious when looking at his action during his first two weeks on the job. His action plan (Figure 2.16) met all of the desired goal characteristics. Also, the Quality Cost Control Matrix (Figure 2.15) was far more detailed than most plans for assigning responsibility for quality defect prevention.

Case 2-9 AJAX Technologies

Goal characteristic	Was characteristic met?
Actually set	Yes
Quantitative	Yes
Obtainable	Yes
Timeline	Yes
Responsibility set	Yes

The Tactical Plan: We will forego developing a separate detailed TP for AJAX because Figure 2.16 contains all the normal elements of a good tactical plan except the start and completion dates.

Chapter 3

Figure 3.23 Control Chart for Tracking Monthly Defect Costs)

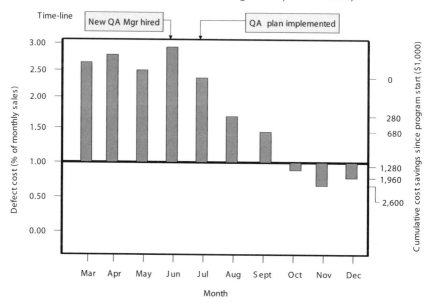

The Control Chart: Figure 3.23 shows a CC for tracking quality defect costs for the remainder of 2003. Significant improvement was made in reducing defect costs during the last half of 2003. A new goal was set for 2004:

- Reduce defect cost to 0.4 percent of monthly sales.

3.6 A FEW ADDITIONAL COMMENTS ON MONITORING GOALS

The tactical plans and control charts used in this chapter are, of course, not the only ways to plan activities and chart performance against goals. Experience has shown that unless the action plan to achieve a goal is clearly spelled out, getting the desired result can be evasive. There's an old saying that "people respond to what you **inspect**, no what you **expect**." Using a control chart has a way of conveying to people that you are serious about achieving the goal. Your odds of making the goal are a lot better if you monitor things while they are happening, rather than after they have happened.

Overview of Value-Based Risk Management*

4.1 WHAT THE READER WILL LEARN FROM THIS CHAPTER

- Why ordinary risk management methods yield ordinary results
- The Value-Based Risk Management (VBRM) approach
- The VBRM bubble chart
- Uncertainty benchmarking
- Mitigation analysis
- Uncertainty grading

4.2 INTRODUCTION

This chapter will discuss the third and fourth key tasks of bubble management: identifying opportunities and risks, and developing VBRM bubble charts for improving opportunities and mitigating risks. Let's start by defining risk. Depending on whom you ask, risk can have many definitions:
- the chance or probability of suffering some harm or loss
- unwanted and/or undesirable outcomes
- exposure or openness to possible loss, damage, or danger
- something involving or related to unknown or uncertain danger
- the likelihood, chance, or probability that something bad will occur

*(Material used in this chapter is excerpted and adapted from an article submitted by Kevin M. Curran in 2005 for publication in AACE International's magazine Cost Engineering.)

Chapter 4

To facilitate communication and preclude miscommunication, VBRM relies on terminology familiar to the general public (i.e., common word use). Do you want more risk in your life? Of course not! That's what most people understand about risk – they don't want it. In VBRM, risk is generally defined as the bad stuff we'd like to remove or avoid. In VBRM terminology, risk represents unfavorable results or outcomes (e.g., the amount of potential cost overrun in a capital investment, the amount that sales can fall short of forecast, the amount an ROA can fall short of its goal).

If business offered only risks, things would be dismal and no project or investment would be worth undertaking. Therefore, there must be an upside along the way. The potential favorable outcomes that management always hopes to attain or capture are called opportunities in VBRM.

When looking at the big picture, all decisions and plans have both good and bad potential. That is to say, decisions and plans have opportunities and risks. In VBRM terminology, the collection of opportunities and risks represent the uncertainty in the decision. (See Appendix 4-1 at the end of this chapter for a graphic definition of risk and uncertainty, Figures 4.15 through 4.19.)

Uncertainty contains both risks and opportunities, with risks reflected in the unfavorable side of forecasts (e.g., lower earnings-per-share than forecasted) and opportunities reflected in the favorable side of forecasts (e.g., higher earnings-per-share than forecasted). Technically speaking, the terms "uncertainty management," "uncertainty analysis," and "uncertainty assessment" are more descriptive than "risk management," "risk analysis," and "risk assessment," which imply that management focus should be limited to the unfavorable aspects of a plan or decision. An overwhelming majority of managers have some understanding of what is implied by risk management, for example, than what is implied by uncertainty management. VBRM retains these three risk terms because they are so deeply ensconced in the world of measuring and managing uncertainty.

Many organizations devote serious attention to risk management and its four phases:

- assessment
- analysis
- mitigation
- control

Overview of Value-Based Risk Management

With rare exception, however, organizations have been plagued by:
1) high resource requirements to complete the assessment and analysis phases (i.e., identifying, quantifying, and analyzing uncertainties), 2) quality issues (predicted versus actual results), and 3) difficulties obtaining senior management support. For some, the assessment and analysis phases alone can involve weeks, or even months, of effort. This is especially true for, but not limited to, public sector endeavors. The result has been a lot of frustration.

Then along came Value-Based Risk Management (VBRM). Under VBRM, resources are re-allocated to the mitigation and control phases while simultaneously improving the reliability of the assessment and analysis phase results. In other words, VBRM optimizes resources to improve dramatically an organization's mitigation and control capabilities. VBRM has proven to be a significant benefit to organizations and attractive to senior management for decisions ranging from small to megasize – up to more than $12 billion in value.

In the rest of this chapter we intend to explain VBRM in the context of its application to improving the reliability of business decision making. VBRM can be applied to any decision problem where numbers are combined to determine a bottom line. In Chapter 5, we will show how it quantifies the goal setting and performance appraisal process.

4.3 ORDINARY METHODS GET ORDINARY RESULTS

A typical (i.e., ordinary) assessment and analysis usually succeeds in identifying a forecast's variability and produces a list of risks. Other information is sometimes gathered that might include a risk register (as it is called by many organizations) and some form of risk categorization (e.g., high, medium, and low). Although these efforts surface uncertainties, the majority of those which gain attention and resources do not substantially impact the bottom line.

In many cases, risks are the primary or sole focus of such analyses; The opportunities, which can have even more impact than the risks in some plans, fail to get detailed scrutiny. The high expense incurred in the assessment and analysis phases of a study can greatly diminish the resources available to focus on the more beneficial mitigation and control phases. Consequently, mitigating actions are not usually analyzed in detail for both their negative and positive contribution – certainly not to the level of detail applied to the base forecast.

Chapter 4

Remember that mitigating actions can have the potential to add risk in addition to their desired effect of lowering risk. Furthermore, because of the high resource drain to conduct typical assessments and analyses, many organizations are reluctant to re-assess and re-analyze decisions or plans regularly during implementation. This reluctance severely restricts any control efforts. The initial assessment and analysis at an early stage in planning is often the only such evaluation conducted during the plan's life-cycle. To achieve desired results, uncertainty must be regularly and frequently measured if it is to be managed! Correcting these deficiencies in current risk management practices requires a new approach.

4.4 VBRM – THE EXTRAORDINARY APPROACH

Improving risk management practices presents several challenges. First, the time devoted to the assessment and analysis phases must be reduced – in some cases drastically. Second, the quality of analysis results (recommended forecast adjustments, risk and opportunity rankings, etc.) must be assured. Third, during the mitigation phase, actions must be thoroughly analyzed without impacting resources. Fourth, the approach must improve management's (and thus the organization's) risk management skills. Finally, assessments and analyses must be rapid and reliable so that ongoing monitoring of uncertainties can enable true risk and opportunity control.

4.4.1　How VBRM Addresses These Challenges

VBRM uses a combination of well-known and recently-developed technologies and methods to overcome the five key challenges facing today's risk management efforts.

Reducing Analysis Time.

VBRM employs the original Range Estimating[1] process to reduce assessment and analysis time while not degrading quality. Range Estimating is a synergistic combination of the application of Pareto's Law, Monte Carlo Simulation, and input/output heuristics.[2] Range

---

[1] Curran, M.W. Range Estimating: Measuring Uncertainty and Reasoning with Risk, Cost Engineering 31, 3 (1989): 18-26.

[2] Heuristics is the study of methods that are valuable for empirical research, but are unproven or incapable of proof.

Overview of Value-Based Risk Management

Estimating, as it was first conceived, developed, and coined by Decision Sciences Corporation (DSC) in the early 1970s, included both a proprietary simulation algorithm (partly based on Monte Carlo Simulation) and a methodology for identifying and quantifying uncertainty. The methodology applied the Critical Variance Matrix (also a development of DSC) in order to surface key uncertainty drivers. Range Estimating and the Critical Variance Matrix have been the topic of numerous articles over the past three decades and are not covered here. The reliability of Range Estimating, however, has been proven over more than 35 years of application.

VBRM relies on a proven method for gathering the right information regarding forecast uncertainty – including hidden risks and opportunities that decision makers typically don't realize exist. The methodology applied to gathering this information is called Provoke-To-Evoke®.[3] Persons involved in the plan and its forecasts are "provoked" in order to "evoke" the correct information. The process is based on the psychology of how estimates and forecasts are prepared and, as such, leads those involved to identify and come to terms with the various unintentional biases that creep into virtually all forecasts. In the majority of cases, uncertainties even unknown to the decision makers are uncovered. These are hidden uncertainties and, if not exposed, often lead to lackluster bottom lines.

Let's track a VBRM data gathering session. The session typically occurs over a one-to-two day period, regardless of decision size or type. (The amount of time required for VBRM sessions depends on the depth of analysis desired by management and the number of business areas to be assessed; more than two days are required in some cases.) All information required for a VBRM study is gathered during this session. The first result of the session is a *probabilistic analysis* which provides:

- the probability (expressed as a percentage) of achieving the forecast goal
- the realistic worst-case financial scenario (e.g., how low the ROA can realistically get)
- the amount of forecast or bottom line adjustment necessary to achieve management's desired level of confidence in the plan

---

[3]Provoke-To-Evoke® is a registered service mark of Decision Sciences Corporation, Saint Louis, Missouri.

Chapter 4

Figure 4.1 VBRM Bubble Chart

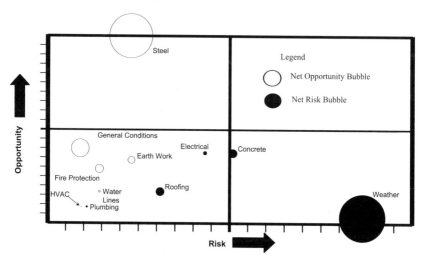

* a ranking of risks and opportunities that guide management's actions for mitigating and controlling uncertainty
* how to allocate any required adjustments among the key risk or opportunity elements within the plan

In addition to these traditional results, VBRM provides a bubble chart (Figure 4.1). All of this will be demonstrated in Case Study 4-1.

4.4.2 VBRM Bubble Chart

The VBRM bubble chart (Figure 4.1) shows each uncertainty driver as a bubble. The diameter of each bubble represents the amount of net risk or net opportunity associated with the driver. For each driver, the amount of risk the driver contributes is subtracted from the amount of opportunity it contributes. If the result is negative, the driver has net risk. If the result is positive, the driver has net opportunity.

Net opportunity and net risk are somewhat analogous to profit and loss on business income statements (P&Ls). If there is more risk than opportunity, then there is a net risk (loss). If there is more opportunity than risk, then there is a net opportunity (profit).

A driver having net risk contributes more unfavorable than favorable potential. Such drivers are depicted as solid bubbles on the bubble chart. On the other hand, a driver having net opportunity contributes more favorable than unfavorable potential. These drivers appear as unfilled bubbles on the bubble chart. (Determination of net risk and net opportunity is not a simple calculation. It takes into account a myriad of variables: the driver's input range, the sensitivity of the bottom line to changes in the driver, the probability the driver will experience an overrun or underrun, etc.)

The horizontal axis (Risk) shows each driver's relative contribution to total risk – its potential for creating an unfavorable result at the bottom line. The vertical axis (Opportunity) shows each driver's relative contribution to total opportunity – its potential for creating a favorable result at the bottom line. The risks and opportunities are calculated based on a variety of measures including the driver's probability of inducing a favorable or unfavorable bottom line, amount of the driver's potential variation, and its impact at the bottom line.

A driver whose bubble appears close to the origin has a small potential impact on the bottom line's variability. One whose bubble appears far from the origin has a large potential impact on bottom line variability. In Figure 4.1, Steel appears at the maximum level on the opportunity scale. Weather, although being the largest risk, does not reach the maximum level along that axis. This means that steel contributes slightly more to total opportunity than weather contributes to total risk. Management should focus first and foremost on capturing the opportunity in steel (its net opportunity bubble is just slightly larger than weather's net risk bubble) and only then address the risk in weather (if at all controllable by changing the overall construction schedule, the build sequence, moving toward prefabrication, etc.). Those drivers toward the middle of the chart contain a mixture of favorable and unfavorable potential.

The bubble chart, derived from data collected during the VBRM session, is the primary tool used by management to identify mitigation actions. This example is based on an actual VBRM analysis. Management decided to capture the potential opportunity in steel by purchasing nearly all steel for this three-year capital investment on the first day of implementation. This mitigation action avoided the rapid increase in steel prices that occurred shortly thereafter. Knowing the probability of this occurring, its potential impact on the bottom line, its relationship with other costs in the decision, and a probabilistically-determined profile of potential costs due to steel changes provided crucial information not generally available to management. This decision saved substantially more capital than the carrying cost of ordering the steel early. This decision would not have been made had management not known the bottom line impact this opportunity provided and its true likelihood of occurring. From the discussion above, the reader can see why the VBRM bubble chart is a core element of the bubble management process.

Ensuring Reliability of Results.
To ensure reliable analyses, VBRM applies an "uncertainty benchmark". The uncertainty benchmark is a proprietary concept developed by DSC based on more than four thousand analyses. VBRM's uncertainty benchmark sets a minimum level of bottom-line uncertainty (variation) that should be expected from an analysis. This benchmark amount is known for virtually all types of capital investments across all industries and sectors (new plants, information technology projects, facility rebuilds, etc.). The benchmark is custom developed for individual organizations when it's applied to ongoing processes such as operating budgets, sales forecasts, etc.

If an analysis' results pass the uncertainty benchmark, then the management team has likely identified and adequately quantified the forecast's key uncertainties. Analyses that fail the uncertainty bench-

Figure 4.2 The Uncertainty Benchmark Horn

Uncertainty Benchmarks of the control estimates of two different projects

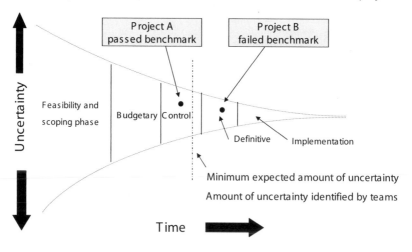

mark most likely understated the uncertainties – often significantly. An overwhelming majority of analyses that fail the uncertainty benchmark wind up with actual results that are even beyond the worst-case scenario predicted by the analysis.

If an analysis fails benchmark, management has some recourse. It can readily revisit its assumptions and logic in order to uncover overlooked or understated uncertainties. The uncertainty benchmark provides a valuable early warning system so that unreliable analysis results are not used for decision making. With very few exceptions, analyses passing the uncertainty benchmark met their budgetary goals without having to alter the original intent of the plan (i.e., without redefining or restructuring the plan).

Uncertainty benchmark results are conveyed to management using two graphics. The first is an uncertainty benchmark horn (Figure 4.2). The horn represents the decision or planning life-cycle beginning from the left side of the horn. The height of the horn at any given point represents the amount of uncertainty that can be expected from an analysis at that stage of the planning life-cycle. The far right hand represents the actual – when the plan is complete and there is no uncertainty. Here, the horn comes to a point indicating no potential bottom line variation.

Figure 4.2 depicts the uncertainty benchmark of the capital portion of two facility improvement projects (A and B). Both were evaluated when they were in a control estimate phase (i.e., estimates where equipment specification and quotes were available).

The dashed, vertical line in Figure 4.2 represents the minimum amount of uncertainty that the management team should have identified and quantified during their assessment and analysis. Location of this particular uncertainty benchmark line is based on the capital investment size, type of project, stage in planning and execution life-cycle, portions of the capital investment under lump-sum contract, etc. For this reason, the uncertainty benchmark line does not usually appear at the boundary of a particular stage but, rather, some place between the boundaries.

Passing uncertainty benchmark scores (we will discuss scores shortly) are to the left of the uncertainty benchmark line. Failing scores are to the right of the uncertainty benchmark line and indicate that the team failed to identify the minimum amount of uncertainty expected from their assessment and analysis. In other words, scores to the right of the benchmark line represent less uncertainty than should be expected from the analysis.

Failing the uncertainty benchmark is one of the strongest indicators that problems are in store if the analysis results are used for decision making. More important, it indicates that management is likely unaware, or is choosing to ignore, significant uncertainty! It is also often an indicator that the plan itself is in jeopardy.

Because Project A passed the benchmark, the team has likely identified and correctly quantified the significant uncertainties. Unfortunately, Project B failed the benchmark. Its management team has either missed significant uncertainties (risks and/or opportunities) or understated the impact of the uncertainties that they have identified, or some combination of both. In short, their assessment and analysis results are likely understating the uncertainties for this plan. Using Project B's faulty analysis for decision making is a risk in itself.

The second uncertainty benchmark graphic is the bar chart shown in Figure 4.3, which quantifies the difference between the minimum amount of uncertainty expected from the analysis and the amount which was identified by management. This information, provided when an analysis fails the uncertainty benchmark, is critical for notifying the decision team and the decision makers of the extent of the potential error in their results.

Here, the minimum amount of uncertainty (in this case, total cost variation) expected for Project B is $13.8 million. However, the assessment and analysis identified only $11.5 million in potential cost variation. Therefore, there is a minimum of $2.3 million in bottom line variation which likely has not been identified and/or quantified. This information warns decision makers that the analysis is likely understating uncertainty by at least $2.3 million. This missing uncertainty could belong to the unfavorable side (risk), the favorable side (opportunity), or some mixture of both.

At this point, management must re-evaluate the information they provided during the VBRM session in order to locate the missing uncertainty or, at the least, they must provide very specific information as to why this particular plan is less uncertain than others of similar nature (i.e., why they are better in controlling uncertainty than others). In most cases, management uncovers one or more errors in their evaluation of uncertainties.

Overview of Value-Based Risk Management

Figure 4.3 The Uncertainty Benchmark

Project B - Control level estimate

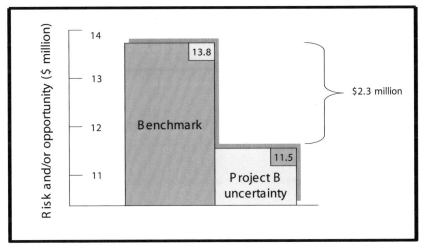

Project B uncertainty analysis failed to identify a minimum of $2.3 million in risk and/or opportunity

Incorporating Mitigation Analysis.

VBRM helps management identify potential mitigating actions regarding risks and opportunities; then probabilistically analyzes the impact of those actions. During the VBRM data-gathering session, quantitative information is gathered concerning mitigating actions, options, or alternatives. This data is subsequently analyzed to provide a detailed, probabilistic mitigation analysis.

Such analyses often expose actions which actually introduce more potential problems rather than less, or which demonstrate that the mitigating action is not likely to provide a benefit favorable enough when compared to its cost. Because mitigating data is gathered during the VBRM session, the impact on the organization's resources is negligible.

There are two common flaws related to mitigation: 1) management taking credit for mitigating actions before they are realized, and 2) not probabilistically analyzing the impact of the mitigating actions at all. The first of these flaws is often seen in analyses that fail uncertainty benchmark. In these cases, the decision team has taken credit for mitigating actions during the analysis. In so doing, they truncate the amount of potential risk or opportunity. The outcome is predictable: an analysis that understates the real amount of bottom line variability. The second flaw is also common – the analysis is completed, everyone assumes that the mitigating actions will work to the extent assumed, and no further analysis is conducted.

VBRM incorporates mitigation analysis during the assessment and analysis phases, thus protecting against the aforementioned flaws. Like the assessment and analysis of the base plan, the mitigation analysis is probabilistic. Keeping with our capital investment example, Figure 4.4 illustrates the result of a mitigation analysis derived from a VBRM session; the figure shows two mitigating actions and their combined effect.

Notice that the first mitigating action "Contracting Alternative" has potential not only for positive savings, but negative as well. In other words, it has the potential to increase cost as well as reduce it. This potential increase is equivalent to a negative savings. There is roughly a 65% probability that implementing the Contracting Alternative option will reduce cost and a 35% probability that it will increase cost. Decision makers need to evaluate this mitigation action in order to determine whether it is worth its potential risk.

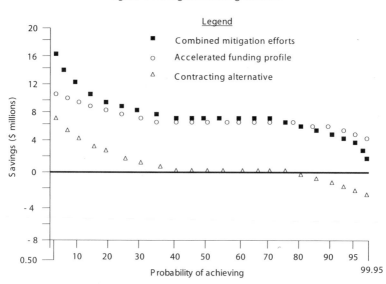

Figure 4.4 Mitigation Savings Profiles

Overview of Value-Based Risk Management

The second mitigation action is "Accelerate Funding Profile" (i.e., to front-load the infusion of capital to take advantage of some early purchases, thereby hedging various market prices). This action has a 65-70 % probability of saving roughly $7 million, and a 10% probability of saving $10 million.

Finally, the "Combined Mitigation Efforts" curve shows the potential savings if both actions are taken. This curve shows that there is a potential savings from across the spectrum of probabilities. However, there is roughly a 20% probability that the Combined Mitigation efforts will be less favorable than the Accelerated Funding Profile alone. (The Combined Mitigation Efforts curve falls below the Accelerated Funding Profile curve at and to the right of the 80% probability.) At its worst case, the Combined Mitigation Efforts option diminishes the potential savings by approximately $4 million. The Combined Mitigation Efforts curve crosses over the Accelerated Funding Profile curve because of the potential for the Contracting Alternative to induce cost overruns, thus reducing the savings in some scenarios.

The information provided by this mitigation analysis resulted in the U.S. Department of Energy significantly modifying the funding profile for this particular project in order to implement these mitigating actions. Unlike many projects where hundreds of millions of dollars are being invested, this project is on time and on budget.

Improving Risk Management Skills.

Reducing assessment and analysis phase resources enables management to refocus their effort on improving their ability to identify and quantify uncertainty. A feedback mechanism is required to enable this ongoing improvement process. VBRM introduces "Uncertainty Grading" to meet this need.

Uncertainty grading compares the plan's current analysis results with one or more prior analyses conducted for the same plan – typically, those used to check regularly the status of the plan's uncertainties. Using various algorithms, management's ability to identify and quantify uncertainty is reported using terms familiar to anyone – percentile and letter grades. Uncertainty grading provides a "lessons learned" feedback to management while the plan is still in progress. This improves current and future analyses in which management participates. An interpretation of uncertainty grading scores is shown in Figure 4.5.

Chapter 4

Figure 4.5 Uncertainty Grading

Numerical grade	Letter grade	Interpretation
90 ...100%	A	SUPERIOR ...Even hidden, uncontrollable , and global Issues do not escape the team s scrutiny. Team has good grasp of probabilities of achieving forecasts in key variables.
80 - 89%	B	ABOVE AVERAGE ...Team possesses ability to correctly assess uncertainty when facilitated. Assessment of probabilities of achieving forecasts is above average.
70 - 79%	C	AVERAGE ...Team has some difficulty identifying and quantifying the most extreme risks and opportunities. Team has some difficulty identifying the true probability of achieving forecasts.
60 - 69%	D	BELOW AVERAGE ...Team has difficulty identifying and/or considering issues not fully under its control. Over-optimism and/or over-pessimism frequently come into play.
0 ...59%	F	POOR ...Team has difficulty imagining that actuals can vary from forecasts by other than minor degrees and/or the team has difficulty understanding its overall exposure to uncertainty.

The uncertainty grading process evaluates the consistency of management's assessments and its tracking toward the actual. All plans have potential variation; simply comparing the analysis to the actual does not provide a correct grading of management ability. Therefore, tracking against prior analyses of the same plan is essential in measuring skills development. Uncertainty grading cannot be delayed until the completion of each plan. Otherwise, valuable management improvement opportunities would be lost during that time.

Uncertainty grading involves complex algorithms. Although these algorithms can generate an "F" grade under various conditions, there is one scenario that is easy to understand. The algorithms will automatically generate an "F" for any area where the current range (low-to-high potential outcome) provided by management exceeds one already provided in a prior analysis. In most such cases, management failed to quantify adequately the real uncertainty in that particular area during the prior analysis. Mathematically, this is saying that the experience management is gaining as the plan is implemented is making them more uncertain about the plan itself.

With extremely rare exception, however, uncertainty decreases over time – not increases! Receiving an "F" in these cases means that managers have fallen into a familiar trap. They aren't comfortable putting a wide-enough range on the area's potential outcomes in the earlier stage of planning. Stated in clear yet painful words, management is actually saying: "I don't know enough about it to provide a wide range. I only know enough to provide the original single-point forecast." Such thought processes are the bane of successful planning and require a change in corporate mindset. The new paradigm of thinking, however, will help achieve great future success.

The grading process does not simply involve determining how well, or poorly, a team assesses uncertainty. If the decision's scope does not significantly change (or if scope changes can be separated from the originally analyzed plan), the grading can be applied to specific types of uncertainties such as sales forecasting, capital investment estimating, and production cost forecasting, in addition to the overall plan's grade.

In one case, for example, an organization was consistently pessimistic concerning a certain type of capital cost. This pessimism generated additional, unneeded contingency allowances that detracted from other investment opportunities. Applying VBRM uncertainty grading to a few of the organization's decisions identified this flaw and its impact on the bottom line. Subsequent decisions benefited from management's knowledge of this pessimism and its quantitative impact on the bottom line. Management's ability to assess this particular uncertainty improved the overall organization because it was then able to free up valuable capital.

An added benefit to uncertainty grading is its ability not only to identify those who might be attempting to "game" the process for their own purposes, but also to quantify by how much they are attempting to sway the results. This benefit protects the integrity of the overall process.

Frequent And Regular Analyses.
Like other forecasting characteristics (time, quantities, prices, etc.), uncertainty cannot be effectively managed unless it is periodically measured. Decisions are made, actuals materialize, and new information is gained during the plan's life-cycle. Uncertainty profiles are directly affected by these events; decision makers need to be informed of what lies ahead at critical points in the plan's progress.

By reducing assessment and analysis cost and time, ensuring the reliability of analysis results, and analyzing mitigating actions, VBRM enables decision makers to re-assess uncertainty regularly. This benefit ensures that risks and opportunities will be effectively controlled by giving decision makers the most up-to-date information available while expending minimal resources. In addition, this benefit provides for easy assessment of the impact of various mitigation ideas and plan alternatives (i.e., options) throughout the plan's life-cycle.

4.4.3   To Sum Up

The purpose of risk management is not to identify, quantify, mitigate, and control every iota of uncertainty. Senior managers know and appreciate the fact that a sensible balance must be met – a balance between the amount of effort applied and the amount of benefit obtained. More is not better when it comes to risk management. In fact, the opposite is true – more effort often degrades the results and the subsequent outcome.

Value-Based Risk Management re-allocates resources to those most critical phases while simultaneously improving the quality and reliability of the assessment and analysis. VBRM can significantly improve an organization's ability to manage uncertainties rather than simply measure them. That's where the real value of risk management lies.

Now let's look at a case study implementing VBRM.

CASE STUDY 4-1 AJAX REFINING (Implementing VBRM)

The Situation: AJAX Refining is a large petroleum company operating six refineries throughout the United States and Canada. Recent marketing analysis indicated that conditions were right to build new refinery capacity for handling heavier crude oil supplies expected over the next decade. However, large cost overruns for a recent major refinery upgrade left the senior management gun-shy about the company's ability to estimate and bring projects in on schedule and budget. The VP of Marketing had a solution.

The Proposed Solution: The Marketing VP had heard about a concept called Value-Based Risk Management (VBRM) that had proven very helpful in avoiding project cost overruns. After the consultants made a presentation to the senior management of AJAX, they were hired to

Overview of Value-Based Risk Management

perform an analysis of the planned new refinery. The scope of the analysis included cost-only data gathering, evaluation, and reporting of recommendations. Deliverables included:

- The probability of not exceeding the new refinery budget
- An estimate of the best and worst case actual cost for the project
- A prioritized list of critical cost elements and the dollar amount each contributed to the project
- The amount of budget contingency needed for an acceptable level of confidence
- An estimate of expected minimum versus actual amount of uncertainty identified by the AJAX decision team
- The minimum amount of unreported uncertainty if the project team's inputs failed benchmark

A decision team of eight AJAX employees was assigned to work with the consultants.

The Numbers: The data gathering and analysis phases consisted of the following activities: 1) identifying the critical cost elements, 2) collecting essential data on the critical elements, 3) development of the simulation model, 4) simulations applying the model, and 5) initial review, benchmarking, and interpretation of results. Activities 1 and 2 above took between one and two days with the decision team and consultants constantly engaged. The Monte Carlo aspects of the simulation process were closely monitored by the consultants to avoid expanding the analysis into too many cost elements because including too many uncertainty drivers understates true uncertainty (risks and opportunities) and introduces iatrogenic risk. Iatrogenic risk is the understatement of true risk in a plan. It is relatively common and is often caused by ad hoc risk analysts applying faulty risk analysis practices. (For those interested in why, see Appendix 4-2 at the end of this chapter).

Figure 4.6 summarizes the cost uncertainty inputs reached during data gathering. For simplicity, the number of initial cost elements has been reduced to twelve and each designated simply as "cost element 1", "cost element 2", etc. Obviously, cost element 1 (total installed equipment cost) is the biggest hitter of all the cost elements. It has the highest overrun potential, carries the highest contingency, and, as we shall see shortly, has a substantial cost-mitigating potential compared to the other options.

Chapter 4

Some readers might be initially concerned that the probabilities provided by the decision team are not all 50%. The fact is this: forecasts are not prepared at the 50% percentile values. Almost all forecast elements have more than a 50% chance of meeting their goal or less than a 50% chance. This has been proven over several thousand assessments. Management's belief that the forecasts which they provide, or which are provided to them for review, are completely "unbiased" is fatally flawed. In many cases, risk analysts will choose 50% for most or all elements because they simply haven't aggressively addressed the issue of confidence in the numbers in the depth that is required for today's decision making environment. Worse yet, because of the combinatorial nature of forecasting, the bottom line would not have a 50% chance of success even if all the inputs to it are at that level of confidence.

Figure 4.7 lists some key information gathered from the team prior to the VBRM analysis compared to those determined by the consultants' analysis. Notice that the project team thought they had at least an 85 percent chance of bringing the project in within the initial $423 million estimate plus $25 million contingency; the VBRM analysis showed substantial pessimism in the estimate (i.e., why they are better in controlling uncertainty than others). Notice also the

Figure 4.6 Initial Cost Inputs

Cost element	Units	Original target estimate	Probability (%)	Cost low	Cost high
1	$1000	261,000	0	268,830	275,000
2	$1000	10,401	0	10,700	11,000
3	$1000	15,076		15,076	15,076
4	$1000	4,793	50	4,543	5,293
5	$1000	4,537	85	4,000	4,837
6	$1000	10,178	75	9,178	10,928
7	$1000	6,892	40	6,592	7,392
8	$1000	5,203	75	4,683	6,504
9	%	5	50	4	6
10	%	9	50	8	11
11	$1000	9,677		9,677	9,677
12	$1000	12,137		12,137	12,137

☐ No significant uncertainty   ▢ Equally likely to overrun and underrun

▢ More likely to underrun   ▢ More likely to overrun

Probability = Probability the cost element's actual will not overrun its target
Cost low   = Value where the element's actual has < 1% chance of being lower
Cost high = Value where the element's actual has < 1% chance of being higher

Overview of Value-Based Risk Management

estimate of accuracy identified by the team indicated about an equal negative and positive accuracy. Figure 4.8 shows that the team passed benchmark because the amount of uncertainty identified was left of the minimum amount of expected uncertainty line on the uncertainty benchmark horn. Note that this team had extensive experience in preparing project cost estimates and that the

Figure 4.7 Values Determined by Decision Team vs. Analysis

Issue	Decision team s belief	Determined by VBRM
Initial project estimate (no contingency)	$ 423,000,000	$ 423,000,000
Contingency amount needed	$ 25,000,000	$ 14,865,000 (for 90% confidence)
Estimated total project cost	$ 448,000,000	$ 437,865,000
Confidence of not over running	85%	90 %
Estimate accuracy	-5% to + 5%	+0.6% to + 5.2%
Lowest possible cost	$ 420,000,000	$ 426,559,000
Highest possible cost	$ 450,000,000	$ 445,777,000

Figure 4.8 The Uncertainty Benchmark Horn

Uncertainty Benchmark of the control estimates for AJAX Refining project

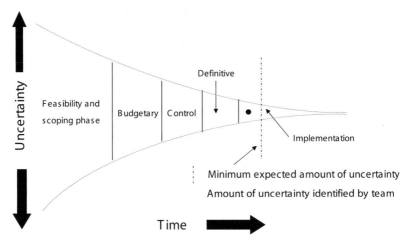

Chapter 4

Figure 4.9 Project Overrun Profile

Probability of overrun	Cost ($1000)
99.95%	426,659
95%	429,986
90%	430,726
80%	431,850
70%	432,647
60%	433,289
50%	433,919
40%	434,691
30%	435,662
20%	436,727
10%	438,763
5%	440,990
0.05%	445,777

Figure 4.10 Project Contingency Profile

Desired confidence of not overrunning project	Required contingency ($1000)	Contingency percentage
99.95 %	21,879	5.2
95 %	17,092	4.0
90 %	14,865	3.5
80 %	12,892	3.0
70 %	11,764	2.8
60 %	10,793	2.6
50 %	10,021	2.4
40 %	9,108	2.2
30 %	8,749	2.1
20 %	7,952	1.9
10 %	6,828	1.6
5 %	6,088	1.4
0.05 %	2,661	0.6

Overview of Value-Based Risk Management

disparity between their assessment of confidence and VBRM's assessment are typical – even for teams with extensive experience in their industry.

Figure 4.9 shows the project overrun profile. From the table it can be seen that there is a 99.95 percent probability the project will not exceed $445.777 million and a 50 % chance it can be brought in for under $434 million. Figure

Figure 4.11 Project Contingency Allocation

Based on 90% chance of not overrunning project cost

Cost element from Fig 4.6	Percent of total contingency (%)	Contingency allocation ($1000)
1	82.3	12,234
2	5.2	773
3	3.4	505
4	3.2	476
5	2.2	327
6	1.4	208
7	0.7	104
8	0.5	74
11	0.4	59
12	0.3	46

Figure 4.12 VBRM Bubble Chart

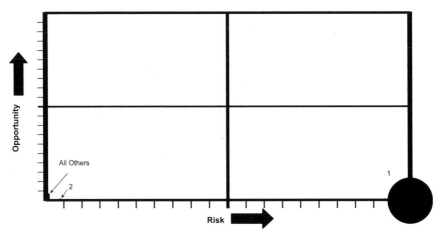

Figure 4.13 Mitigation Savings Profiles

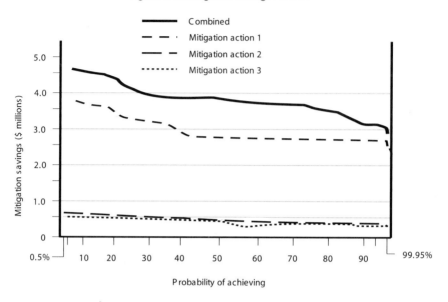

Figure 4.14 Unmitigated vs. Mitigated Uncertainty Profiles

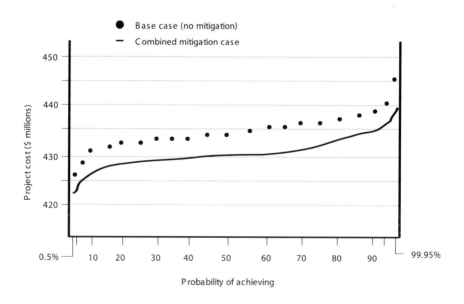

Overview of Value-Based Risk Management

4.10 shows the project contingency profile. To have a 90 percent confidence the project will not overrun the base estimate, a contingency of $14,865,000 is required (3.5 %); for a flip of the coin probability (50 %), $10,021,000 needs to be added. Of the twelve cost elements listed initially in Figure 4.6, element 1 requires most of the contingency (about 82%), with each of the other cost elements requiring significantly less (Figure 4.11). The allocation algorithm is complex and the sum of these adjustments does not add to exactly $14,865,000 due to rounding during the allocation calculations.

The VBRM bubble chart (Figure 4.12) shows that, of the twelve costs elements, two (elements 1 and 2) account for nearly all of the risk. None of the twelve cost elements contain significant opportunity. Clearly, the overrun potential for cost element 1 far outweighs all others.

Using data supplied by the project team during the data gathering session, the consultants analyzed the impacts of potential mitigation actions and developed new uncertainty profiles for the project cost based on those impacts (Figure 4.13). Mitigation savings curves for three potential actions are shown. None of the mitigation options introduced additional risk to the project; that is, none of the mitigating action profiles extended below the zero dollar savings line on Figure 4.13.

Figure 4.14 shows curves for the base case and the mitigated case using the combined mitigation values. Implementing the mitigation actions will not introduce additional risk and lowers total project cost under all levels of confidence. For most potential outcomes, there is the potential to save roughly $4 million by implementing the mitigation actions.

Conclusion: Armed with the analysis supplied by the consultants, the project team drafted tactical plans for the mitigation actions to get the benefits projected for mitigating some of the cost elements. (Some of the mitigating actions impact more than one cost element simultaneously.) In addition, control charts were prepared to track actual costs versus budget for all cost elements. Meetings were held each week with the senior managers to review status against budget. When the project was finally completed and all outstanding invoices paid, the project final cost tally was $ 434,212,000 – about a 53 percent probability level. By identifying and quantifying the uncertainties in this plan, VBRM also guided management to release approximately $11 million from this appropriation to be used in other investments.

Chapter 4

APPENDIX 4-1 Graphic Definition of Risk and Uncertainty

The five figures in Appendix 4-1 show a graphic definition of risk and uncertainty: 1) Figure 4.15 defines what we mean by a forecast – a single-point number, 2) Figure 4.16 conveys the concept of uncertainty, 3) Figure 4.17 defines the concept of risk and opportunity, 4) Figure 4.18 illustrates what we mean by net risk, and 5) Figure 4.19 shows the difference between uncertainty and net risk.

APPENDIX 4-2 Critical Element Uncertainty Identification

Monte Carlo Simulation (MCS) is a premier tool for performing analyses, particularly in its application to budget estimates. Like

Figure 4.15 The Forecast (target/goal) Defined

Figure 4.16 Uncertainty Defined

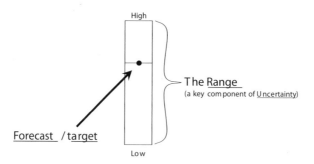

This g raphic is designed to convey the <u>concept</u> of u ncertainty. The qua ntification of uncertainty is <u>no t</u> simply a ma tter of cons idering an el ement's high a nd low value s (i.e., uncer tainty is no t equivalent to the ra nge). F or conceptual purpose's, h owever, the r ange (a m ajor component of calcula ting u ncertainty) can be thought of as a physical re presen tation of uncertainty.   More sophi sticated an alys es are req uired to determine uncertainty which include not only the range itsel f but bottom line se nsitivity, the loca tion of the f orecast within the range, and other critical de terminants. Fo r example, two eleme nts coul d hav e the sam e r ange   but the secon d element could hav e m ore uncertainty because it ca uses a wider varia tion at the bottom line than the first eleme nt. The use of simpl e ari thmetic does no t co rrectly quantify uncertainty and sho uld not be applied when a ssessing a plan' s uncertainties.

Overview of Value-Based Risk Management

Figure 4.17 Risk and Opportunity Defined

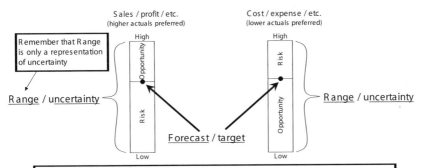

This graphic is designed to convey the concept of risk and opportunity. The determination of how much risk and / or opportunity an item or element in the plan contributes is a proprietary algorithm within VBRM and is not simply a matter of considering the range endpoints from the single-point forecast. The proprietary algorithms used to calculate risk and opportunity include adjustments for the sensitivity of the bottom line, the probability of the actual being higher or lower than forecast, the location of the forecast within the range, and other critical determinants. The use of simple arithmetic does not correctly quantify risk or opportunity and should not be applied to risk/opportunity ranking.

Figure 4.18 Net Risk and Net Opportunity Defined

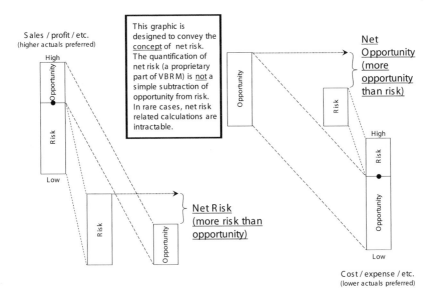

Chapter 4

Figure 4.19 Uncertainty vs. Net Risk

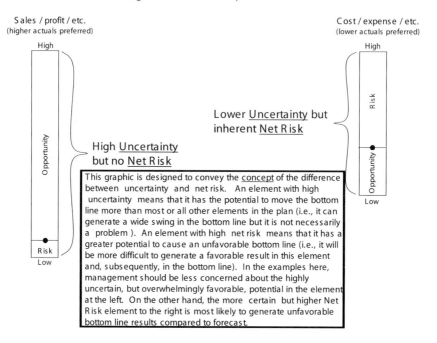

Figure 4.20 Just Right Inputs

Cost element	Target estimate ($)	Probability (%)	Low estimate ($)	High estimate ($)
A	19,000,000	50	8,000,000	30,000,000
B	38,000,000	50	16,000,000	60,000,000
C	30,000,000	50	15,000,000	45,000,000
Total	87,000,000	-	39,000,000	135,000,000

many highly-sophisticated analytical tools, errors can be made in applying MCS. One of the most frequent is assigning probability density functions (PDFs)ʹ, or probability distributions as they are more commonly known, to too many elements, typically resulting in serious understatement of both risk and opportunity.

The following cost example will demonstrate the magnitude of this iatrogenic risk. Two cases were considered: 1) a "just right" situation

Overview of Value-Based Risk Management

Figure 4.21 Too Many Inputs

Cost element	Target estimate ($)	Probability (%)	Low estimate ($)	High estimate ($)
A -1	10,000,000	50	5,000,000	15,000,000
A -2	4,000,000	50	2,000,000	6,000,000
A -3	5,000,000	50	1,000,000	9,000,000
B -1	15,000,000	50	10,000,000	20,000,000
B -2	11,000,000	50	2,000,000	20,000,000
B -3	7,000,000	50	2,000,000	12,000,000
B -4	5,000,000	50	2,000,000	8,000,000
C -1	10,000,000	50	8,000,000	12,000,000
C -2	7,000,000	50	4,000,000	10,000,000
C -3	13,000,000	50	3 ,000,000	23,000,000
Total	87,000,000	-	39,000,000	135,000,000

Figure 4.22 "Too Many" Verses "Just Right Analysis"

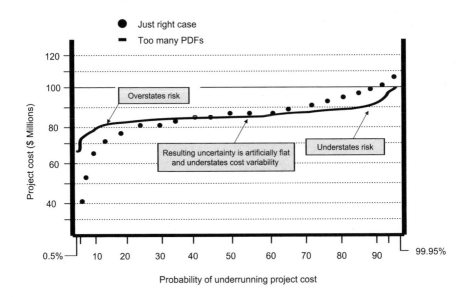

where three cost elements were used (Figure 4.20), and 2) a "too many" elements case (Figure 4.21).

In the first case, MCS was applied to cost elements A, B, and C. Values were selected so that the target estimate was the midpoint of each range and the confidence level of not overrunning the target was set at 50 percent (the probability). Although forecasts rarely have a 50% likelihood of occurrence, setting these restrictions ensures that the resulting differences for this example are not skewed. The second case dealt with the same plan, but was broken down into ten cost elements. Total costs and probabilities remained the same.

Simply breaking down the analysis from three items to ten causes the uncertainty profile to flatten dramatically (see Figure 4.22). As the number of PDFs increases, this flattening effect tends to overstate risk at low probabilities and understate risk at high probabilities. The result is inaccurate statistics and a plan likely to overrun the cost estimate.

An even more serious consequence is the tendency to low-ball the budget contingency (single-digit contingencies on projects of a hundred million dollars or more are common). Attempts to circumvent the problem of dealing with artificially low contingencies have misdirected some to apply PDFs to the contingencies rather than to the cost element dollars. Such an approach can often exclude the possibility of achieving negative contingency – commonly known as a "cost underrun" or, in VBRM terminology, "opportunity."

In short, the best approach is to restrict the analysis to the most critical uncertainty elements – let our old friend Pareto's rule work for us. VBRM ensures that the correct elements of a forecast, and the appropriate number of them, are evaluated in order to avoid this iatrogenic ("self-induced") risk[4]. There are other sources of iatrogenic risk. However, in-depth coverage of these sources is beyond the scope of this book.

---

[4] Iatrogenic Risk is a term coined by Decision Sciences Corporation to describe the understatement of uncertainty which results from analyzing the wrong or too many forecast elements. The understatement of uncertainty is in itself a risk and the term iatrogenic risk was originally defined as "analyst-induced" or, "analyst-caused" or "self-induced" risk. This type of risk (the understatement of true risk) occurs frequently when persons not steeped in the psychology of forecasting and the nuances of Monte Carlo Simulation begin applying off-the-shelf Monte Carlo software packages to their forecasts.

The Bubble
Management Approach

5.1 WHAT THE READER WILL LEARN FROM THIS CHAPTER:

- How the original appraisal concept was structured
- Flaws in the original concept
- How VBRM overcomes the flaws
- How the Bubble Management concept works, with some case study illustrations
- The use of Performance Translation Tables

5.2 INTRODUCTION

This chapter pulls together all the elements of the Bubble Management process, ending with rating the performance of executives.

Those who have done it know that appraising the performance of subordinates frequently ends up as a traumatic experience for both the boss and subordinate. It need not be. The secret to conducting an effective performance appraisal that avoids conflict or misunderstandings lies in developing mutually acceptable quantitative performance measurement standards.

In this chapter we will show how to evaluate managers against performance in a way that will improve the overall performance of the organization. Recall that in Chapter 2 we showed the merits of setting two levels for each goal: a commitment level and a target level. We discussed the need for different goals for top corporate executives versus middle managers. We covered the need to set short-range, mid-range and long-range goals.

In this chapter, we will discuss the problem of measuring and rating performance for individual managers, including situations where several managers share a common goal. We will show how each can get a fair and equitable quantitative performance rating that reflects both the results achieved and also individual contribution toward obtaining the results. Finally, we will describe how to use the quantitative performance rating from this concept and translation tables to illustrate potential rewards to employees for their contribution to business unit performance (the actual level of award would, of course, be decided by the company's management in consultation with their compensation consultant).

5.2.1 Organizational Basis for Applying the Appraisal Concept

To illustrate how the Bubble Management approach works, we will use a business unit organization structure. Traditionally, the business unit consists of functional departments like sales and marketing, engineering, manufacturing, and accounting, each managed by a senior manager reporting to the business unit manager (see Figure 5.1). If the business unit markets more than one product, it might be organized along a matrix-structure, with one or more product line managers also reporting to the business unit manager.

In this structure, the product line managers act like the coaches of

Figure 5.1 Typical Business Unit Organization Structure

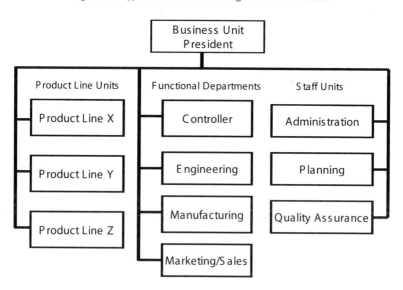

a football team. They send in the sales and marketing players in the first half of the game (pre-contract phase), whereas the engineering, manufacturing, and project management teams are deployed in the second half of the game (post-contract phase). The product line managers must coach both halves of the game, coordinating and controlling as necessary to maximize the performance of the product line team. Other staff managers such as quality assurance, planning, and administration could also make up the senior staff and report to the business unit manager. What we have then is a management team, with each manager responsible for a given assignment. And, as with a football team, the outcome will likely depend not only on individual performance, but also on shared performance.

5.2.2 Ingredients for an Effective Performance Appraisal

Three ingredients are essential for developing an effective performance appraisal:

- Setting quantitative goals
- Monitoring results against goal
- Evaluating performance against the goals

When these three elements are developed and documented, much of the subjective judgment can be eliminated from the performance appraisal because now both the boss and subordinate know:

- What results are expected
- By when
- How performance will be measured

Let's discuss each briefly.

Setting Goals

As discussed earlier (Chapter 2), one convenient way to set goals is to divide them into categories such as:

- Primary goals
- Secondary goals
- Management skills

The primary goal should be selected to concentrate on a single metric that significantly impacts the financial performance of the business

Chapter 5

unit. Examples are revenues, market share, return-on-assets (ROA), return-on-equity (ROE), earnings per share (EPS), and turnover. We will discuss suggested goals for organizations later in Chapters 6, 7, and 8.

Recall from Chapter 2 that secondary goals can be selected to concentrate on additional financial goals or other goals for improving performance of each business unit. Examples are budget, productivity improvement, inventory, and affirmative action. Secondary goals are somewhat tailored to each department. For example, if the sales department had recently experienced high attrition of sales personnel, it might need a vigorous new recruitment and training program as a secondary goal. Likewise, if factory productivity traditionally slips prior to a new labor contract, then a special program and goal may be needed by the manufacturing manager to offset or avoid productivity deterioration. Affirmative action goals to meet minority hiring targets might be an appropriate goal for all organizations.

There is no simple solution to the problem of setting the quantitative value for each primary and secondary financial goal. Later in this chapter, we will discuss some approaches that can help set goals that are reasonable. Remember that the goal can be impacted by factors that are outside the control of the people being measured against the goal. Usually, a thorough analysis of recent performance trends is needed, coupled with judgment as to what constitutes a fair and reasonable degree of improvement from recent performance. For example, a 20 percent improvement in booking might be a reasonable goal for the sales management if the forecast predicts a seller's market, whereas it would be unrealistic in the face of a pending recession. Consider the following case study concerning setting an unreasonable goal.

CASE STUDY 5-1 AJAX NUCLEAR*
(Setting an unreasonable goal)

The Situation: AJAX Nuclear was a 985-megawatt nuclear-fueled generating station in the eastern United States. Unscheduled outages had caused the station to shut down, once for eight days in January, and again for fourteen days in March. During these times, the utility was

---

*This case study is from *Production Spare Parts*, E. C. Moncrief et al, Industrial Press (2005), with permission.

The Bubble Management Approach

required to purchase replacement power, often at prices far in excess of their own cost to generate. The effect was putting a financial strain on the company, so a directive was sent down from top management to cut all possible corners to offset the revenue loss by year-end. The station supply-chain manager, who was given an edict to cut inventory by 18 percent, reacted as follows, "I don't know who came up with that number, but they must be out of their mind. Our inventory moves too slowly to just wave a magic wand and make it disappear."

The Proposed Solution: The supply-chain manager decided to put some numbers together to prove the goal was unattainable. He made two assumptions: 1) all current open purchase orders could be canceled, and 2) no new purchase orders would be written unless urgent. Investment recovery of excess inventory was not an option because of the write-off cost; therefore, all of the inventory decrease would have to come from working down existing stocks over the next eight months.

The Numbers: The station storeroom contained 46,665 stock items with a current inventory value of $38.2 million. To meet the 18-percent decrease, the stock would have to get down to $31.3 million. An item-by-item analysis showed that only about $2.9 million of current inventory could possibly work-off by year-end, not the $6.9 million required to meet the goal. Even more alarming was the conclusion that over 3,500 stock items would be in a backorder condition by year end if procurements were stopped. No estimate was made of the cost of these back orders.

The Conclusion: When presented with the numbers, the management cut the goal from 18 to 5 percent. The supply-chain manager put a poster on the office wall. It read "Don't Set Impossible Goals". Rating management skills is more subjective than rating primary and secondary goals. Later, in Chapter 6, we will list some management skills that could be considered during the appraisal process.

Monitoring results

We discussed this subject in detail in Chapter 3, so we won't repeat ourselves here. Remember that many factors can come into play when deciding how often a goal should be monitored, including: 1) whether you are monitoring a fast-moving or slow-moving event, 2) how useful more frequent feedback would be for taking corrective action, 3) whether the data base is adequately designed to capture frequent measurements, 4) the response time between making decisions on the information, and 5) how often management would really look at the results.

Setting Performance Standards

A key ingredient of the appraisal concept must be established – the performance standards. Too often, immature managers make the mistake of believing that they should be evaluated on "how hard they try" to achieve a goal, not on the results. Many are quick to disavow poor results, especially if they can conjure up a credible excuse. Most top managers will not accept excuses; most just want results. Basically, performance standards are used to translate actual performance into a rating scale that can be used for awarding merit increases or other compensation. We will cover that in detail in the following section.

5.3 THE ORIGINAL PERFORMANCE APPRAISAL CONCEPT

Back in the late 1970s, your lead author developed and used an appraisal concept for rating managers in a division of a Fortune 500 company. The organization of the division was essentially identical to the business unit structure shown in Figure 5.1. In the rest of this chapter, we will describe how the appraisal concept worked, discuss some of its flaws (section 5.4), and how it was improved significantly by applying Value-Based Risk Management techniques (section 5.7).

In our original appraisal concept, the overall rating focused on primary and secondary goals, and management skills. The primary and secondary ratings judged actual results, pure and simple. Some allowance or adjustment was made when results were impacted by events beyond the control of the manager. For example, if a shipment goal for the year was set based on a firm order backlog, say in January, and then a customer canceled an order in March (before shipment), the manufacturing manager was entitled to an adjustment on his shipment goal for the year. However, he could still be judged on how successful he was in offsetting the shop-scheduling void. This is where the management skills rating applied.

5.3.1 The Translation Table

Figure 5.2 shows an example of a translation table used for converting factory shipments into a rating scale. Any numerical rating scale can be used, but we liked the 1 to 6 scale. The procedure for translating shipments would be as follows:

    •First, actual shipments were compared to planned shipments.

    •Next, a percent of goal was calculated by dividing actual shipments by planned shipments and multiplying by 100.

    •Then, the percent of goal was converted to a rating using the predetermined translation table.

For example, if actual shipments were 102.5 % of goal (actual exceeds goal by 2.5 %), the results rating would be a 4.

Care must be used in establishing the translation table for each goal. Usually, this involves an analysis of recent variability in the goal under consideration. For example, a translation table for budget control might cover a range of only two or three percent of goal over the entire 1-to-6 rating scale; bookings (new orders) might justify spanning twenty or thirty percent of goal. Later, we will show how it is pos-

Figure 5.2 Translation Table for AJAX Factory Shipments

Shipments

Percent of goal	Results rating
Over 106.0	6
103.0 – 105.9	5
97.0 – 102.9	4
94.0 – 96.9	3
90.0 – 93.9	2
Under 90.0	1

Chapter 5

sible to avoid setting a translation table for each goal by using what we call the Performance Translation Table. But for now, take a look at the following case study for a manufacturer of electronic components:

CASE STUDY 5-2 AJAX ELECTRONICS
(Appraising a marketing manager)

The Situation: AJAX Electronics is a medium-size supplier of circuit boards to the general industry. It designs the circuit boards to customer specifications and bids for contracts against both domestic and foreign competitors. AJAX's only factory is in Indiana from where it ships finished components to both domestic and international markets. The business unit president was about to begin his annual appraisal of the performance of the marketing manager against goals for the last year. Before the year began, they had agreed to focus the appraisal on one primary goal (net bookings), three secondary goals (market share, sales and marketing budget, and proposal success rate), and three management skills (customer relations, communications, and quality of advice).

Figure 5.3 Translation Table for AJAX Electronics Sales
(Primary Goal: Increase Net Bookings)

Sales goal for 2004:	$162 million
Actual net sales:	$189 million
Percent of goal:	116.7

Percent of goal	Results rating
Over 115.0	6
106.0 – 114.9	5
95.0 – 105.9	4
85.0 – 94.9	3
80.0 – 84..9	2
Under 80.0	1

The Bubble Management Approach

Figure 5.4 Translation Table for AJAX Electronics Market Share
(Secondary Goal: Increase Market Share!)

Market share goal for 2004: 28 %
Actual market share: 31 %
Percent of goal: 110.7

Percent of goal	Results rating
Over 125.0	6
110.0 – 124.9	5
90.0 – 109.9	4
75.0 – 89.9	3
60.0 – 74..9	2
Under 60.0	1

Figure 5.5 Translation Table for AJAX Electronics Marketing Budget
(Secondary Goal: Meet Annual Budget!)

Budget goal for 2004: $ 12.6 million
Actual budget: $ 13.2 million
Percent of goal: 104.8

Percent of goal	Results rating
Under 97.0	6
97.0 -100.0	5
100.1 -103.0	4
103.1 -105.0	3
105.1- 107.0	2
Over 107.0	1

Chapter 5

They also agreed to the following weighting:
- Performance against primary goals = 50% of overall rating
- Secondary goals = 30%
- Management skills = 20%

The Numbers: Figures 5.3 through 5.6 show the year-end actual results against goal and the translation tables for the primary and three secondary goals. Ratings were 6 for bookings (sales), 5 for market share, 3 for budget and 5 for proposal award rate.

Figure 5.6 Translation Table for AJAX Electronics Proposals Awarded
(Secondary Goal: Meet Proposal Award Goal)

Proposal award goal for 2004:	25 %
Actual award:	27 %
Percent of goal:	108.0

Percent of goal	Results rating
Over 120.0	6
100.0 -119.9	5
85.0 - 99.9	4
75.0 - 84.9	3
65.0 - 74.9	2
Under 65.0	1

Figure 5.7 Management Skills Ratings

Management skills category	Marketing manager self-rating (a)	Business unit president rating
Customer relations	5	5
Communications	5	4
Quality of advise	5	5
Average rating	5.0	4.7

(a) as part of the appraisal process the marketing manager was asked by the president to rate his management skills.

The Bubble Management Approach

Figure 5.8 Calculation of Overall Performance Rating

Overall rating = (Primary goal weighting) (Primary goal rating)
+ (Secondary goal weighting) (Secondary goal rating)
+ (Management skills weighting) (Management skill rating)

= (0.50) (6.0) + (0.30) (4.3)* + (0.20) (4.7)

= 3.00 + 1.29 + 0.94

= 5.23

---

* Average rating of three secondary goals

Figure 5.9 Conversion Table for Compensation Determination

Overall performance rating	Salary increase potential (%)	Bonus potential (%) (a)
5.5 - 6.0 (Level 1)	8 - 10	10 - 20
4.9 - 5.4 (Level 2)	6 - 7	6 - 9
4.2 - 4.8 (Level 3)	4 - 5	2 - 5
3.6 - 4.1 (Level 4)	2 - 3	None
3.0 - 3.5 (Level 5)	None	None
Under 3.0 (Level 6) (b)	None	None

(a) Award recommended by president requires Board of Directors approval.
(b) Managers with ratings below 3.0 are placed on probation and are reviewed semi-annually. A second rating of 3.0 or less during the following year means automatic dismissal.

> The salary and bonus levels used in this and subsequent charts are for illustrative purposes only. Actual levels would be set by company management in consultation with their compensation consultant

Figure 5.7 shows the marketing manager's self-ratings for management skills as well as the president's ratings. Unless there was mutual agreement to change, the president's skills ratings were used in the final overall rating.

The Conclusion: Figure 5.8 summarizes the overall rating for the marketing manager, using the agreed upon weighting. The overall rating was determined to be 5.23, entitling the market manager to a salary increase of 6-7 percent and a bonus award of 6-9 percent (Figure 5.9).

Chapter 5

Critique of Case Study 5-2

The weighting of the three performance areas was somewhat arbitrary. However, to really get the manager to focus on the primary goal it had to carry a significant proportion of the overall rating, in this case 50 percent (Figure 5.8). Notice that the range of the "percent of goal" values corresponding to the same results rating varied considerably in the translation tables. This reflects the volatility of each goal as observed from recent history. In Figure 5.7, the marketing manager's self-rating on all three skills categories was 5; the president only rated a 4 on communications. That determination was based on feedback from the field sales force that they were frequently unaware of the marketing manager's directives. Notice footnote (b) in Figure 5.9. Many top executives look for ways to weed out low-performers. We know of situations where some companies simply terminate the lowest rated 10% of their employees, and, where necessary, rehire those who they think are better performers. That's all the more reason for having a results-oriented appraisal system that is based on quantitative goals.

5.3.2 Shared Goals

One complication in trying to appraise the performance of managers is that seldom is the achievement of a goal entirely the work of

Figure 5.10 Shared Contribution to a Factory Shipment Goal

Business unit manager	Contribution to meeting annual shipment goal
Engineering	Timely issue of error-free shop drawings
Manufacturing	On-schedule manufacture of product
Purchasing	On-time procurement of product supplies and components
Accounting	Timely tracking of actual costs against budget
Sales	Negotiating reasonable ship dates and necessary delays
Product line	Effective overview of product costs and schedule

any one manager alone. Suppose a goal had been set to lower the internal time by 20 percent for ordering and receiving replacement spare parts. In all likelihood, purchasing, stores, maintenance, administration, and shipping/receiving managers all played a part in achieving that goal. That doesn't mean that each department contributed equally, nor must they be rewarded or penalized equally.

Therefore, the rating of managers against shared goals needs to consider an additional appraisal factor – we call it the contribution factor, or how much each manager or their department contributed to achieving the actual results. Look at Figure 5.10. It lists some ways that each of six different departments of a business unit could support the unit's shipment goal for the year. Although each manager's department played a role, their contribution was not equal.

Consider the following case study for AJAX Manufacturing:

CASE STUDY 5-3 AJAX MANUFACTURING
(Evaluating managers against a shared goal)

The Situation: AJAX designs and manufactures package boilers for the industrial and small utility markets. The company controller had recently completed the financial statements for 2004. At the same time, the president was compiling the performance of the company against its primary goals (one of which was to ship $250 million of boilers) in preparation for conducting the annual performance review with his direct reports. Prior to 2004, a translation table for converting factory shipments into a rating was agreed upon by six of his key managers who played a part in achieving the shipments goal (Figure 5.2). A weighting between the results rating and the contribution rating was also set, with the manufacturing manager carrying the highest results weighting (80%).

The Numbers: Final shipments for 2004 came in at $254.2 million. Although above the commitment goal of $250 million, it was below the company's target goal of $265 million. Achieving the target goal would have rated a solid "6" on the company's 1 to 6 rating scale. Figure 5.11 summarizes the weighting for each manager between results and contribution, the ratings against each, and the overall rating for compensation purposes. The overall ratings ranged from 4.2 for the manufacturing manager to 5.2 for the engineering manager.

Chapter 5

Figure 5.11 Rating Managers Against A Shared Shipment Goal

Shipments goal for 2004: $ 250 million
Actual shipments: $ 254.2 million
Actual % of goal: 101.7 %

Manager	Weighting (%)		Rating (scale 1 to 6)		Overall rating
	Results	Contribution	Results (a)	Contribution (b)	(1 to 6)
Engineering	20	80	4	5.5	5.2
Manufacturing	80	20	4	4.8	4.2
Purchasing	30	70	4	5.0	4.7
Controller	30	70	4	5.5	5.1
Sales	15	85	4	5.0	4.9
Product Line	50	50	4	5.0	4.5

(a) All managers get same results rating using Figure 5.2
(b) Rating based entirely on business unit presidents evaluation

The President presented these comments on the ratings at the next staff meeting: "I gave engineering the highest contribution rating because all shop drawings were delivered on-time, within budget, and drawing errors were less than one percent. I rated manufacturing down, even though the shipment goal was made, because product rework costs were way above normal due to quality problems. I thought the controller did a very good job in monitoring costs and bringing potential overruns to the attention of everybody; I thought the rest of you did a commendable job in supporting the factory in getting the product out the door during the year. Without all the rework cost and delays, a '5' on shipments results could easily have been obtained."

Conclusion: The president used the translation table (Figure 5.9) to award salary increases and recommended bonuses for the year to the Board of Directors. None of the managers got the highest potential level of compensation (Level 1). The manufacturing manager, purchasing manager, and the product line managers qualified for a level 3 award, whereas the rest of the management team qualified for a level 2 award.

Critique of Case Study 5-3: The case study above illustrates how multiple managers can contribute to a single goal. In a profit center organ-

The Bubble Management Approach

ization, it is not uncommon to expect all senior executives to share in the bottom-line profit result, even though only the top executive can be held totally responsible for profits. Nevertheless, it is desirable to require the entire senior management to share in the profit commitment. This can be done by making gross or operating profit a primary or secondary goal for all of the staff. Some staff managers will argue that it's unfair to hold them accountable for the bottom-line profit because they have very little direct control on it. Although there is a temptation to accept this argument, it should be avoided. Instead, think of it this way – being rated on the profit center bottom-line is the ticket you buy to get on the senior staff.

5.3.3   Implementing the Appraisal Concept

We suggest that the performance appraisal be held as soon as possible in the quarter following the end of the calendar or fiscal year. This allows areas of weak performance to be discussed and corrective action applied to the goals for the current year. We also think it's a good idea to have each member of the senior staff submit throughout the year an assessment of their own performance against goals after results are in each quarter. That way managers will have a benchmark of their performance throughout the coming year, thereby eliminating any surprises when the annual appraisal is held. Obviously, there is no requirement that the boss must formally review the quarterly assessments, but it can certainly be a point of discussion in one-on-one meetings throughout the year.

Reaching agreement between the boss and subordinate is easier during the performance appraisal if the boss evaluates the subordinates and the subordinates evaluate themselves. That way the two ratings can be compared and any significant differences discussed. Experience with this approach has shown that seldom do the independent ratings differ by more than three-tenths (0.3) of a point on a 1 to 6 rating scale. If they do, serious differences of opinion are apparent and should be discussed in detail during the appraisal session.

A key objective of any performance appraisal system is to have the concept applied uniformly across the organization from top to bottom. No appraisal system will work effectively unless the top manager gives it full support. Furthermore, the business unit manager must be willing to devote adequate time to setting the goals, monitoring results,

Chapter 5

and developing the performance standards. It has proved useful in the past to have the financial department collect the business unit results quarterly and compile them for review by all managers.

We believe the appraisal concept works best if implemented first at the top management tier of the company. Our experience indicates that it will take about a one-year trial period to achieve acceptance at each tier of management. Thus, if the profit center has three management levels, allow three years to implement the concept fully at all levels, starting from the top and working down the organization. The following case study shows how AJAX Refining accomplished the implementation.

CASE STUDY 5-4. AJAX REFINING
(Awarding bonuses)

The Situation: AJAX Refining is a 320,000-barrel-per-day refinery in the Houston area producing a variety of petroleum products including diesel fuel, which was AJAX's most profitable product. The plant was originally erected in 1967 and has had a few major upgrades to the process over the years. Because of its age, the recent owners were able to purchase the plant at a bargain price. They expect to yield a 16 percent return-on-assets if plant operating expenses and capital expenditures can be held to current levels. But because of the age of much of the equipment, breakdowns have shown an upward trend; backorders

Figure 5.12 Analysis of Refinery Major Capacity Problems

The senior staff identified the following problems and probable causes for the 6 % loss of refinery capacity:

- Bearing failures in pumps used to transfer crude oil from tankers into storage tanks and move crude from storage to desalting units. Preliminary analysis attributed the cause to stress corrosion cracking, probably due to higher than normal chloride levels in recent crude shipments.
- Loss of capacity in atmospheric distillation towers due to corrosion of tower bubble caps. Probable cause also thought to be due to chloride stress corrosion cracking.
- Loss of capacity in the diesel fuel hydro-treating units that remove sulfur and improve quality. Suspected cause was inadequate use of catalyst during hydro-treating.
- Minor breakdowns of various refinery components attributed to inadequate preventive maintenance.

---

of replacement spare parts have been high, and maintenance repairs have been overrunning cost and schedule. The net effect was a 6 percent loss of capacity over the last year. The plant manager put it this way, "We've got to get a handle on our operating and maintenance problems or we're not going to be in business very long. I'm working with the senior refinery staff to set some clear goals for turning our situation around; I plan to cascade the goals down to all senior managers and see that they all get rated and rewarded appropriately. Because of the importance of this project, the general manager had convinced the Board of Directors to establish a $120,000 bonus pool for a successful completion of the forthcoming capacity upgrade.

The Proposed Solution: Working together, the senior staff identified the problem areas and likely causes for the capacity loss (Figure 5.12). Next, they created tactical plans that identified actions needed to fix the main maintenance/operating problems. Figure 5.13 shows the tactical plan for correcting the crude oil pump bearing problem; plans were also written to cover the other two major problems (bubble cap corrosion, and loss of capacity for diesel hydro-treating), but are not

Figure 5.13 Tactical Plan For Bearing Failure Problem

TACTICAL PLAN 2004-7

Title: Crude pump bearing failure correction   Date of Issue: June 21, 2004

Prime Responsibility: Maintenance superintendent   Reference: Causal report 04-12

Purpose: Replace present austenitic stainless steel bearings with new alloy to prevent chloride stress corrosion cracking in crude pump bearings.

Measure of Performance: Improve crude transfer operations to 100% of 1Q 2004 capacity.

Key milestones

	Event	Responsibility	Planned completion	Actual completion
1.	Prepare new drawings and specs for bearings	Engineering	June 28, 2004	June 28, 2004
2.	Cast/machine bearing prototype	AJAX Bearing	Jul 7, 2004	Jul 8, 2004
3.	R&D test bearing in loop for 7 days	Development	Jul 15, 2004	Jul 18,2004
4.	Mfg/ship replacement bearings	AJAX Bearing	Jul 27, 2004	Jul 29, 2004
5.	Install in pumps	Maintenance	August 10, 2004	August 11, 2004

shown here. Control charts were used to monitor performance against plan and track refinery capacity and budget against goals (Figure 5.14 and 5.15). Overall corrective actions were expected to take up to six weeks to complete. Overtime was authorized as necessary to minimize

Figure 5.14 Control Chart For Monitoring Refinery Capacity Improvement

Measurement	Processing unit capacity (% of goal for unit)			Overall refinery capacity	
period	Crude handling	Distillation	Hydro-treating	Target (%) (a)	Actual (%)
Week 0	92.5	96.7	94.7	-	94.1
Week 1	92.7	95.7	95.2	94.0	94.8
Week 2	92.4	95.9	95.1	94.0	95.1
Week 3	92.6	96.2	100.9 (d)	96.0	96.4
Week 4	80.4 (b)	57.9 (c)	101.7	90.0	90.8
Week 5	98.8	59.6	102.1	97.0	96.8
Week 6	100.7	100.7	102.4	100.0	99.7
Week 7	100.7	101.4	103.9	100.0	100.5

(a) The target was to bring overall refinery capacity up to 320,000 bbl/day
(b) Capacity loss due to removing pumps from production to install new bearings
(c) Capacity loss due to shutting down units to replace bubble caps
(d) Capacity improved after catalyst mix adjustment

Figure 5.15 Control Chart for Monitoring Budget Performance

Manager	Cumulative performance against budget goal through week shown (%)						
	Week 1	Week 2	Week 3	Week 4	Week 5	Week 6	Week 7
Supply chain	98.6	102.5	103.5	103.8	105.9	109.4	107.4
Engineering	102.1	101.7	101.4	101.2	100.3	100.7	100.7
Development	94.9	102.4	103.9	103.6	103.6	103.6	103.6
Operations	102.1	101.3	104.1	103.8	103.7	103.3	102.4
Maintenance	100.2	100.1	100.8	100.2	99.6	98.3	98.9

For performance rating the following scale was used:

Actual budget less than 102.0 % of goal = 6
Actual budget from 102.1 - 104.0 % of goal = 5
Actual budget from 104.1 - 106.0 % of goal = 4
Over 106.1% = 3

The Bubble Management Approach

time span at both the refinery and bearing vendor. Overnight shipment of replacement parts was also approved.

The Numbers: For performance evaluation purposes, the plant manager developed a performance ranking system covering five of his senior managers: 1) maintenance, 2) supply chain, 3) engineering, 4) development, and 5) refinery operations. Figures 5.16 and 5.17 show the ratings of the managers against results and contribution for capacity improvement and budget control. Figure 5.18 converts the ratings for bonus purposes. Finally, Figure 5.19 shows how the maintenance manager recommended the split of his department's 25 % share of the bonus pool.

Critique of Case Study 5-4: The refinery manager decided to limit his performance rankings to only the three major problem areas identified by the senior staff (Figure 5.12). Each tactical plan recognized that, once replacement parts were received from the vendors, there would be a temporary loss of additional capacity as pumps and operating units were removed from service for repairs. Figure 5.14 shows the impact on crude handling (one week), and on distillation (two weeks) as each of the two fractionators was taken out of service. Overall refin-

Figure 5.16 Rating Refinery Managers Against Shared Capacity Goal

Capacity goal for 2004:   320,000 barrels per day (bbl/day)
Actual capacity achieved: 321,600 bbl/day
Actual % of goal: 100.5 %

Manager	Weighting (%)		Rating (Scale 1 to 6)		Overall Rating
	Results	Contribution	Results (a)	Contribution (b)	(1 to 6)
Supply chain	50	50	5	5.0	5.0
Engineering	50	50	5	5.5	5.3
Development	50	50	5	4.5	4.8
Operations	30	70	5	5.0	5.0
Maintenance	70	30	5	5.5	5.2

(a) All managers get same results rating of 5 (capacity needed to be greater than 101 % to rate a 6)
(b) Rating based entirely on refinery managers evaluation

ery capacity was restored to 100.5 percent of previous capacity, only 0.5 % below the level that would have rated a "6" on the refinery manager's rating scale (Figure 5.16).

All managers rated at least a 4.8 on budget control except the supply chain manager who received a 3.8 because of vendor cost overruns (Figure 5.17). For the purpose of translating results to bonus share, the

Figure 5.17 Rating Refinery Managers Against Shared Budget Goal

Total budget goal for project: $ 964,000
Actual budget: $ 989,500
Actual % of goal: 102.6 %

Manager	Weighting (%)		Rating (Scale 1 to 6)		Overall rating
	Results	Contribution	Results (a)	Contribution (b)	(1 to 6)
Supply chain	60	40	3	5.0	3.8
Engineering	50	50	6	5.5	5.8
Development	50	50	5	4.5	4.8
Operations	50	50	5	5.0	5.0
Maintenance	70	30	6	5.5	5.9

(a) All managers were rated against the their budget performance shown on Figure 5.15
(b) Rating based entirely on refinery managers evaluation

Figure 5.18 Conversion Table for Bonus Determination

Department	Rating		Weighting (%)		Overall rating and ranking	Bonus share (%)
	Capacity improvement	Budget control	Capacity improvement	Budget control		(a)
Engineering	5.3	5.8	80	20	5.40 / 1	30
Maintenance	5.2	5.9	80	20	5.34 / 2	25
Operations	5.0	5.0	80	20	5.00 / 3	20
Development	4.8	4.8	80	20	4.80 / 4	15
Supply chain	5.0	3.8	80	20	4.76 / 5	10

(a) Each department manager was requested to submit to the refinery manager recommendations for sharing the bonus award with other personnel in their departments (see Figure 5.19 for the maintenance managers recommendation).

The Bubble Management Approach

refinery manager choose to weight each manager 80 percent against achieving the capacity improvement goal and 20 percent on budget control (Figure 5.18). Overall, the engineering manager ranked number 1 mainly because of performance on getting the drawings and specifications to the vendors ahead of schedule and within budget. Another factor was the lack of any rework by the vendors due to faulty drawing or specification errors. This was the first time the refinery had ever awarded bonuses for performance on a specific project. Speaking to the Board of Director's on their next visit, the refinery manager commented, "I think two things made the program a success: 1) the bonus incentive award, and 2) the shared goal concept used to rate the managers and dispense the bonuses."

5.4 FLAWS IN THE ORIGINAL APPRAISAL CONCEPT

Although the original appraisal concept worked very well, over the years we've recognized that it contained several flaws that needed to be corrected: 1) the goal was set using only management judgment, without factoring in any modern-day approaches for predicting the expected results, 2) the concept was based on setting a single-value goal that seldom, if ever, was meet exactly, and 3) the translation tables were based on a step-wise (stratified) rating – barely missing a goal could have a large impact on the results rating.

Figure 5.19 Maintenance Manager's Bonus Sharing Recommendation

Total maintenance award = $30,000

Manager	Recommended bonus ($)	Basis for bonus award
Maintenance manager	5,000	Meet schedule and beat budget
First shift superintendent	4,000	Excellent overtime and budget control
Second shift superintendent	4,000	Excellent overtime and budget control
Third shift superintendent	4,000	Maintained high productivity on third shift
Maintenance planner	3,000	Excellent coordination of materials and services
First shift weld foreman	2,500	Very low weld defect rates

Chapter 5

The remainder of this chapter will be devoted to discussing things we've done to correct these deficiencies. We will look first at the use of statistical forecasting models to improve on flaw 1 above; next show how VBRM not only will correct flaw 2, but also add a whole new dimension to the appraisal process; then finish by introducing the Performance Translation Table (PTT) (which is possible now because of VBRM) to offset flaw 3.

But before we do, let's summarize where we are at this point in the book. In Chapter 1 we talked about why the management appraisal process needs a new approach. In Chapter 2 we discussed the various types of goals and pointed out that setting a goal carries with it a certain level of uncertainty. In Chapter 3 we showed two convenient ways to monitor goals: the tactical plan and the control chart. Chapter 4 is where we introduced Value-Based Risk Management and how it provides some key tools for the Bubble Management approach. And earlier in this chapter we introduced the original appraisal concept and noted that it had a few flaws like focusing on a single-value goal. Now, we are ready for the coup de grace – refining the original appraisal process to bring it into the twenty-first century.

5.5 PUTTING IT ALL TOGETHER

Very simply, we need to restructure the original appraisal concept to make it: 1) easy to understand, 2) quantitative, 3) easy to apply, and 4) not too time consuming to implement. That's a tall order, but we're going to try. But there are some obstacles we must overcome such as:

- Most goals are single-valued, for example, "Make of profit of $15 million." One thing for certain, you are unlikely to make **exactly** $15 million. It's a little like owning a cheap watch, it's never exactly right, except twice per day when it's broken.
- Goals have uncertainty. There's a risk of falling short of them, as well as an opportunity to exceed them.
- Most people prefer not to be measured. That can add stress, and we're told all the time to avoid that.
- The process of setting goals takes time. We never have enough of that.

The Bubble Management Approach

5.6 PREDICTING QUANTITATIVE VALUES FOR FUTURE EVENTS

In our quest to predict operating profit, ROA, or simply the budget for performing some service, we usually find that actual results differ significantly from predicted results. That difference can usually be attributed to the use of a single-value estimate even though we know that an infinite number of other values are possible. Consider the case of trying to estimate the ROA for next year. A look back at Figure 2.1 shows the numerous factors that contribute to the calculation of ROA. Because each factor can vary widely from estimate, the number of possible ways they can combine to impact on the ROA estimate is extremely large. Many of the factors don't vary that much from estimate either because the costs are well defined, or because constraints can be placed on the item to keep it within tight control. However, factors like sales or revenues estimates do vary widely and can be beyond the reasonable control of management.

One answer then seems to be to let our old friend, the Pareto principle (the 80/20 rule) help us simplify our job. Vilfredo Pareto was an economist who studied the distribution of wealth. In his own country, he found that approximately 80% of the wealth was controlled by roughly 20% of the population. Pareto had found that, in most cases, something of interest (wealth, poor driving accident records, etc.) is represented disproportionately within the population. In the early 1900s, Dr. Joseph M. Juran (considered by many to be the father of quality management) applied the Pareto principle to business (i.e., 80% of product defects can be found in 20% of the produced products, etc.). Juran named this application to business problems as the Pareto principle in recognition of our friend Vilfredo. It has also been called the rule of the "vital few and trivial many."

The simplification of the Pareto principle to the term 80/20 Rule, however, is often misunderstood to mean that the values 80 and 20 apply to all things. In reality, the proportions can be almost anything and don't even have to add up to 100. For example, 12% of the elements in a forecast might account for 93% of the bottom line. Stated simply, the Pareto principle (and thousands of actual forecast analyses) says that a majority of the variability in a forecast can be attributed to a small percentage of the factors in Figure 2.1.

It is not unusual to find that, out of the hundreds of factors which go into a detailed ROA forecast, only 10 to 15 of those factors contribute much more than 80% of the variability. That's not an 80/20 ratio, but more like "greater than 80 / less than 1" ratio. Therefore, we need to focus most of our attention on these few key-items when trying to set the ROA goal. But one way or another, we need to start the process by setting a goal.

We do have one advantage when we set goals for corporate financials – we have plenty of history to start from unless it's a brand new company. Certainly, other factors need to be considered like: 1) are we entering a recessionary period, 2) will our new plant startup on schedule and meet production goals, 3) will the competition bring out a new product line that impacts our sales? In other words, we must apply some judgment to the financial history when we try to set our goals. But we've got to start somewhere, and one logical way is to apply statistical forecasting models to the recent results to see how good the models are in forecasting results for the coming year. That's what we've done in the following case study for AJAX Machinery.

 CASE STUDY 5-5 AJAX MACHINERY (Using statistical forecasting models to set initial goals for next year)

The Situation: AJAX Machinery is a modest-sized custom-assembly company located in Charleston, West Virginia. They mainly buy parts and components from other suppliers and assemble them into custom-made assemblies for general industry clients. Their business is derived from two major product lines: 1) air compressors, and 2) air heaters. The company president was holding his bi-weekly staff meeting and made the following remark: "It's getting close to the time to start our planning process for next year. I'd like to see if we can do a better job of setting our financial goals. We haven't been very accurate in the past two years. Any suggestions?"

The Proposed Solution: The controller made the following suggestion: "Maybe we should try some statistical forecasting models to set the initial targets for next year, using the last two or three years of financial history. We can always override the statistical results if they seem out-of-line." The controller agreed to collect the data to try the approach.

The Bubble Management Approach

The Numbers: Table 5.1 is an Excel spreadsheet showing 24 quarters of financial history for sales, cost of sales (COS), operating profit (OP), net income (NI), cash flow from operations (CF/O), total assets (ASSETS), operating profit (OP %), net income as a percent of sales (NI %), turnover ratio (TO), and return-on-assets (ROA) on both operating income (OI) and net income (NI). The approach used to set the goal targets for next year was as follows:

- Fifteen different statistical forecasting models were used including variations of moving average, seasonal, trend, linear regression, and exponential smoothing.
- The data from the oldest twelve quarters (periods -13 to -24) were run through each model to see which model produced the best fit for the following twelve quarters, where results were known.
- Then the best model (one with the least standard error) was used with all twenty-four quarters of known results to forecast the next 12 quarters.
- The forecast for the first four quarters of the twelve-quarter forecast was adjusted by management to set the goals for next year.

Figure 5.20 shows the forecasts for the four quarters of next year (actual results after the year was over are inserted for comparison and the

Figure 5.20 Comparison of Forecast and Actual Results for AJAX Machinery

Element	Units	Quarter 1			Quarter 2			Quarter 3			Quarter 4		
		F	A	%	F	A	%	F	A	%	F	A	%
Sales	$ 1000	5,184	5,696	-9.0	5,184	6,092	-14.9	5,184	5,997	-13.6	5,184	5,715	-9.3
COS	$ 1000	4,150	4,438	-6.5	4,150	4,807	-13.7	4,150	4,787	-13.3	4,150	4,168	-0.4
Oper Inc	$ 1000	439	619	-29.1	439	742	-40.8	439	578	-24.0	439	472	-7.0
Net Inc	$ 1000	249	355	-29.9	249	404	-38.4	249	283	-12.0	249	268	-7.1
Cash flow	$ 1000	342	70	388.6	938	560	67.5	1,728	1,407	22.8	0	161	-
Assets	$ 1000	31,157	32,099	-2.9	32,462	31,667	2.5	33,838	32,308	4.7	35,214	31,100	13.2
Oper Inc	%	8.46	10.87	-22.2	8.47	12.18	-30.5	8.47	9.67	-12.4	8.47	8.32	1.8
Net Inc	%	4.80	6.23	-23.0	4.80	6.63	-27.6	4.80	4.74	1.3	4.80	4.69	2.3
Turnover	Ratio	0.17	0.19	-10.5	0.16	0.19	-15.8	0.15	0.18	-16.7	0.15	0.20	-25.0
ROA (OI)	%	1.44	1.85	-22.2	1.36	2.31	-41.1	1.27	1.74	-27.0	1.27	1.49	-14.8
ROA (NI)	%	0.82	1.06	-22.6	0.77	1.26	-38.9	0.72	0.85	-15.3	0.72	0.84	-14.3

F = Forecast amount using statistical best fit model (lowest standard error)
A = Actual
% = Deviation (F-A)/A

Table 5.1 AJAX Machinery Historical Financial Data

PERIOD	SALES ($1000)	COS ($1000)	OP ($1000)	NI ($1000)	CF/O ($1000)	ASSETS ($1000)	OP (%)	NI (%)	TO (ratio)	ROA (%)	ROA/NI (%)
-24	3445	2618	460	210	239	14173	13.35	6.09	0.24	3.20	1.46
-23	3587	2760	447	207	417	17576	12.46	5.77	0.20	2.49	1.15
-22	4109	3198	441	218	635	17893	7.79	5.30	0.23	1.79	1.22
-21	3862	3083	455	218	907	17463	11.77	5.65	0.22	2.59	1.24
-20	3985	3129	415	221	336	17103	10.41	5.55	0.23	2.39	1.28
-19	4033	3140	481	240	461	17098	11.93	5.60	0.24	2.86	1.34
-18	4052	3119	512	259	720	16865	12.63	6.39	0.24	3.03	1.53
-17	3801	2781	363	334	719	17066	8.78	8.76	0.23	2.02	2.01
-16	4531	3332	749	355	416	17110	16.53	7.83	0.26	4.30	2.04
-15	5569	4216	795	377	1106	30832	14.28	6.77	0.18	2.57	1.22
-14	6298	4798	835	368	1100	30735	13.26	5.84	0.21	2.78	1.21
-13	5612	4263	397	385	184	31691	7.07	6.84	0.17	1.20	1.16
-12	6176	4713	862	404	342	29967	13.96	6.54	0.21	2.93	1.37

The Bubble Management Approach

		COS	OP	NI	CF/O						
-11	5991	4607	589	307	938	28423	9.83	5.12	0.21	2.06	1.08
-10	5511	4228	651	339	1728	28669	11.81	6.15	0.19	2.24	1.17
-9	4255	3510	312	142	-597	28335	7.33	3.33	0.15	1.10	0.50
-8	4983	4044	404	218	237	28412	8.11	4.37	0.18	1.46	0.79
-9	4255	3510	312	142	-597	28335	7.33	3.33	0.15	1.10	0.50
-8	4983	4044	404	218	237	28412	8.11	4.37	0.18	1.46	0.79
-7	5245	4196	485	232	667	28897	9.25	4.42	0.18	1.67	0.80
-6	5222	4165	430	193	1009	29175	8.23	3.70	0.18	1.48	0.67
-5	4484	3523	-134	-223	2	29810	-2.99	-4.97	0.15	-0.45	-0.74
-4	5112	4073	451	151	-30	30356	8.82	2.30	0.17	1.39	0.39
-3	5460	4347	489	216	1215	30771	8.98	3.96	0.18	1.61	0.71
-2	5322	4213	504	280	1697	30989	9.47	5.26	0.17	1.60	0.89
-1	5198	4121	342	291	456	31711	6.58	5.60	0.16	1.05	0.90

COS = Cost of sales

OP = Operating profit

NI = Net income

CF/O = Cash flow from operations

TO = Turnover

ROA = Operating profit return on Assets

ROA/NI = Net income return on assets

Chapter 5

actual-to-forecast deviations calculated). Quarterly deviations varied widely and were sometimes large. However, in 29 of 44 comparisons (66 percent) the actual results were within plus or minus one standard error of the forecast, with actual exceeding forecast about 70% of the time. The forecast modeling approach worked best for sales, cost of sales, and assets where deviations were all less than 15 percent each quarter. The deviations for all goals based on a "percentage" (e.g., ROA) varied widely from quarter to quarter, as did the deviations for the cash flow goal.

Figure 5.21 shows the best fit model for each goal forecast, along with the standard error and what percent the standard error was of the first quarter forecast amount. Notice that six different forecast models turned out to be the best fit for the eleven goal areas.

Figure 5.22 shows the final goals for the year set by the president with the concurrence of the management team. Because the economy was coming out of a recessionary period, and business was expected to improve, it was decided to set the individual goals for next year at a level to achieve a 5-10 percent improvement over the forecasted val-

Figure 5.21 Summary of Statistical Forecasting Analysis

Goal area	Best fit model	Standard error (a)	Std. error as % of first quarter forecast amount
Sales ($ 1000)	Exponential smoothing	534	10.3
Cost of sales ($ 1000)	Exponential smoothing	357	8.6
Operating income ($ 1000)	12 month trending	234	53.3
Net income ($ 1000)	12 month moving average	82	32.9
Cash flow ($ 1000)	Seasonal (no trend)	647	189.2
Total assets ($ 1000)	Linear regression	9,128	29.3
Operating income (%)	Seasonal (12 month trend)	3.65	43.1
Net income (%)	Seasonal (12 month trend)	1.70	35.4
Turnover (Ratio)	Linear regression	0.02	11.8
ROA (OI) (%)	Seasonal (12 month trend)	0.80	55.6
ROA (NI) (%)	Seasonal (12 month trend)	0.37	45.1

(a) The notation for standard error is $\sigma\sqrt{}$ square root of n, where σ is the standard deviation and n is the sample size. The standard error is calculated on the most recent twelve quarterly differences between the forecasted and actual results where the actual results are known.

The Bubble Management Approach

ues. Results for the year showed that eight of the eleven goals were met or exceeded for the year; two goals came in at 95-99.9 %; and one was below 70 % (cash flow). Prior to the start of the year, a translation table was developed for each goal converting the "% of goal" measure to a quantitative value for appraisal purposes. Figure 5.23 shows the translation table for four of the goals. From Figure 5.22 and the translation table, it can be seen that the results ratings were as follows:

Sales	4
Cost of sales	4
Operating income	4
Turnover	4

Figure 5.24 shows the final calculation of performance for the senior managers by the president. Two goals (operating income and turnover) were designated as shared goals, whereas the sales goal was assigned

Figure 5.22 Final Goals for AJAX Machinery

Annual results for 2004

Goal area	Forecast	Actual (A)	Final goal (G)	Achieved % of goal	Basis (a)
Sales ($1000)	20,736	23,500	22,800	103.1	A/G
Cost of sales ($1000)	16,600	18,200	18,000	98.9	G/A
Oper income ($1000)	1,756	2,410	2,000	120.5	A/G
Net income ($1000)	996	1,310	1,100	119.1	A/G
Cash flow ($1000)	3,008	2,198	3,300	66.6	A/G
Assets	35,214	31,100	31,500	98.7	G/A
Oper inc (%)	8.47	10.26	8.77	116.9	A/G
Net inc (%)	4.80	5.58	4.80	116.3	A/G
Turnover	0.63	0.76	0.72	105.6	A/G
ROA (OI) (%)	5.34	7.75	6.35	122.0	A/G
ROA (NI) (%)	3.02	4.02	3.46	116.2	A/G

A/G = Actual/goal   G/A = Goal/actual   [ ] Final goal exceeded

Chapter 5

Figure 5.23 Translation Table for Selected AJAX Machinery Goals

2004 goal year

Sales ($)		Cost of sales ($)		Operating income ($)		Turnover (Ratio)	
Percent of goal	Results rating	Percent of goal	Results rating	Percent of goal	Results rating	Percent of goal	Results rating
Over 110	6	Over 105.0	6	Over 150.0	6	Over 120.0	6
106.0-109.9	5	100.0-104.9	5	125.0-149.9	5	110.0-119.9	5
95.0-105.9	4	95.0- 99.9	4	100.0-124.9	4	100.0-109.9	4
85.0-94.9	3	85.0- 94.9	3	75.0- 99.9	3	90.0- 99.9	3
75.0-84.9	2	75.0- 84.9	2	50.0- 74.9	2	80.0- 89.9	2
Under 75.0	1	Under 75.0	1	Under 50.0	1	Under 80.0	1

to the sales manager and cost-of-sales goal to the manufacturing manager. The split of results versus contribution was set by the president depending on a number of factors including the control each manager had over achieving the assigned goal. The performance ratings were later used as the basis for rewarding salary increases and distributing the management bonus pool.

The Conclusion: After reviewing the results from using statistical forecasting models, the president concluded that the process was helpful in setting goals for AJAX. He especially liked the longer-range aspect of being able to get an independent forecast twelve quarters out, even though he wasn't sure how much credence could be placed on the second- and third-year estimates. It was decided to have the controller update the forecasting process after results for each quarter were available.

Critique of Case Study 5-5: The use of statistical forecasting models shows promise as a starting point for setting goals for the coming year. For many businesses like paper production that have had historical business cycles, some of the models like 12-month trending or seasonal may work well for picking up such trends. Some management override of the raw forecast is advisable, especially for those goals that have large deviation between forecast and actual results.

The Bubble Management Approach

Figure 5.24 Rating Manager Performance at AJAX Machinery

Manager	Basis of goal rating	Weighting (%)		Rating (Scale 1 to 6)		Overall rating
		Results	Contribution	Results (a)	Contribution (b)	(1 to 6)
Sales	Sales	80	20	4	4.5	4.1
Manufacturing	Cost of sales	80	20	4	4.0	4.0
Sales	Operating income (c)	70	30	4	5.0	4.3
Manufacturing	Operating income (c)	70	30	4	5.0	4.3
Controller	Operating income (c)	70	30	4	5.3	4.4
Sales	Turnover (c)	75	25	4	4.2	4.1
Manufacturing	Turnover (c)	75	25	4	4.6	4.2
Controller	Turnover (c)	60	40	4	4.5	4.2

(a) Determined from Figures 5.22 and 5.23
(b) Rating based entirely on presidents evaluation of each manager contribution to achieving goal
(c) Shared goal among managers shown

5.7 APPLYING VBRM TO THE GOAL SETTING PROCESS

Back in Chapter 4, we gave an overview of the VBRM process. Here we will show how we modified the process to handle performance appraisals.

In section 5.5, we said our objective was to make the use of VBRM easy to understand. To this end, we have simplified our coverage of the process for most of the following case studies by eliminating: 1) the uncertainty benchmark horn, 2) the uncertainty benchmark, 3) mitigation analysis, and 4) the contingency profile (applicable only to capital investment decisions). But we still need to: 1) develop goal-uncertainty inputs, 2) determine the probability of meeting the goals, and 3) calculate a total risk and opportunity contribution for each goal. Once this is done, the use of the Performance Translation Table will yield our desired appraisal rating. Let's illustrate all of this by taking another look at the AJAX Machinery case, but this time using VBRM and Bubble Management. But before this we want to list the sequence

Chapter 5

of flow used when discussing all cases in the rest of the book:

- Recent historical financial data
- Goals for the next year
- VBRM analysis of goals
- Actual results for the next year
- Translation of actuals into results ratings and suggested compensation

In some tables and figures we have inserted the actual results along with the goal (forecast) to allow the reader to compare the probability of meeting both on the same figure.

CASE STUDY 5-6 AJAX MACHINERY
(Using VBRM to set goals and appraise management performance)

The Situation: When the results from using statistical forecasting models to set goals showed fairly large standard errors for many situations, the controller decided to try another approach for setting goals. He contacted a consulting company which applies Value-Based Risk Management that used probability theory to set goals. After reviewing the AJAX situation, the consultants proposed the following solution.

The Proposed Solution: The principles of Value-Based Risk Management would be used to quantify the probability of achieving each goal planned by AJAX. A team of financial and operating managers from the company was assembled to work with the consultants to collect and define the data inputs for the VBRM process.

The Numbers: The end product from the data gathering session is shown in Figures 5.25 and 5.26. First, the original target goal for each goal element from Case Study 5-5 was selected along with the team's estimate of the probability of improving on each goal. Next, low and high estimates were made wherein the actual value of each goal's endpoint (highest and lowest estimates) was expected to have less than a 1% chance of happening (Figure 5.27).

The Bubble Management Approach

Figure 5.25 ROA Goals for AJAX

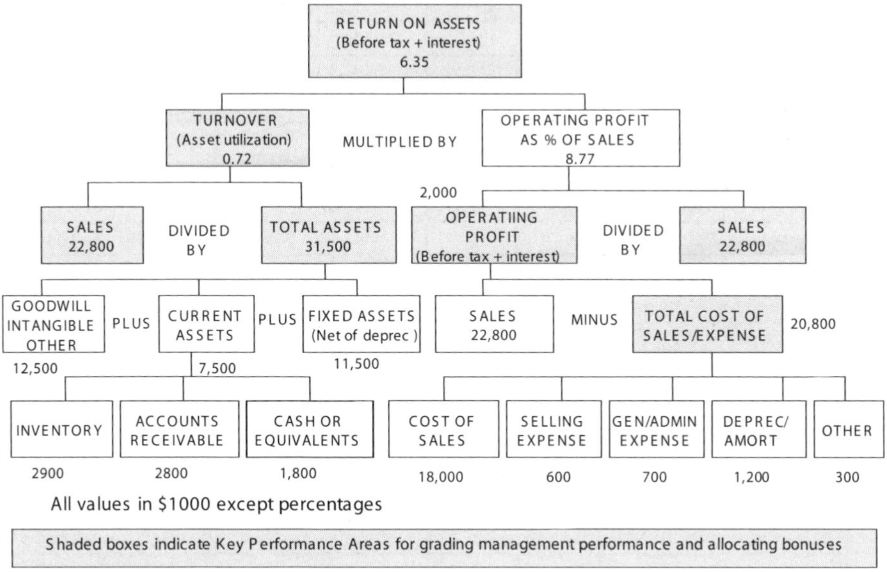

```
                    RETURN ON ASSETS
                   (Before tax + interest)
                          6.35
        ┌───────────────────┴───────────────────┐
    TURNOVER                              OPERATING PROFIT
  (Asset utilization)   MULTIPLIED BY       AS % OF SALES
        0.72                                     8.77
                                                2,000
  ┌─────┬──────────┐                ┌──────────┬─────────┬─────────┐
SALES  DIVIDED  TOTAL ASSETS      OPERATIING  DIVIDED   SALES
22,800   BY       31,500            PROFIT       BY     22,800
                                 (Before tax + interest)
```

| GOODWILL INTANGIBLE OTHER | PLUS | CURRENT ASSETS | PLUS | FIXED ASSETS (Net of deprec.) | | SALES 22,800 | MINUS | TOTAL COST OF SALES/EXPENSE | 20,800 |
| 12,500 | | 7,500 | | 11,500 | | | | | |

| INVENTORY | ACCOUNTS RECEIVABLE | CASH OR EQUIVALENTS | | COST OF SALES | SELLING EXPENSE | GEN/ADMIN EXPENSE | DEPREC/ AMORT | OTHER |
| 2900 | 2800 | 1,800 | | 18,000 | 600 | 700 | 1,200 | 300 |

All values in $1000 except percentages

Shaded boxes indicate Key Performance Areas for grading management performance and allocating bonuses

Figure 5.26 Key Performance Data Inputs and Calculations

Key Performance Boxes (KPBs). KPBs must be calculated values - not inputs.
Input value - not a calculation.

(1000) Unless stated otherwise

Revenues			Expenses		
Product Line A sales	$ 5,500		Product Line A labor cost (% of sales)	38.18%	$ 2,100
Product Line B sales	12,400		Product Line B labor cost (% of sales)	36.29%	4,500
Product Line C sales	4,900		Product Line C labor cost (% of sales)	44.90%	2,200
Total sales	$ 22,800		Labor Cost		$ 8,800
Operating profit	$ 2,000		Product Line A material cost (% of sales)	41.82%	$ 2,300
(Operating profit as % of sales)	8.77%		Product Line B material cost (% of sales)	25.00%	3,100
			Product Line C material cost (% of sales)	40.82%	2,000
Assets			Material cost		$ 7,400
Inventory	$ 2,900				
			Factory overhead		1,800
Product Line A (% of sales)	12.73%	$ 700			
Product Line B (% of sales)	12.10%	1,500	Cost of sales		$ 18,000
Product Line C (% of sales)	12.24%	600			
Accounts receivable		$ 2,800	Product Line A (% of sales)	2.73%	$ 150
			Product Line B (% of sales)	2.82%	350
Cash or equivalents		1,800	Product Line C (% of sales)	2.04%	100
			Selling expense		$ 600
Current assets		$ 7,500			
			Gen/admin expense		$ 700
Goodwill/intangible/other		$ 12,500	Depre/amort (% of fixed assets)	10.43%	1,200
Fixed assets		11,500	Other 300		
Total assets		$ 31,500	Total cost of sales/expense		$ 20,800
Turnover (asset utilization)	0.72				
ROA (Operating profit)	6.35%				

123

Chapter 5

Figure 5.27 AJAX Uncertainty Inputs

Input element	Units	Target	Probability*	Low	High
Product Line A sales	$1000	5,500	60	3,500	7,500
Product Line B sales	$1000	12,400	40	10,000	14,500
Product Line C sales	$1000	4,900	45	3,500	6,000
Labor cost - Product Line A	%	38.18		38.18	38.18
Labor cost - Product Line B	%	36.29		36.29	36.29
Labor cost - Product Line C	%	44.90		44.90	44.90
Material cost - Product Line A	%	41.82	35	38.00	42.00
Material cost - Product Line B	%	25.00	40	23.00	27.00
Material cost - Product Line C	%	40.82	30	38.00	43.00
Factory overhead	$1000	1,800	65	1,700	2,000
Selling expense - Product Line A	%	2.73		2.73	2.73
Selling expense - Product Line B	%	2.82	45	2.00	3.20
Selling expense - Product Line C	%	2.04		2.04	2.04
Gen/admin expense	$1000	700	60	600	800
Fixed assets	$1000	11,500	55	10,000	13,000
Deprec/amort	%	10.43		10.43	10.43
Other	$1000	300	50	100	500
Inventory	$1000	2,900	35	2,500	5,000
Accounts receivable - Product Line A	%	12.73		12.73	12.73
Accounts receivable - Product Line B	%	12.10		12.10	12.10
Accounts receivable - Product Line C	%	12.24		12.24	12.24
Cash or equivalents	$1000	1,800	35	1,000	3,700
Goodwill/intangible/other	$1000	12,500	55	10,000	14,500

*Probability of achieving or improving compared to Target

Keep in mind that this is a simplified example of VBRM and that our remaining case studies have also been simplified for sake of brevity. However, VBRM's applicability to the appraisal process has not been lost through this simplification. Some values, like labor cost, are entered as percentages of other inputs, such as percent of sales. This is a requirement to ensure that they are synchronized because they are dependent on other inputs. Also, notice that some of the inputs have been entered with no variability (no probability or range). Although these values can vary to some extent, they cannot vary enough to cause significant change to the bottom line ROA. Entering probabilities and

The Bubble Management Approach

Figure 5.28 Probability Forecast Table for AJAX Goals

Probability of Achieving	ROA (%)	Turnover ratio	Sales ($1000)	Total COS ($1000)	Operating Profit ($1000)	Total assets ($1000)	Shading indicates location of single-point forecast (Target)
0.05%	11.13	0.91	27,056	16,379	3,390	27,601	
5%	8.69	0.80	25,291	18,695	2,766	29,629	
10%	7.95	0.78	24,613	19,207	2,552	30,155	
15%	7.62	0.76	24,155	19,484	2,437	30,580	
20%	7.30	0.76	23,876	19,763	2,334	30,825	
25%	7.04	0.74	23,619	19,997	2,256	31,098	
30%	6.78	0.73	23,409	20,176	2,190	31,271	
35%	6.60	0.72	23,232	20,311	2,115	31,535	
40%	6.41	0.72	23,076	20,447	2,060	31,734	
45%	6.24	0.71	22,907	20,621	2,005	31,922	
50%	6.04	0.70	22,740	20,760	1,952	32,110	
55%	5.90	0.70	22,553	20,920	1,885	32,342	
60%	5.72	0.69	22,330	21,040	1,825	32,516	Expected results … each value has 50% chance of being improved
65%	5.51	0.68	22,163	21,149	1,762	32,742	
70%	5.28	0.68	21,881	21,310	1,714	32,938	
75%	5.09	0.67	21,668	21,461	1,645	33,127	
80%	4.82	0.66	21,434	21,619	1,565	33,460	
85%	4.50	0.65	21,065	21,845	1,451	33,713	
90%	4.15	0.64	20,566	22,169	1,340	34,030	
95%	3.60	0.62	20,009	22,623	1,144	34,695	
99.95%	1.81	0.53	17,175	24,003	564	38,519	

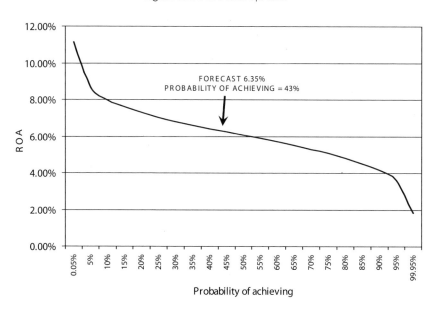

Figure 5.29 AJAX ROA profile

FORECAST 6.35%
PROBABILITY OF ACHIEVING = 43%

Chapter 5

Figure 5.30 AJAX Sales Profile

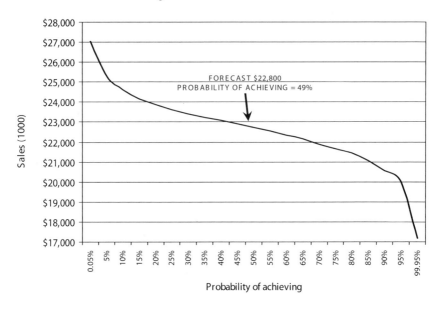

Figure 5.31 AJAX Total Assets Profile

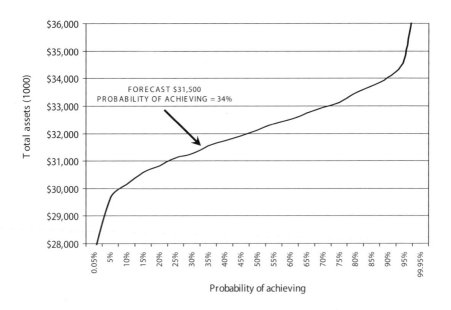

The Bubble Management Approach

Figure 5.32 AJAX Total COS Profile

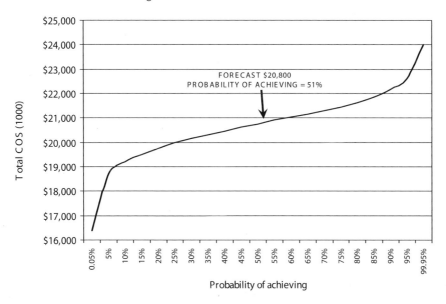

Figure 5.33 AJAX Operating Profit Profile

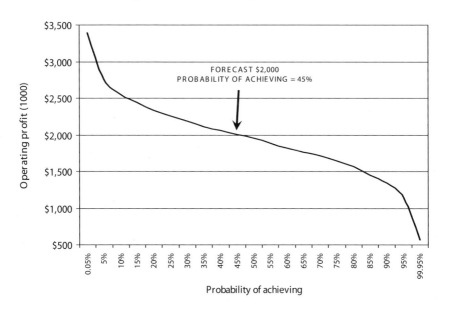

Chapter 5

Figure 5.34 AJAX Turnover Ratio Profile

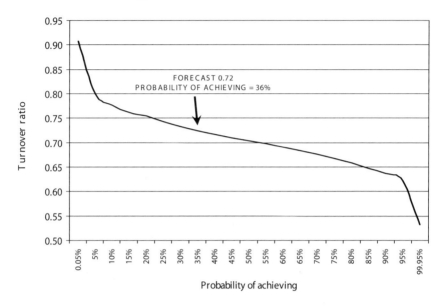

ranges for these inputs would introduce iatrogenic risk and understate the total ROA uncertainty.

At this point, the consultants processed the data, arriving at the probability ranges for achieving each goal shown in Figure 5.28 (graphs of the uncertainty profile for ROA, sales, total assets, cost-of-sales, operating profit, and turnover are shown in Figures 5.29 through 5.34).

The consultants next developed a VBRM bubble chart for recommending where AJAX management focus its attention to have the best chance of capturing opportunities and reducing risks (Figure 5.35). Notice that Product Line B Sales overwhelms all other ROA factors. This factor contributes the most opportunity and risk to the bottom line. Because it is also the largest contributor of net risk, it is also more likely to create a problem at the bottom line by falling short of goal. The AJAX management must focus heavily on this factor in order to ensure that its actual does not fall substantially short of goal. In general, management should focus first on uncertainty drivers having the most net risk and net opportunity. Once those drivers have been improved, the focus should move to those remaining drivers which are furthest from the origin.

The Bubble Management Approach

Figure 5.35 VBRM Bubble Chart

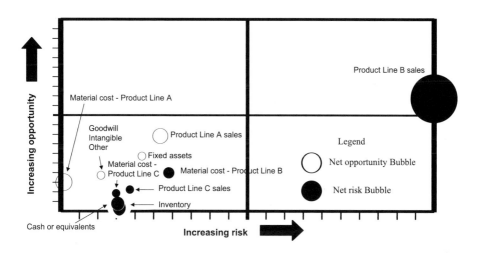

Figure 5.36 Actual Results for AJAX

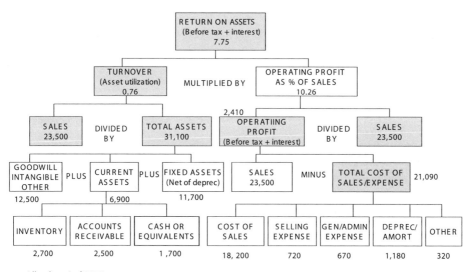

Figure 5.37 The Performance Translation Table (PTT)

Values in cells are performance rating (1 to 6 scale) based on probability of meeting the actual result

First digit (s) of probability	Next digit of probability									
↓	0	1	2	3	4	5	6	7	8	9
0.	6.0	6.0	6.0	6.0	6.0	6.0	6.0	6.0	6.0	6.0
1	5.5	5.5	5.4	5.4	5.3	5.3	5.2	5.2	5.1	5.1
2	5.0	4.9	4.8	4.7	4.6	4.5	4.4	4.3	4.2	4.1
3	4.0	4.0	3.9	3.9	3.8	3.8	3.7	3.7	3.6	3.6
4	3.5	3.5	3.4	3.4	3.3	3.3	3.2	3.2	3.1	3.1
5	3.0	3.0	2.9	2.9	2.8	2.8	2.7	2.7	2.6	2.6
6	2.5	2.5	2.4	2.4	2.3	2.3	2.2	2.2	2.1	2.1
7	2.0	1.9	1.8	1.7	1.6	1.5	1.4	1.3	1.2	1.1
8	1.0	1.0	0.9	0.9	0.8	0.8	0.7	0.7	0.6	0.6
9	0.5	0.5	0.4	0.4	0.3	0.3	0.2	0.2	0.1	0.1
9.9	0.1	0.1	0.1	0.1	0.1	0.1	0.1	0.1	0.1	0.1

As an illustration, if the probability of meeting the goal was determined to be 47 %, the rating would be 3.2; if 89 %, the rating would be 0.6.

Figure 5.38 Comparison of AJAX Results Rating

Goal	Results rating using VBRM (a)		Results rating using traditional concept (from figure 5.23)
	Probability (%)	Rating	
Sales	28	4.2	4.0
Cost of sales	63	2.4	4.0
Operating income	18	5.1	4.0
Turnover	15	5.3	4.0

(a) Using figures 5.30, 5.32, 5.33 and 5.34 for sales, cost of sales, operating income and turnover. Probability of achieving actual results determined and translated to the results rating using PTT figure 5.37

Product Line A Sales is the next largest contributor of ROA opportunity. Because it also has one of the largest net opportunities, this factor should be managed to meet or exceed its goal. The net opportunity in Material cost – Product Line A should also then be addressed. Inventory, material cost – Product Line B, and cash or equivalents should be the next factors to receive attention. Although they do not contribute substantial risk or opportunity, they do contribute a sizable por-

The Bubble Management Approach

tion of net risk indicating that they are potential problem areas. Figure 5.36 shows the actual results for the year superimposed on the ROA chart.

The final step in the exercise was to recommend a Performance Translation Table (Figure 5.37) to the president for translating the actual results to a results rating for performance appraisal purposes. Figure 5.38 shows the results rating comparison for sales, cost of sales, operating income, and turnover using the traditional appraisal approach (Figure 5.23) and the VBRM approach. In this case, except for cost of sales, ratings using VBRM came in higher than by the traditional approach.

The Conclusion: After seeing the presentation of the VBRM approach to goal setting, the president decided to use the Bubble Management approach as the basis for performance appraisal in the coming year. He also planned to use statistical forecasting to help set the initial goals.

Critique of Case Study 5-6: Several aspects of Case Study 5-6 are unique: 1) determining the probability of achieving goals rather than relying on a single-value goal for appraising performance, 2) developing the VBRM bubble chart that identifies priorities for capturing opportunities and reducing risk, and 3) using the Performance Translation Table for converting goal probability to a results rating for appraising performance and awarding compensation. It is interesting that the results ratings using Bubble Management tended to be higher in general than the rating obtained using the traditional concept, but that will not always be the case. We think the convenience of having a single basis for translating actual results into a performance rating works well with the Bubble Management approach.

As predicted, Product Line B Sales was problematic, falling short of its $12.4 million goal by $400,000. Without attention to this specific factor, the results could have been considerably worse. Management succeeded in capturing the opportunity available in Product Line A sales and exceeded the goal of $5.5 million by $800,000 (nearly 15% higher than the goal). Overall, the sales division succeeded in capturing opportunities and mitigating risks (this is reflected in their bonus allocation as shown in the next case study).

The net risk in Material Cost – Product Line B was not substantially mitigated and was a major cause of the $200,000 overrun in total materials cost. This, along with below average performance compared to the expected (50%) forecast resulted in a zero bonus for managers working in this area (see case study 5-7). Cash or cash equivalents was managed below its forecast. Inventory was also managed well as risks were mitigated here.

This is a good place to explain, in simpler terms, how the VBRM bubble chart should be used to focus management attention. First, the largest bubbles should be addressed – regardless of whether they are net risks (solid) or net opportunities (unfilled). Addressing these uncertainty drivers means that management should apply any viable alternatives or options in order to capture available opportunities and mitigate risks. After those uncertainty drivers have been addressed, focus should next go to those which appear furthest from the origin – those that do not appear in the lower left quadrant of the chart. Although these might be very small bubbles (very small net risks or net opportunities), they do contribute to the total risk and opportunity. Their smaller diameter simply means they are more balanced (they contribute nearly the same amount of opportunity as they do risk).

Management's goal should be to implement any viable options or alternatives available to reduce the size of the larger bubbles and move all bubbles into the lower left quadrant. Put quite bluntly, management should take action so that the only things appearing on the VBRM bubble chart are small bubbles in the lower left quadrant! This will not be possible under all circumstances, but it is still the goal in order to effectively manage uncertainty.

5.8 THE PERFORMANCE TRANSLATION TABLE

Earlier in this chapter, Figures 5.2 through 5.6, we showed typical translation tables for converting shipments, sales, market share, budgets, and proposal awards into quantitative performance ratings. In other words, each goal needed to have its own translation table. Not any more. By applying probabilities when rating results, and setting the translation values carefully so that the steep slopes at the high and low end of the probability profile curves are captured properly, we can now perform the translation using a single table, the Performance Translation Table (PTT) we showed earlier (Figure 5.37).

For example, if after applying VBRM to a goal we found that the probability of achieving the result was 47%, that would rate a 3.2 regardless of which goal we were measuring. We have selected the probability ranges to reflect a degree of difficulty, somewhat similar to the way Olympic divers or gymnasts are rated – the more difficult the dive or routine, the higher the point total for achieving it. Because a rating of 3.0 is considered average, we think that fits well with a 50% probability of achievement; to get a 6.0, we think the probability should be less than 10%. However, if you don't like the probability ranges we chose, then pick your own.

5.9 USING BUBBLE MANAGEMENT TO SET BONUS AWARDS

Most corporations set up bonus pools to reward executives for outstanding performance against certain goals such as net income or earnings-per-share.

Usually the determination of which executives get a bonus tends to be a judgment call on the part of the president or CEO, or maybe a compensation committee of the Board of Directors. Here again is a situation where Bubble Management can help quantify the award process.

We believe that the overall financial performance of the corporation should determine the maximum amount of the bonus pool available. Also, we believe that if the probability of achieving an actual financial result is greater than 50 per cent, there should be no bonus based on that goal. Once the corporate-level bonus pool is determined, the available pool can be allocated based on individual business units' risk and opportunity contribution to the goal. In other words, each business unit is allocated a percentage of the total pool based on its ability to impact the goal. Some units would get a bonus, others may not.

Some organizations might, as part of their regular management appraisal process, exclude general economic conditions such as fluctuations in overall raw materials prices, commodity prices, etc. Although not covered in the context of this book, VBRM allows these general economic conditions (which some managers refer to as "swing money") to be removed from the appraisal process.

To illustrate the use of Bubble Management when awarding bonuses, we will use the data from Case Study 5-6. See also Appendix 5-1 for a suggested procedure for setting goals.

Figure 5.39 Key Performance Actual Results for AJAX

Key Performance Boxes (KPBs). KPBs must be calculated values - not inputs.
Input value - not a calculation.

($ 1000 unless otherwise indicated)

Revenues	
Product line A sales	$ 6,300
Product line B sales	12,000
Product line C sales	5,200
Total sales	$ 23,500

Assets	
Inventory	$ 2,700
Accounts receivable	2,500
Cash or equivalents	1,700
Current assets	$ 6,900
Goodwill/intangible/other	12,500
Fixed assets	11,700
Total assets	$ 31,100

Expenses	
Labor cost	$ 8,700
Material cost	7,600
Factory overhead	1,900
Cost of sales	$ 18,200
Selling expense	$ 720
Gen/Admin expense	670
Deprec/amort	1,180
Other	320
Total cost of sales/expense	$ 21,090

Turnover (Asset utilization)   0.76

ROA(Operating profit)   7.75%

Operating profit $ 2,410
(Operating profit as % of sales)   10.26%

CASE STUDY 5-7   AJAX MACHINERY
(Using VBRM to determine bonus awards)

The Situation: The president of AJAX Machinery was sufficiently pleased with the use of Bubble Management in the appraisal process that he decided to consider setting up a bonus pool to reward units of the company for outstanding performance. He asked the Bubble Management consultants to propose a program for awarding bonuses on improving ROA by looking especially at two financial factors: 1) operating income before taxes and interest and 2) total assets. (From these two factors and the sales results for the year, the ROA could be calculated, as shown in Figure 2.1).

The president believed that excluding taxes and interest from the ROA goal was appropriate because the impact of those factors was usually outside of the control of the operating units. He also decided to set the maximum bonus pool at 25 percent of the difference between the profit forecast at 0.05 percent probability and 50 percent probability ($ 1,438,000), or $359,500 as determined from Figure 5.28.

The Bubble Management Approach

Figure 5.40 Ajax ROA Profile

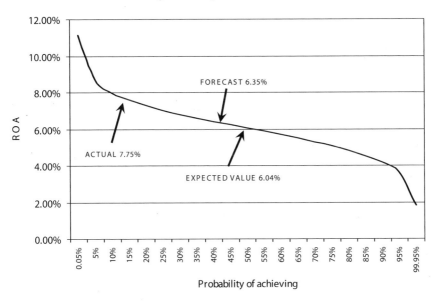

Figure 5.41 Probability of Achieving ROA Goals

ROA	Probability of achieving
11.13	0.05%
8.69	5%
7.95	10%
7.62	15%
7.30	20%
7.04	25%
6.78	30%
6.60	35%
6.41	40%
6.24	45%
6.04	50%
5.90	55%
5.72	60%
5.51	65%
5.28	70%
5.09	75%
4.82	80%
4.50	85%
4.15	90%
3.60	95%
1.81	99.95%

Actual = 7.75%

ROA Target = 6.35%

ROA Expected Value is 6.04%

Chapter 5

The Proposed Solution: Using data from their previous case study (Figure 5.22, and Figures 5.25 through 5.28), the consultants inserted the actual results from Figure 5.39 on the probability profiles for ROA, sales, cost-of-sales, and total assets. From these they determined the amount of the bonus pool that could be awarded.

Figure 5.42 The Performance Translation Table for Bonus Award

(Values in cells are percent of available bonus based on probability of meeting the goal)

First digit of probability	Next digit of probability									
	0	1	2	3	4	5	6	7	8	9
0.	100	95	90	85	80	75	70	65	60	55
1	50	49	48	47	46	45	44	43	42	41
2	40	39	38	37	36	35	34	33	32	31
3	30	29	28	27	26	25	24	23	22	21
4	20	18	16	14	12	10	8	6	5	5
> 5	0	0	0	0	0	0	0	0	0	0

As an illustration, if the probability of meeting the goal was determined to be 13%, the award would 45% of the available bonus pool.

Figure 5.43 Business Area Contributions to ROA Total Uncertainty

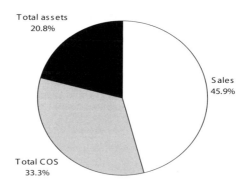

Total assets
20.8%

Sales
45.9%

Total COS
33.3%

Manager overseeing operating profit has total uncertainty of 79.2% (Sales + Total COS)	Manager overseeing turnover ratio has total uncertainty of 66.7% (Sales + Total Assets)

136

The Bubble Management Approach

Figure 5.44 Maximum Bonus Available to Qualifying Business Areas
(The Maximum Bonus Pool For Achieving The 7.75% ROA Was $168,965)

Area of uncertainty	Percent contribution to Ajax ROA total uncertainty	Maximum amount of bonus potential
Sales Area	45.9	77,555
Total COS Area	33.3	56,265
Total Assets Area	20.8	35,145

Total $ 168,965

Management decided that if the corporation could achieve an operating profit of $3,390,000 (less than 1% chance of being achieved), a maximum potential bonus pool of 25% of the improvement over the expected operating profit at %50 probability (equal to $359,500) would be made available for the maximum bonus pool. This does not imply that a straight-line 25% of any improvement over the expected operating profit is available for bonus. It is significantly more difficult for managers to improve performance the further they are away form the 50th percentile. For example, improving from 15% achievable result to the 10% achievable is considerably more difficult than improving from the 45% achievable to the 40% achievable result. Therefore, manager performance must take into consideration not only the amount of improvement but the level of difficulty in achieving that improvement. Therefore, incremental movements closer to the top-level of performance should be compensated more than the same incremental movement near the expected value (50% value).

Figure 5.45 AJAX Sales Profile

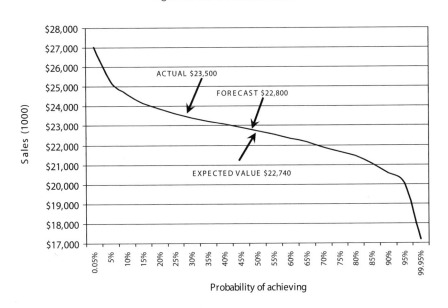

137

Figure 5.46 Determination of Maximum Sales Bonus

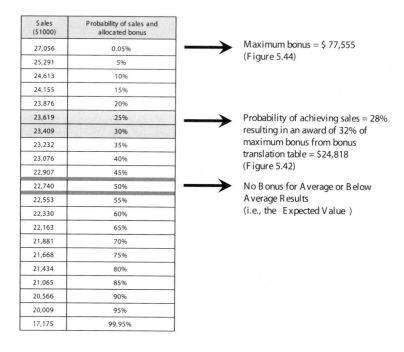

Sales ($1000)	Probability of sales and allocated bonus
27,056	0.05%
25,291	5%
24,613	10%
24,155	15%
23,876	20%
23,619	25%
23,409	30%
23,232	35%
23,076	40%
22,907	45%
22,740	50%
22,553	55%
22,330	60%
22,163	65%
21,881	70%
21,668	75%
21,434	80%
21,065	85%
20,566	90%
20,009	95%
17,175	99.95%

Maximum bonus = $ 77,555
(Figure 5.44)

Probability of achieving sales = 28%
resulting in an award of 32% of
maximum bonus from bonus
translation table = $24,818
(Figure 5.42)

No Bonus for Average or Below
Average Results
(i.e., the Expected Value)

Figure 5.47 AJAX Total COS Profile

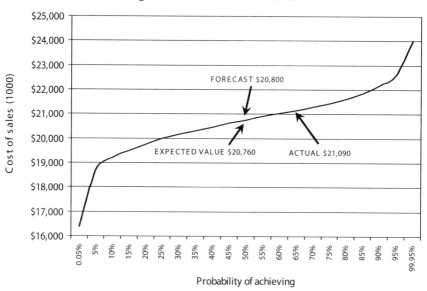

The Bubble Management Approach

Figure 5.48 Determination of Maximum COS Bonus

Total COS ($1000)	Probability of Total COS and allocated bonus
16,379	0.05%
18,695	5%
19,207	10%
19,484	15%
19,763	20%
19,997	25%
20,176	30%
20,311	35%
20,447	40%
20,621	45%
20,760	50%
20,920	55%
21,040	60%
21,149	65%
21,310	70%
21,461	75%
21,619	80%
21,845	85%
22,169	90%
22,623	95%
24,003	99.95%

Maximum bonus = $ 56,265
(Figure 5.44)

No bonus since probability of meeting Cost of Sales greater than 50%

Figure 5.49 AJAX Total Assets Profile

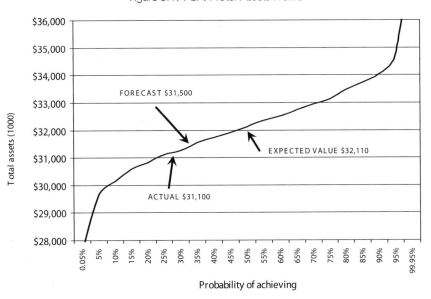

FORECAST $31,500

EXPECTED VALUE $32,110

ACTUAL $31,100

Total assets (1000)

Probability of achieving

Chapter 5

Figure 5.50 Determination of Maximum Total Assets

Total assets ($1000)	Probability of total assets and allocated bonus
27,601	0.05%
29,629	5%
30,155	10%
30,580	15%
30,825	20%
31,098	25%
31,271	30%
31,535	35%
31,734	40%
31,922	45%
32,110	50%
32,342	55%
32,516	60%
32,742	65%
32,938	70%
33,127	75%
33,460	80%
33,713	85%
34,030	90%
34,695	95%
38,519	99.95%

→ Maximum bonus = $35,145

→ Probability of achieving total assets = 28% resulting in an award of 32% bonus from bonus translation table = $ 11,246

↘ No Bonus for Average or Below Average Results (i.e., the Expected Value)

Figure 5.51 Summary of Total Bonus Paid

Area of uncertainty	Percent contribution to Ajax ROA total uncertainty	Maximum amount of bonus available	Amount of bonus paid
Sales Area	45.9	$ 77,555	$24,818
Total COS Area	33.3	$ 56,265	No bonus
Total Assets Area	20.8	$ 35,145	$11,246
TOTAL	100.0	$168,965	$36,064

$36,064 (slightly more than 21%) bonus payout on the Operating profit goal of $2 million.

The Numbers: The AJAX ROA uncertainty profile is shown graphically in Figure 5.40 and tabulated in Figure 5.41. The probability of achieving the actual ROA goal of 7.75% was 13 percent, which set the maximum bonus potential at 47 percent of $359,500, or $168,965, using the Performance Bonus Translation Table (Figure 5.42). Using their propri-

The Bubble Management Approach

etary VBRM codes, the consultants determined the amount of contribution to the total uncertainty of the ROA (Figure 5.43).

Sales contributed about 46% of the ROA uncertainty, followed by cost-of-sales (33%) and total assets at about 21%. That set the amount of the maximum bonus potential for the three areas of uncertainty as shown in Figure 5.44.

Next, the amount of actual award for the managements involved in sales, cost-of-sales, and total assets was determined (Figures 5.45 and 5.46 shows the result for sales; Figures 5.47 and 5.48 for cost-of-sales; Figures 5.49 and 5.50 for total assets). The summary of the total awards (Figure 5.51) shows that 21.3 percent of the maximum bonus was earned, but only by the management in functions contributing to sales and managing total assets.

The Conclusion: The president of AJAX was extremely pleased with the program presented by the consultants. He thought the maximum bonus of $359,500 was a fair incentive for a company of their size, and thought the actual earned award of $36,064 was appropriate. He was certain that the managers involved in controlling cost-of-sales would see the need to do a better job of controlling costs in the coming year. He asked the VPs of Sales and Operations to submit a listing of their proposed allocation of the bonus award.

Critique of Case Study 5-7: We like the idea that the performance for the entire company be the basis for setting the maximum bonus pool. We also believe that if the actual result for the primary corporate goal (ROA in this case) had a 50% or greater probability of being achieved there should be no corporate bonus pool for that year. Providing a bonus for average (i.e., 50%) or less than average performance is poor management. In other words; bonuses should only be available when above-average results are achieved. That statement, of course, runs somewhat counter to what seems to be happening in companies these days, as executives who "run their company into the ground" end up walking away with exorbitant bonuses.

One unique feature of the Bubble Management approach is its ability to determine the degree of uncertainty (risk plus opportunity), and assign it to the various business functions, as shown in Figure 5.43. That allows whatever bonus is available for award to go to those managers

Chapter 5

that have the most impact on achieving corporate results. As this case demonstrates, it is possible to award certain units of a company for above average performance without awarding all units. Business units that perform below average within their own uncertainty profile should not be entitled to a bonus award. Another advantage of using Bubble Management is that bonuses are based on value added by the business units rather than some simplistic calculation based on a percentage of current salaries.

5.10 AN IMPORTANT COMMENT ABOUT COMPENSATION AWARDS

The authors of this book, although experts in assessing and appraising uncertainty and risk/opportunity contributions in business plans, acknowledge that they are not experts in setting compensation levels for management salary increases or bonuses. Accordingly, compensation tables like Figure 5.9 and Performance Translation Tables like Figure 5.37, as well as award levels shown in other case studies, are for illustrative purposes only. Companies considering adopting the VBRM Appraisal concept should consult closely with their Human Resource expert and/or compensation consultant, such as those certified by the American Compensation Association (ACA), who can recommend more appropriate levels for rewarding management against performance depending on the business environment within which the company operates.

APPENDIX 5-1 Procedure for Setting and Analyzing Goals

Organizations interested in setting and analyzing goals using the Bubble Management approach process should consider the following procedure:

1. Review the last year or two of financial history.
2. Determine which goals (e.g., product line A, sales, turnover, etc.) are to be used for measuring performance. (A goal can be set at any level in the organization – corporate, division, department, group, etc.)
3. Set the tentative goals for next year.
4. Establish a team to participate in the VBRM data gathering session. The team should consist of several

individuals having knowledge of the goal areas. Very small groups of just two or three people should be avoided when possible. The dynamics of very small groups lack the variety of discussion and challenges offered by larger groups and also limit synergy. This team will be the one that participates in the facilitated VBRM session in order to provide the goal inputs (such as Figure 5.27).

5. The selected team participates in the facilitated VBRM session. Internally-facilitated sessions are generally not recommended because the facilitator must be intimately familiar with the psychology and nuances prevalent in all forecasts and estimates (e.g., iatrogenic risk, types of numerical bias, origins of hidden assumptions). Focus on the wrong, or too many, goal input elements by ad hoc facilitators have led to disastrous results.

6. Evaluate the results of the probabilistic results which are derived from modeling the information provided through the facilitation. If the uncertainty profiles are reasonable, adopt the goals for next year; otherwise re-evaluate the goals inputs and revise the goals. Uncertainty benchmarking helps separate the two.

7. Once the goals are set, the Tactical Plans, Control Charts, and Performance Translation Tables are developed for monitoring progress and determining performance against goals for appraisal rating and compensation awards.

8. Have the analysis results, Tactical Plans, and Control Charts updated against goals periodically throughout the year.

Applying The Bubble Management Approach to Production Companies

6.1 WHAT THE READER WILL LEARN FROM THIS CHAPTER:

- Suggested goals for appraising production executives
- How to set probability goals using VBRM for production companies
- How to apply the Performance Translation Table
- Conclusions concerning the appraisal process for production companies

6.2 INTRODUCTION

In this chapter will apply the principles of Bubble Management to three companies in production industries.

Again, let's summarize where we are at this point in the book. In Chapter 1 we talked about why the management appraisal process needs a new approach. In Chapter 2 we discussed the various types of goals and pointed out that setting a goal carries with it a level of uncertainty. In Chapter 3 we showed two convenient ways to monitor goals: the tactical plan and the control chart. We introduced the VBRM concept in Chapter 4. Then in Chapter 5, we showed how we broadened the goal setting and rating process, eliminating some of its flaws by bringing probability into the equation.

Now, in this chapter, we are ready to pull all these elements together using the Bubble Management approach to set quantitative goals that can be used to rate executive performance in production companies. As we do, we want to make one thing crystal clear. The cases in this and subsequent chapters are designed to illustrate how the Bubble Management approach can be applied to set goals using prob-

145

ability and reward performance quantitatively. Any company using the approach will need to set its own standards for setting goals and awarding compensation.

6.3 SUGGESTED GOALS FOR APPRAISING PRODUCTION EXECUTIVES

6.3.1 Primary Goals

Back in Chapter 2, we discussed primary goals and suggested that they should be focused on metrics that have a significant impact on the financial performance of a company, or a business segment of a company. In Figure 6.1, we list some primary goals that we believe are appropriate for measuring performance of selected corporate executives in production or manufacturing companies. Notice that we assigned earnings per share only to the CEO because, in many cases, that's the main metric used by many company boards to determine CEO compensation. As we move down the corporate management hierarchy, we have suggested other goals for assignment to business unit and departmental managers.

6.3.2 Secondary Goals

Recall that secondary goals are selected to concentrate on areas where the company needs to improve performance if its primary goals are to be achieved. We have listed several secondary goals for measuring performance of the CEO including net income, stockholder equity, return-on-equity, and share price. At least one or two should be included by the Board of Directors when they set compensation guidelines for the CEO. We have also listed some suggested secondary goals for various executives and managers in Figure 6.1.

6.3.3 Shared Goals

In section 2.3.7, we noted that no single manager or executive is usually solely responsible for achieving any goal. Therefore, we must consider shared goals. When setting shared goals, recognize that each

Applying The Bubble Management Approach

Figure 6.1 Summary of Primary and Secondary Goals for Executives

Title	Performance measurement	Primary goal	Suggested secondary goals
Chief Executive Officer (CEO)	Overall corporate financial performance	Earning per share	Net income, stockholder equity, capital expenditures, share price, Return-on-Equity (ROE)
Chief Operating Officer (COO)	Operating income before minority Interest and taxes	Operating income	Sales growth, operating budgets, total assets, turnover, ROI
Chief Financial Officer (CFO)	Cash flow growth from continuing operations and financial activities	Cash flow growth	Cash flow from operations, cash flow from financial activities, turnover
Chief Admin Officer (CAO)	Overall corporation administrative expenses	Overhead control	General & Administration expense
Business Unit President	Business Unit operating income	Operating income	Sales growth, total assets, market share, business unit turnover
Marketing VP	Net sales	Sales growth	Market share, sales expense, proposal award rate, sales margin
Manufacturing VP	Cost of products sold	Cost of goods	Cost of goods sold, plant productivity, current assets (inventory)
Engineering VP	Quality of product design	Product cost	Recall cost, engineering budget
Product Line Mgr	Product line cost	Product cost	Budget, product line rework costs, accounts receivable, admin expense, product line turnover
Controller	Business Unit operating costs	Cash flow from operations	Account receivable, cash, turnover
Human Resource Mgr	Employee salaries and wages	Labor cost control	Employee diversity, training budget, work stoppages, salary and wage control, labor costs
Quality Assurance Mgr	Overall product quality	Product rework cost	Product design change cost, Manufacturing rework cost

executive or manager sharing in the goal does not have the same level of control over achieving the goal. For that reason, in Figures 6.2 and 6.3, we have chosen to rank the level of control we think each executive might have over the goal shown. We have sorted the shared goals into two categories: 1) those related to core financial factors such as inventory, cash management, and factory overhead, and 2) those related to calculated financial factors such as turnover, operating profit as a percent of sales, and ROA.

6.3.4 Management Attributes

No discussion of goals would be complete without including certain management skills or attributes when designing a package of goals for appraisal purposes. In Figure 6.4 we have listed about a dozen skill

Figure 6.2 Sharing of Goals Among Executives

Core Financial Factors

Factor	Suggested executives sharing the goal	Level of control over goal achievement
Product labor cost	Business Unit President Manufacturing VP HR Mgr	Medium High Medium
Product material cost	Business Unit President Manufacturing VP Purchasing VP Engineering VP	Medium Medium High Low
Factory overhead	Business Unit President Manufacturing VP	Medium High
Inventories	Business Unit President Manufacturing VP	Medium High
Accounts receivable	Controller Product Line Managers	Medium High
Cash	CFO Controller	High High
General expense	CAO Product Line Managers	High Medium
Administrative expense	Business Unit President CAO Product Line Mgr	Medium High Medium
Selling expense	Business Unit President Marketing VP	Medium High
Permanent assets	CFO Business Unit President Manufacturing VP	High High Medium
Sales/revenue	Business Unit President Manufacturing VP Marketing VP	Medium Medium High

areas we think are worthy of consideration. Notice that we list *quality of advice* at the top of our list. We think it is one of the most important management attributes. Furthermore, we pay dearly to get it from our attorneys, doctors and financial advisors – why not also get it from our subordinates?

6.4 SELECTED GOAL AREAS FOR PRODUCTION COMPANIES

In Chapter 5, we used a case study for AJAX Machinery to show how VBRM can be applied to the appraisal process. In this chapter, we will apply VBRM to real data from a Fortune 500 company in the

Applying The Bubble Management Approach

Figure 6.3 Sharing of Goals Among Executives

Calculated Financial Factors

Factor	Suggested executives sharing the goal	Level of control over goal achievement
Cost of goods sold	Business Unit President Manufacturing VP Purchasing VP	High High Medium
Current assets	Business Unit President Manufacturing VP Controller Product Line Mgr	Medium Medium High Medium
Sales and general expenses (SG&A)	Business Unit President CAO Controller Product Line Mgr Marketing VP	High High Medium Medium High
Total assets	CFO Business Unit President Manufacturing VP	High Medium High
Operating profit	COO Business Unit President CFO	High High High
Turnover	COO Business Unit President CFO Marketing VP	High High Medium High
Operating profit as % of sales	COO Business Unit President Manufacturing VP Marketing VP CAO	High High Medium High Low
Return on investment (ROI)	COO Business Unit President Manufacturing VP Marketing VP CFO	High High Medium High High
Share Price	CEO COO CFO	High High High

paper, chemical, and utility industry using published data from annual reports or 10-K statements to the SEC (see Tables 6.1, 6.2 and 6.3). In the next two chapters, we will look at some case studies for service companies and for not-for-profit organizations where we will focus on some different goals customary to those industries.

In this chapter, when collecting company financial data from annu-

Figure 6.4 Suggested Management Skills for Rating Executives

Management skill	What to consider
Quality of advice	Is advice sound and well thought out?
Communication	Are oral and written communications clear?
Time management	Is time well managed?
Team-building	Attracts and motivates people?
Problem solving	Solves problems effectively?
Decision making	Generally makes good decisions?
Planning	Shows good planning skills?
Customer relations	Well respected by clients?
Contract negotiations	Is effective in negotiating with others?
Personnel relations	Has good people skills?
Meeting management	Manages meetings efficiently?
Appraising others	Conducts effective appraisals of subordinates?
Delegation	Is not afraid to delegate?

al reports and 10-K statements, we have tried to apply a format that will conform to the scope of the ROA factors in Figure 2.1. For example, cost of sales includes only costs of making product; it does not include selling expense, G&A, and depreciation. Likewise, Operating Profit (income, contribution, or whatever you want to call it) is calculated before interest expense and taxes.

In some cases, we have had to adjust the data in the 10-K statements shown in Tables 6.1 through 6.3 in order to arrive at the data in the context we wanted. Remember, data shown in these tables were gathered only for use in illustrating our concepts for setting goals and appraising performance presented in this book. Errors, or misinterpretations of the data, if any, are strictly those of the authors, and should have no bearing on our intended use from applying the data. For example, it is not uncommon to have 10-K financial data restated from one year to the next, even though it can lead to some inconsistency in reporting results.

In each of the data tables, we have chosen selected goals areas and shown results for 2001, 2002, and in two cases for 2003. Results consist of total sales, cost of sales, operating income, net income, income per share, cash flow from operations, total assets, turnover, and

Applying The Bubble Management Approach

Table 6.1 Selected Goal Areas and Results for Alpha Paper

GOAL AREA:	Unit of Measure	Actual Results 2001	2002	2003
TOTAL SALES	Million Dollars	24,344	22,715	19,656
Business Unit 1		3,290	3,328	3,830
Business Unit 2		2,485	2,599	2,671
Business Unit 3		5,310	5,345	5,430
COST OF SALES	Million Dollars	18,755	17,685	15,376
OPERATING INCOME	Million Dollars	732	309	1,252
(Before Tax + Interest)				
Business Unit 1		83	129	378
Business Unit 2		387	321	345
Business Unit 3		663	851	601
NET INCOME	Million Dollars	-477	-735	254
INCOME PER SHARE	$ Per Share	-2.01	-3.09	1.01
CASH FLOW/OPERATIONS	Million Dollars	1,481	1,007	1,792
TOTAL ASSETS:	Million Dollars	26,364	24,629	24,405
Business Unit 1		2,398	2,278	2,315
Business Unit 2		2,386	2,329	2,284
Business Unit 3		10,925	11,412	11,246
OPER INCOME (% OF SALES)	Percent	3.01	1.36	6.37
NET INCOME (% OF SALES)	Percent	-1.95	-3.24	1.29
TURNOVER	Ratio	0.92	0.92	0.81
(Total Sales/Total Assets)				
RETURN ON ASSETS	Percent	2.77	1.25	5.16
(Turnover times Oper Income				
as Percent of Sales)				
RETURN ON ASSETS	Percent	-1.80	-2.98	1.05
(Turnover times Net Income as Percent of Sales)				

Note: Data based on 2004 10-K statement unless earlier needed to capture 2001 results.

return-on-assets. In the three cases in this chapter, we have also listed recent results for two or three of the top product line segments for each company.

Where necessary to have sufficient data to run our probabilistic financial model, we have had to allocate certain financial information, such as cost-of-sales, to the business units where the data are not available to that level in the 10-K statements. In those situations, we

Table 6.2 Selected Goal Areas and Results for Beta Petrochemical Company

GOAL AREA:	Unit of Measure	Year		
		2001	2002	2003
TOTAL SALES	Million Dollars	5,390	5,320	5,800
Business Unit A		1,132	1,023	1,098
Business Unit B		535	528	559
Business Unic C		1,587	1,510	1,756
COST OF SALES	Million Dollars	4,497	4,541	4,990
OPERATING INCOME	Million Dollars	-120	208	-634
(Before Tax + Interest)				
Business Unit A		-60	21	-45
Business Unit B		51	34	63
Business Unit C		-187	35	62
NET INCOME	Million Dollars	-175	61	-270
INCOME PER SHARE	$ Per Share	-2.28	0.79	-3.5
CASH FLOW/OPERATIONS	Million Dollars	397	801	244
TOTAL ASSETS:	Million Dollars	6,092	6,287	6,230
Business Unit A		1,249	1,617	1,685
Business Unit B		925	763	762
Business Unit C		1,379	1,208	1,351
OPER INCOME (% OF SALES)	Percent	-2.22	3.91	-10.93
NET INCOME (% OF SALES)	Percent	-3.25	1.15	-4.66
TURNOVER	Ratio	0.88	0.83	0.93
(Total Sales/Total Assets)				
RETURN ON ASSETS	Percent	-1.95	3.25	-10.17
(Turnover times Oper Income				
as Percent of Sales)				
RETURN ON ASSETS	Percent	-2.86	0.95	-4.33
(Turnover times Net Income				
as Percent of Sales)				

Note: Data based on 2004 10-K statement unless earlier needed to capture 2001 results.

Applying The Bubble Management Approach

Table 6.3 Selected Goal Areas and Results for Gamma Utility

		Year	
GOAL AREA:	Unit of Measure	2001	2002
TOTAL SALES	Million Dollars	17,889	15,860
Business Segment A		5,746	4,875
Business Segment B		5,203	3,197
Business Segment C		6,940	7,788
COST OF SALES	Million Dollars	13,967	13,120
OPERATING INCOME	Million Dollars	3,922	2,740
(Before Tax + Interest)			
Business Segment A		1,626	1,595
Business Segment B		607	1,044
Business Segment C		1,689	101
NET INCOME	Million Dollars	1,898	1,034
INCOME PER SHARE	$ Per Share	2.59	1.53
CASH FLOW/OPERATIONS	Million Dollars	4,357	4,199
TOTAL ASSETS:	Million Dollars	49,624	60,122
Business Segment A		14,193	14,642
Business Segment B		5,047	15,189
Business Segment C		30,384	30,291
OPER INCOME (% OF SALES)	Percent	21.92	17.28
NET INCOME (% OF SALES)	Percent	10.61	6.52
TURNOVER	Ratio	0.36	0.26
(Total Sales/Total Assets)			
RETURN ON ASSETS	Percent	7.90	4.56
(Turnover times Oper Income			
as Percent of Sales)			
RETURN ON ASSETS	Percent	3.82	1.72
(Turnover times Net Income			
as Percent of Sales)			

Note: Data based on 2004 10-K filling

assumed that the business unit financial ratios were equivalent to the overall corporate ratios.

6.5 DISGUISING THE CASE STUDY DATA

Although the data used in the case studies in this and the next two chapters are real, the names of the production companies, service companies, and not-for-profit organizations have been disguised. In addition, much of the Situation section of each case study is simulated to focus on the goal setting or appraisal issue desired by the authors. We believe that, by disguising the data, we also have more latitude in discussing the results of each case without possibly embarrassing the management of any of the companies.

6.6 EVALUATING PRODUCTION RESULTS USING BUBBLE MANAGEMENT

In the following case studies, we will focus on a paper company, a chemical company, and an electric utility. We will vary the situation in each case study to highlight the use of the Bubble Management approach to focus on a different issue of the company management. After each case, we will offer a critique. We will also use the flow sequence for each case listed in section 5.7.

CASE STUDY 6-1 ALPHA PAPER COMPANY
(Evaluating business unit managers in a paper company)

The Situation: Alpha Paper is a large paper company operating primarily in the United States, but with several off-shore plants. The Board of Directors recently narrowed the list of candidates to replace the CEO, who was nearing the required retirement age, to three executives. In 2002, they assigned each to manage one of the company's major business segments. The company had used the Bubble Management approach for several years to rate and reward executive performance. The Board was anxious to see the latest ratings of the three executives

Applying The Bubble Management Approach

against the 2004 goals to reach a final decision on the CEO's replacement. They also requested the CEO to have each business unit executive prepare a 30-minute presentation of their unit's 2004 performance.

The Proposed Solution: For the purpose of evaluating the three executives, the Board decided to limit the appraisal process to comparing the performance of each business segment on return-on-assets (ROA) before interest and taxes. It planned to base the final rating on 75 percent results and 25 percent contribution, with the Board Compensation Committee setting the contribution ratings after listening to the performance presentations and questioning each executive. The Board instructed the CFO to limit the financials to the three business units, allocating overhead and other corporate costs to each business unit as appropriate.

Because Alpha Paper had been using VBRM for a while, an operating budget uncertainty benchmark had been developed from history. The initial inputs provided by the Alpha Paper assessment team failed benchmark (Figure 6.5), indicating that there was less uncertainty in their ROA forecast ranges (20%, as shown in Figure 6.6) than should be expected from the benchmark (at least 27%). In other words, the range used for the low and high uncertainty inputs was too narrow, thereby

Figure 6.5 Alpha Paper Uncertainty Benchmark Horn

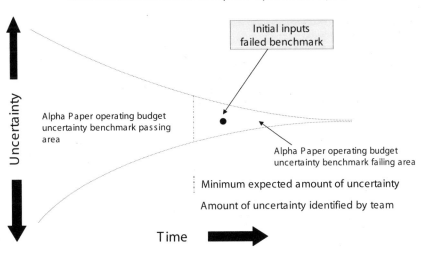

Chapter 6

Figure 6.6 Alpha Paper Uncertainty Benchmark

Alpha Paper – operating budget – Initial inputs risk benchmark failure

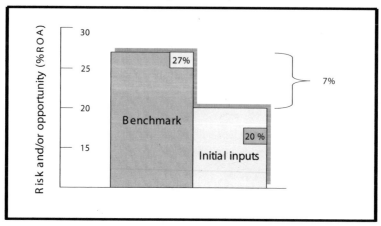

Alpha Paper ROA initial inputs failed to identify at least 7% of ROA risk and /or opportunity.

Figure 6.7 Alpha Paper Goals for 2004

($ million)	(Actual results from 2003 and Goals for 2004)						Data directly from 10-K
Goal area	Business Unit 1		Business Unit 2		Business Unit 3		Basis for Allocat'ng to Business units
	Actual	Goal	Actual	Goal	Actual	Goal	
Sales	3,830	4,000	2,671	3,000	5,430	5,700	-
Inventory	154	160	152	160	749	800	Assets
Receivables	146	140	144	140	708	700	Assets
Cash/equiv	117	120	115	115	567	700	Assets
Current assets	417	420	411	415	2,024	2,000	Calculated
Goodwill/other	1,088	1,080	1,073	985	5,286	4,800	Assets
Fixed assets	810	800	800	800	3,936	4,000	Assets
Total assets	2,315	2,300	2,284	2,200	11,246	10,800	Calculated
Cost-of-sales	2,987	3,000	2,083	2,150	4,235	4,400	Sales
Selling expense	253	225	176	165	358	320	Sales
G&A	165	175	115	125	233	250	Sales
Depreciation	163	180	163	175	378	400	Sales
Other	19	20	13	15	27	30	Sales
Total cost	3,587	3,600	2,550	2,600	5,231	4,900	Calculated
Operating profit	379	400	345	400	601	800	Calculated
Turnover	1.65	1.74	1.17	1.36	0.48	0.53	Calculated
OP as % of sales	9.89	10.0	12.92	13.3	11.07	14.0	Calculated
ROA		17.4		18.2		7.4	Calculated

Applying The Bubble Management Approach

Figure 6.8 ROA Goals For Alpha Paper Business Units

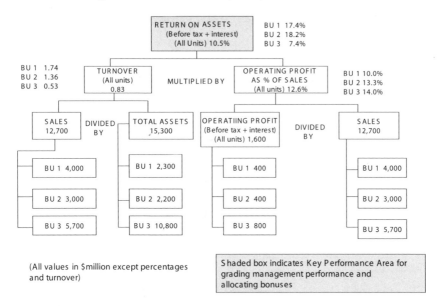

(All values in $million except percentages and turnover)

Shaded box indicates Key Performance Area for grading management performance and allocating bonuses

failing to capture at least 7% of the ROA uncertainty. After the team revisited the inputs and overcame their "tunnel-vision" approach to forecasting uncertainty, new inputs were arrived at that passed benchmark and were used in the results shown below.

The Numbers: Table 6.1 shows selected historical results for Alpha Paper for 2001-2003. At the end of 2003, the CEO and the business segment executives agreed on the goals for 2004 (see Figures 6.7, 6.8, and 6.9) and set the probability uncertainty inputs shown in Figure 6.10. The uncertainty-input data from Figure 6.10 was then processed through VBRM to develop the probabilities shown in Figure 6.11 for the business units. Figures 6.12 through 6.15 show the ROA uncertainty profiles for the overall corporate ROA as well as the three business units (actual results are inserted for simplicity of comparing against goal). Figure 6.16 shows the actual results for 2004. Figure 6.17 shows the VBRM bubble chart (prepared at the beginning of the year) suggesting the priority areas where management needs to focus its attention to capitalize on opportunities and reduce risk.

Chapter 6

Figure 6.9 Key Performance Boxes for Alpha Paper

Key Performance Boxes (KPBs). KPBs must be calculated values - not inputs.
Input value - not a calculation.

($ million unless shown otherwise)

Business unit 1

Revenues		Assets	
Sales	4,000	Total assets	$ 2,300

Expenses	
Total cost of sales/expense	$ 3,600

Operating profit	$ 400	Turnover (asset utilization)	1.74
(Operating profit as % of sales)	10.0%	ROA (operating profit)	17.4%

Business unit 2

Revenues		Assets	
Sales	3,000	Total assets	$ 2,200

Expenses	
Total cost of sales/expense	$ 2,600

Operating profit	$ 400	Turnover (asset utilization)	1.36
(Operating profit as % of sales)	13.3%	ROA (operating profit)	18.2%

Business unit 3

Revenues		Assets	
Sales	5,700	Total assets	$ 10,800

Expenses	
Total cost of sales/expense	$ 4,900

Operating profit	$ 800	Turnover (asset utilization)	0.53
(Operating profit as % of sales)	14.0%	ROA (operating profit)	7.4%

Corporate

Revenues		Assets	
Sales	12,700	Total assets	$ 15,300

Expenses	
Total cost of sales/expense	$ 11,100

Operating profit	$ 1,600	Turnover (asset utilization)	0.83
(Operating profit as % of sales)	12.6%	ROA (operating profit)	10.5%

Applying The Bubble Management Approach

Figure 6.10 Alpha Paper Uncertainty Inputs

Input element	Units	Target	Probability*	Low	High
Business Unit 1 - Sales	$ millions	4,000	30	3,800	7,000
Business Unit 1 - Total COS/Expense	$ millions	3,600	35	3,400	6,000
Business Unit 1 - Total assets	$ millions	2,300	40	2,200	2,700
Business Unit 2 - Sales	$ millions	3,000	55	2,500	3,600
Business Unit 2 - Total COS/expense	$ millions	2,600	50	2,300	3,000
Business Unit 2 - Total assets	$ millions	2,200	60	1,900	2,600
Business Unit 3 - Sales	$ millions	5,700	40	4,800	6,000
Business Unit 3 - Total COS/expense	$ millions	4,900	50	4,700	5,200
Business Unit 3 - Total assets	$ millions	10,800	45	9,000	12,000

*Probability of achieving or improving compared to target

Figure 6.11 Probability Forecast Table for Alpha Paper Goals

Probability of achieving	Corporate ROA (%)	BU1 - ROA (%)	BU2 - ROA (%)	BU3 - ROA (%)
0.05%	33.58	146.73	54.91	12.75
5%	20.91	87.97	42.22	10.27
10%	16.31	56.51	37.51	9.53
15%	14.30	37.87	33.45	8.82
20%	12.85	25.09	30.55	8.49
25%	11.67	21.27	27.40	8.11
30%	10.89	18.71	25.49	7.80
35%	10.15	16.91	23.58	7.56
40%	9.25	15.17	21.43	7.29
45%	8.59	13.65	20.03	6.97
50%	7.94	11.11	19.07	6.61
55%	7.05	8.30	17.58	6.23
60%	6.40	3.69	16.24	5.82
65%	5.61	-2.60	14.62	5.45
70%	4.62	-10.43	13.09	4.94
75%	3.36	-19.58	10.77	4.23
80%	1.90	-29.68	8.63	3.35
85%	0.30	-41.60	4.94	2.30
90%	-1.71	-54.49	1.48	1.16
95%	-4.27	-69.16	-2.53	-0.01
99.95%	-10.16	-91.75	-18.53	-3.09

Shading indicates location of single-point forecast (Target)

Expected results .. each value has 50% chance of being improved

159

Figure 6.12 Alpha Paper Corporate ROA Profile

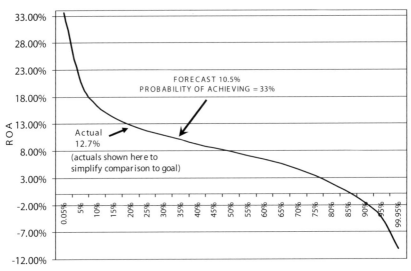

The Conclusion: Clearly, the Business Unit 1 executive achieved the best ROA (41.9 %) during 2004, coming in at a 13% probability of achieving (Figure 6.13) and rating 5.4 on the Performance Translation Table (Figure 6.18). Ratings for BU2 and BU3 executives were 2.2 and 2.9, respectively. After listening to the presentations from the business unit executives, it was the unanimous decision of the compensation committee that the Business Unit 1 executive be selected as the heir-apparent to the CEO. Besides achieving the best actual results, his innovation in improving certain business practices scored heavily on his contribution rating (Figure 6.19).

Critique of Case Study 6-1: We want to cover seven points about the Alpha Paper case, and will discuss them in some detail, but try not to repeat ourselves in future case study critiques.

Point 1: Notice the shape of the ROA profile curves such as Figure 6.12. The curves are much steeper at the very low and very high probability values. As a consequence, it is much more difficult to increase

Applying The Bubble Management Approach

Figure 6.13 Alpha Paper Business Unit 1 ROA Profile

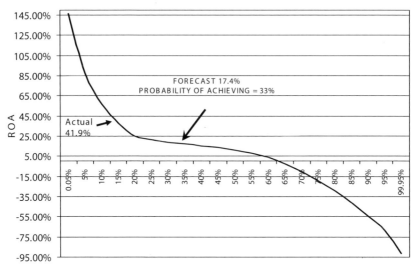

Figure 6.14 Alpha Paper Business Unit 2 ROA Profile

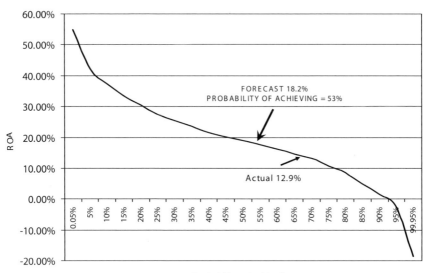

Chapter 6

from a 10% probability to a 5% percent probability than to go from 55% to 50%. This will be true for virtually all budget uncertainty probability curves and will be reflected in all case studies to come later.

Point 2: In order to ensure that goals are set at desired and reasonable probabilities of achievement for all business units, it is recommended that the targets (goals) be run through VBRM before settling on the final goal values. If the target values have too high or low a probability of achieving, they can be adjusted before being set in concrete.

Point 3: The uncertainty inputs, like those shown in Figure 6.10, look simple enough, but companies are cautioned to consider outside training in the process of setting these values. Significant changes can occur in the uncertainty profile curves if inappropriate data are used as uncertainty inputs. Although VBRM, and even basic Monte Carlo simulations, are robust in nature, several organizations have found, painfully, that assessing the wrong elements, too many elements, and too narrow ranges result in fatally flawed, though nice looking results. Selecting the correct elements, and setting their uncertainty inputs, requires a paradigm shift in mindset.

Figure 6.15 Alpha Paper Business Unit 3 ROA Profile

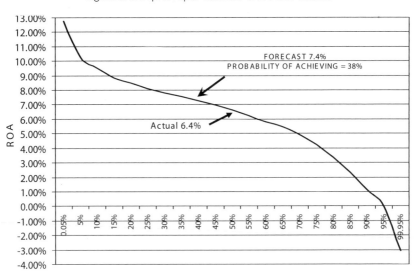

Applying The Bubble Management Approach

Point 4: Probability Translation Tables (PTTs) such as Figure 6.18 can be set by analyzing recent financial data and setting pro forma goals for the last year of available actual results. If a single PTT does not seem to fit all the goal uncertainty profile curves, than an individual PTT can be developed for each goal.

Figure 6.16 Final 2004 Results for Alpha Paper

Goal area	Business unit 1	Business unit 2	Business unit 3	All units
Net sales ($ million)	6,892	2,968	5,656	15,516
Operating profit ($ million)*	997	304	698	1,999
Total assets ($ million)	2,379	2,360	10,968	15,707
Turnover	2.90	1.26	0.52	0.99
Operating profit (% of sales) ($ million)	14.5	10.2	12.3	12.9
Return-on-assets (%)* *Before interest and taxes	41.9	12.9	6.4	12.7

Figure 6.17 VBRM Bubble Chart

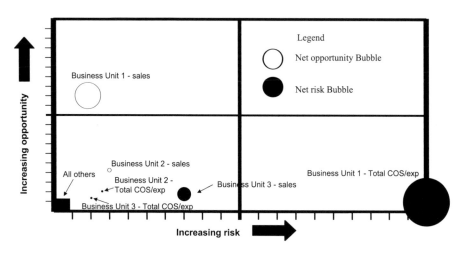

Chapter 6

Point 5: In this case study, we have elected to use only one PTT to rate performance for each business unit of Alpha Paper. A separate PTT could be developed for each business unit, but we found very little value gained in doing that for this case study.

Point 6: A close look at Figure 6.17 shows that Business Unit 1 cost-of-sales carries the highest net risk of any of the goal inputs. Management should focus on this area first because it represents the largest disparity between risk and opportunity for Business Unit 1 performance. After that, Business Unit 1 sales should be the next area to get attention because it contributes the largest net opportunity. Finally, Business Unit 3 sales should be addressed for any potential to mitigate its net risk. The use of the VBRM algorithms to determine net risk is considered highly proprietary by Decision Sciences Corporation and can not be disclosed in more detail here. Suffice it to say that the concept has been proven to be technically correct in several thousand previous applications.

Point 7: A look at Figure 6.11 shows that the 2004 goal set for Business Unit 2 carried an achievement probability of 50-55%, substantially eas-

Figure 6.18 The Performance Translation Table

Values in cells are performance rating (1 to 6 scale) based on probability of meeting the actual result

First digit (s) of probability	Next digit of probability									
	0	1	2	3	4	5	6	7	8	9
0.	6.0	6.0	6.0	6.0	6.0	6.0	6.0	6.0	6.0	6.0
1	5.5	5.5	5.4	5.4	5.3	5.3	5.2	5.2	5.1	5.1
2	5.0	4.9	4.8	4.7	4.6	4.5	4.4	4.3	4.2	4.1
3	4.0	4.0	3.9	3.9	3.8	3.8	3.7	3.7	3.6	3.6
4	3.5	3.5	3.4	3.4	3.3	3.3	3.2	3.2	3.1	3.1
5	3.0	3.0	2.9	2.9	2.8	2.8	2.7	2.7	2.6	2.6
6	2.5	2.5	2.4	2.4	2.3	2.3	2.2	2.2	2.1	2.1
7	2.0	1.9	1.8	1.7	1.6	1.5	1.4	1.3	1.2	1.1
8	1.0	1.0	0.9	0.9	0.8	0.8	0.7	0.7	0.6	0.6
9	0.5	0.5	0.4	0.4	0.3	0.3	0.2	0.2	0.1	0.1
9.9	0.1	0.1	0.1	0.1	0.1	0.1	0.1	0.1	0.1	0.1

As an illustration, if the probability of meeting the goal was determined to be 47 %, the rating would be 3.2; if 89 %, the rating would be 0.6.

ier to achieve than either Business Unit 1 (30-35%) or Business Unit 3 (35-40%). Even though Business Unit 2 only achieved a result at the 66% probability level, it is unwise to let one unit of a company start out with a goal much easier to achieve initially than other units of the company (see point 2 above). Seek consistency when setting goals based on probability.

Figure 6.19 Rating for Alpha Paper Business Unit Executives

Goal	Executive rated	Weighting (%)		Rating (Scale 1 to 6)		Overall rating
		Results	Contribution	Results (a)	Contribution (b)	(1 to 6)
ROA	BU 1	75	25	5.4	5.5	5.43
ROA	BU 2	75	25	2.2	4.2	2.70
ROA	BU 3	75	25	2.9	4.6	3.33

(a) Results rating based on Performance Translation Table Figure 6.18
(b) Rating based on a consensus of Board of Directors compensation committee

Figure 6.20 Tactical Plan for Marketing New Vinyl Composite

Title: TP 6-1   Marketing plan for vinyl composite
Date Issued: Dec 12, 2003
Purpose: Generate $300 million of sales by December 31, 2004
Measure of Performance: Net sales by December 31,2004

Key milestones

	Event	Responsibility	Planned completion	Actual
1.	Complete design of ad program	VP Sales/Mkt	Jan 1	Jan1
2.	Demo models to home centers	VP BU A	Feb 3	Feb 5
3.	Begin phase 1 ad blitz	VP Sales/ Mkt	Feb 10	Feb 11
4.	Complete sales incentive program:			
	Home improvement stores	VP Sales/Mkt	Feb 20	Feb 19
	Builders	VP Sales/Mkt	Feb 28	Feb 28
	Home remodelers	VP Sales/Mkt	Mar 5	Mar 7
5.	Present quarterly sales results	VP Sales/Mkt	Quarterly starting April 5	
6.	Begin phase 2 ad blitz	VP Sales/Mkt	Apr 15	Apr 16
7	Begin phase 3 ad blitz	VP Sales/Mkt	Jul 1	Jul 3
8.	Begin phase 4 ad blitz	VP Sales/Mkt	Sept 15	Sept 13
9.	Submit year-end results	VP Sales/Mkt	Jan 5, 2005	Jan 5

Chapter 6

CASE STUDY 6-2 BETA PETROCHEMICAL COMPANY
(Evaluating the performance of a new Chief Operating Officer)

The Situation: During the fourth quarter of 2003, the CEO of Beta petrochemical replaced the Chief Operating Officer (COO) because he felt operating results were not improving as expected, especially the return-on-assets (ROA). The new COO was given a directive to improve the ROA (based on operating income before interest and tax) to at least 2.00 percent, up from a negative 2003 ROA of 10.17%. The COO knew he had to move fast because the CEO had set the end of 2004 to achieve the goal.

The Proposed Solution: After discussions with his three main business unit executives, it was determined that the upswing in the home improvement market (a market of Business Unit A) represented the best

Figure 6.21 2004 ROA Goal for Beta Petrochemical

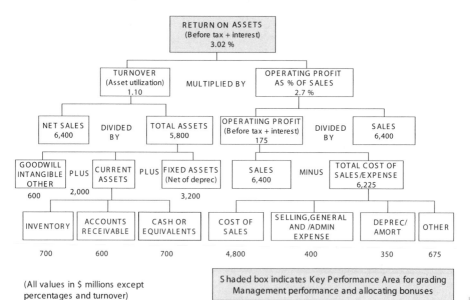

(All values in $ millions except percentages and turnover)

Shaded box indicates Key Performance Area for grading Management performance and allocating bonuses

Applying The Bubble Management Approach

near-term possibility to improve results significantly (the unit had a $45 million loss in 2003). During a two-day strategy meeting involving the VPs of sales, production, and the business units, an aggressive program was devised to improve Business Unit A sales, which typically represented about 20 percent of the total company sales. The core of the program was the introduction of a new vinyl product recently out of development, and the close of some under-performing assets to offset

Figure 6.22 Key Performances Boxes for Beta Petrochemical

Key Performance Boxes (KPBs). KPBs must be calculated values - not inputs.
Input value - not a calculation.

($ million unless shown otherwise)

Revenues	
Total sales	$ 6,400

Expenses	
Cost of sales	$ 4,800
Selling expense and G&A	400
Depre/amort	350
Other	675
Total cost of sales/expense	$ 6,225

Assets	
Inventory	$ 700
Accounts receivable	600
Cash or equivalents	700
Current assets	$ 2,000
Goodwill/intangible/other	600
Fixed assets	3,200
Total assets	$ 5,800

Operating profit $ 175
(Operating profit as % of sales) 2.73%

Turnover (asset utilization) 1.10
ROA (operating profit) 3.02%

Figure 6.23 Beta Petrochemical Uncertainty Inputs

Input element	Units	Target	Probability*	Low	High
Sales	$ million	6,400	40	5,500	7,000
Cost of sales	$ million	4,800	50	4,200	5,500
Selling expense and G&A	$ million	400	40	350	700
Depreciation/amortization	$ million	350	50	275	500
Other	$ million	675	55	550	750
Inventory	$ million	700	60	600	800
Accounts receivable	$ million	600	45	500	700
Cash or equivalents	$ million	700	50	400	850
Goodwill/intangible/other	$ million	600	50	500	675
Fixed assets	$ million	3,200	55	2,800	4,000

*Probability of achieving or improving compared to target

Chapter 6

equipment investment to support the new product. The Business Unit A executives were very excited about the new product, because pilot demonstrations of the new vinyl composite were very successful. The composite, applied in sheets over an improved interlocking particle board substrate (developed with a particle board manufacturer), offered durable seamless finishes for countertops and walls in a variety of colors and designs. The Bubble Management approach was to be used to measure performance.

The Numbers: Table 6.2 shows the historical results for Beta Petrochemical from 2001-2003. Although sales were up in 2003, ROA was extremely volatile from 2001 through 2003. Figure 6.20 shows the tactical plan for increasing Business Unit A sales.

During the strategy meeting, the management agreed on the goals for

Figure 6.24 Probability Forecast Table for Beta Petrochemical

Probability of achieving	ROA (%)
0.05%	22.58
5%	13.45
10%	11.19
15%	8.86
20%	7.22
25%	5.85
30%	4.70
35%	3.45
40%	2.37
45%	1.33
50%	0.38
55%	-0.75
60%	-1.80
65%	-3.06
70%	-4.04
75%	-4.91
80%	-6.34
85%	-8.27
90%	-10.43
95%	-13.96
99.95%	-24.72

Shading indicates location of single-point forecast (Target)

Target = 3.02% (Actual = 2.98%)

Expected results ... each value has 50% chance of being improved

Applying The Bubble Management Approach

2004 (Figures 6.21 and 6.22) and set a target ROA of 3.02 percent. They also set the uncertainty inputs shown in Figure 6.23 (after a little retraining). The uncertainty data from Figure 6.23 was then processed through VBRM to develop the probabilities shown in Figure 6.24. Figure 6.25

Figure 6.25 Beta Petrochemical ROA Profile

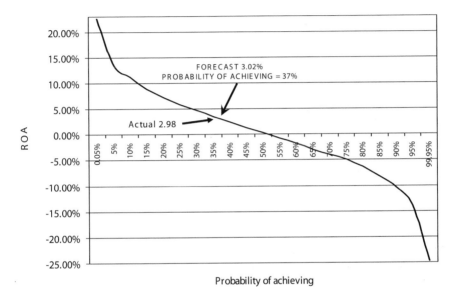

Figure 6.26 VBRM Bubble Chart

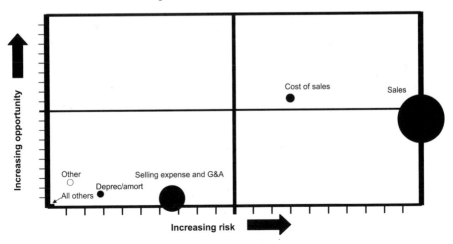

Figure 6.27 Business Area Contribution to ROA Uncertainty

Area of uncertainty	Percent contribution to Beta Petrochemical ROA total uncertainty
Sales	41.5
Cost-of-sales	34.7
Selling expense and G&A	10.6
Depreciation/amortization	6.0
Other	5.5
Fixed assets	0.9
Cash or equivalents	0.4
Inventory	0.2
Accounts receivable	0.1
Goodwill/Intangible/other	0.1

shows the ROA profile, whereas Figure 6.26 shows the bubble chart, which suggests that sales, selling/G&A expenses, and cost-of-sales are the most fruitful areas to focus management attention to improve opportunity and/or reduce risk. Figure 6.27 shows the business area contribution to ROA uncertainty. Finally, Figure 6.28 shows the actual results for 2004 and Figure 6.29 shows the control chart plot of the corporate ROA each quarter during the year (quarterly results annualized).

The Conclusion: Clearly performance improved significantly in 2004 driven by improved sales (up 23 %) and operating income for Business Unit A, helped significantly by the new vinyl product line. Overall company ROA for 2004 improved to 2.98 percent, essentially matching the goal of 3.02. The new COO's job was secure for at least one more year. At the year-end performance appraisal, the COO rated a 3.7 on results and a 5.2 on contribution by the CEO. Based on a pre-set split of 70% results/30% contribution, the COO's final performance rating was 4.15, earning him a 7% salary increase on the company's compensation scale. Bonus awards were yet to be awarded and approved by the Board of Directors.

Critique of Case Study 6-2: Points 1 through 5 from the previous case study critique apply here as well. Setting the ROA goal for 2004 at

Applying The Bubble Management Approach

Figure 6.28 Final 2004 Results for Beta Petrochemical

Goal area	Business unit A	Business unit B	Business unit C	All others	All units
Net Sales ($ million)	1,347	664	2,183	2,386	6,580
Total assets ($ million)	1,640	709	1,418	2,105	5,872
Operating profit ($ million)	16	13	25	121	175
Turnover	0.82	0.94	1.54	1.13	1.12
Operating profit (% of sales) ($ million)	1.18	1.96	1.15	5.07	2.66
Return-on-assets (ROA)	0.97	1.84	1.77	5.73	2.98

3.02% resulted in a probability of achieving the goal of 35%, about what we think is fair and reasonable. The VBRM bubble chart (Figures 6.26) and the uncertainty table (Figure 6.27) show total sales as having the greatest contribution to net risk and uncertainty, respectively. Because overall sales were up 13% from 2003 to 2004, significant ROA improvement from additional sales growth may not be in the cards for 2005, and management may be better off focusing their efforts on cutting cost-of-sales and S/G&A expenses. The tactical goal of $300 million of new sales for Business Unit A was not met, although the new product line contributed all of the $249 million improvement in Business Unit A sales for 2004.

CASE STUDY 6-3 GAMMA UTILITY
(Evaluating a new Chief Executive Officer)

The Situation: Traditionally, Gamma Utility was a regulated utility, but over the last few years it ventured into the non-regulated power business like many other utilities. During 2001 alone, the utility constructed or acquired nearly twenty generating facilities, mostly combustion turbine plants running on natural gas. The strategy was to broaden its mar-

Chapter 6

Figure 6.29 Control Chart for Beta Petrochemical ROA

Goal: Generate $300 million of vinyl composite sales by December 31, 2004

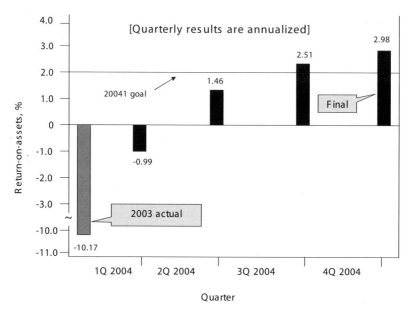

ket and take advantage of energy growth in new markets. As the utility was soon to find out, it's easy to spend money, but a lot harder to improve financial results. Three financial elements told the story from 2001 to 2002: 1) assets grew by $10.498 billion, 2) revenues declined by $2.029 billion, and 3) turnover declined from 0.36 to 0.26.

These were major concerns to the Board of Directors, who decided in June 2003 to ease the current CEO into retirement and promote the president to the job. The directive of the Board was clear – shed non-performing assets and meet goals set by the Board for sales, operating profit, turnover, and ROA. The new CEO was given eighteen months, until the end of 2004, to succeed.

The Proposed Solution: Working with his CFO and senior staff, the new CEO developed a list of assets that were weak-performers. Working with an investment banking firm, a special task force was put together to find buyers for the stations. Cash generated from the station sales would be used to upgrade the company's technology base and

Applying The Bubble Management Approach

Figure 6.30 ROA Goals For Gamma Utility for 2004

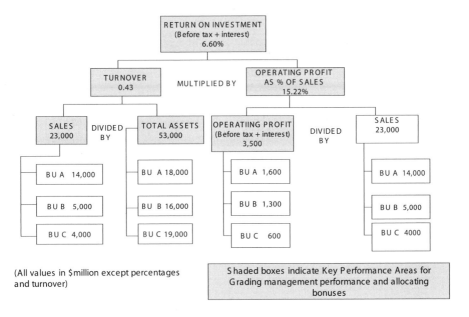

(All values in $million except percentages and turnover)

Shaded boxes indicate Key Performance Areas for Grading management performance and allocating bonuses

Figure 6.31 Key Performance Boxes for Gamma Utility

Key Performance Boxes (KPBs). KPBs must be calculated values - not inputs.
Input value - not a calculation.

2004 ($ million unless shown otherwise)

Revenues	
Business unit A	$ 14,000
Business unit B	5,000
Business unit C	4,000
Total sales	$ 23,000

Assets	
Business unit A	$ 18,000
Business unit B	16,000
Business unit C	19,000
Total assets	$ 53,000

Expenses	
Business unit A	$ 12,400
Business unit B	3,700
Business unit C	3,400
Total cost of sales/expense	$ 19,500

Turnover (asset ytilization)   0.43

ROA (operating profit)   6.60%

Operating profit $ 3,500
(Operating profit as % of sales)   15.22%

Chapter 6

Figure 6.32 Gamma Utility Uncertainty Inputs

Input element	Units	Target	Probability*	Low	High
Business unit A - sales	$ million	14,000	50	12,000	15,000
Business unit A - total COS/expense	$ million	12,400	55	11,500	13,500
Business unit A - total assets	$ million	18,000	40	17,000	19,500
Business unit B - sales	$ million	5,000	55	4,000	6,000
Business unit B - total COS/expense	$ million	3,700	55	3,000	4,500
Business unit B - total assets	$ million	16,000	45	15,500	18,000
Business unit C - sales	$ million	4,000	55	3,000	4,800
Business unit C - total COS/expense	$ million	3,400	45	2,800	4,000
Business unit C - total assets	$ million	19,000	40	18,000	21,500

*Probability of achieving or improving compared to target

Figure 6.33 Probability Forecast Table for Gamma Utility

Probability of achieving	ROA(%)	Turnover ratio	Sales ($million)	Operating profit ($ million)	Total assets ($million)	Operating profit as % of sales
0.05%	12.46	0.492	25,522	6,500	50,630	26.40
5%	9.52	0.456	24,323	5,115	52,166	21.49
10%	8.96	0.451	24,024	4,816	52,471	20.21
15%	8.40	0.446	23,862	4,570	52,702	19.27
20%	8.00	0.443	23,704	4,303	52,856	18.22
25%	7.71	0.439	23,558	4,130	53,010	17.62
30%	7.42	0.436	23,412	4,006	53,148	17.00
35%	7.16	0.433	23,285	3,832	53,347	16.49
40%	6.88	0.431	23,162	3,692	53,502	15.97
45%	6.60	0.429	23,057	3,555	53,633	15.48
50%	6.32	0.426	22,963	3,394	53,792	14.82
55%	6.05	0.424	22,845	3,238	53,929	14.24
60%	5.73	0.420	22,735	3,073	54,127	13.52
65%	5.41	0.418	22,581	2,940	54,259	13.00
70%	5.10	0.415	22,442	2,737	54,427	12.10
75%	4.74	0.412	22,290	2,558	54,646	11.39
80%	4.39	0.408	22,114	2,377	54,827	10.59
85%	3.90	0.404	21,897	2,083	55,092	9.53
90%	3.33	0.399	21,587	1,791	55,461	8.20
95%	2.43	0.391	21,133	1,288	55,869	6.07
99.95%	-1.56	0.360	19,546	-820	57,204	-4.14

Shading indicates location of single-point forecast (Target)

Expected results ... each value has 50% chance of being improved

Applying The Bubble Management Approach

Figure 6.34 Gamma Utility ROA Profile

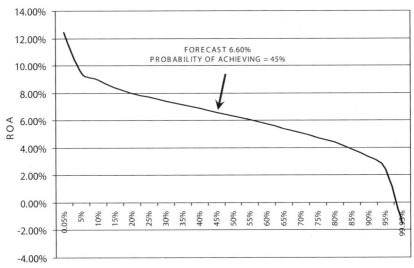

Figure 6.35 Gamma Utility Turnover Ratio Profile

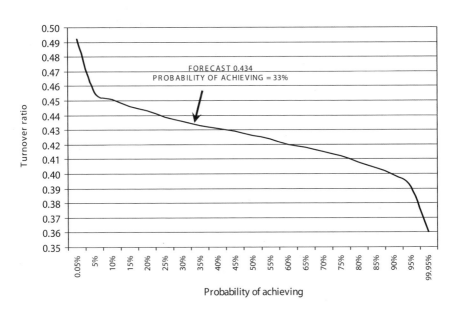

Chapter 6

Figure 6.36 Gamma Utility Sales Profile

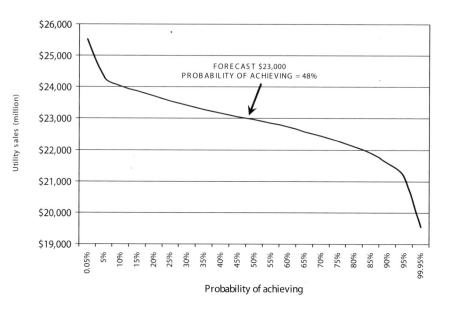

reduce debt. Other actions were taken to improve revenues and cut expenses.

The Numbers: Table 6.3 shows selected results for Gamma Utility for 2001 and 2002. Figures 6.30 through 6.33 show the goals for 2004, the uncertainty inputs and the probability forecast for the goals. Figures 6.34 through 6.39 show the profile curves for the goals. Figure 6.40 provides management with guidance for improving performance.

The Conclusion: Figure 6.41 tells the whole story for Gamma Utility. The bottom line was that by the end of the eighteen months performance period, even though performance improved significantly over 2002, the CEO failed to meet a single one of the goals. The average performance rating on the goals of 1.78 did not help the CEO's case either. After a lengthy discussion in private, the Board unanimously decided to fire the CEO. The chairman of the Board would act as CEO until a replacement from outside the utility was hired.

Applying The Bubble Management Approach

Figure 6.37 Gamma Utility Operating Profit Profile

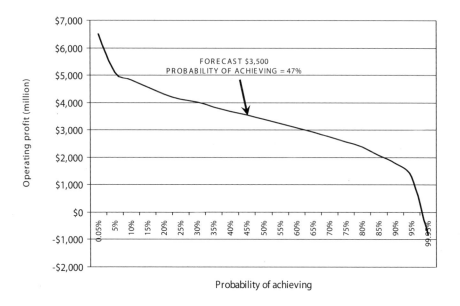

Figure 6.38 Gamma Utility Total Assets Profile

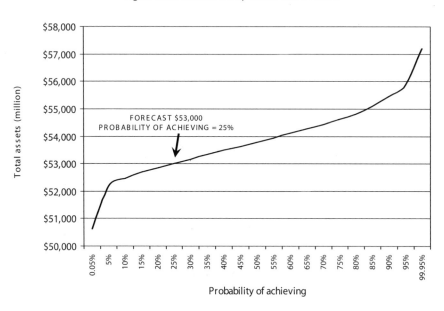

Chapter 6

Figure 6.39 Gamma Utility Operating Profit as Percent of Sales Profile

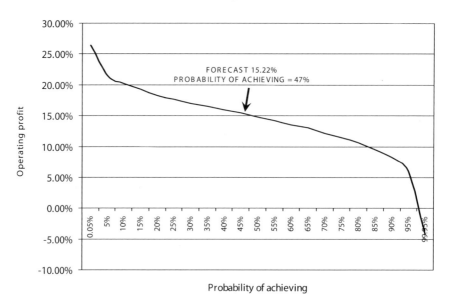

Critique of Case 6-3: Figure 6.38 clearly shows that the asset target was very optimistic, having only a 25% chance of occurring; the other goals were more in-line (33 to 48%). From Figure 6.40, the focus of the new management should have been on Business Unit B and C assets (because they contributed 16% of all the net risk to the ROA), and Business Units A and B sales (largest contributors of net risk, total risk, net opportunity, and total opportunity, respectively).

Some may think that firing the CEO was an extreme action by the Board because significant improvement occurred since 2002. Welcome to the real world of more demanding Boards of Directors! A close look over the last two years at financial publications will show many examples where top executives have been relieved for failing to meet earnings-per-share expectations by only a penny or two. Also, due to corporate scandals recently, many Boards have dropped their cozy relationship with the CEO and have become far more demanding for improved results.

Applying The Bubble Management Approach

Figure 6.40 VBRM Bubble Chart

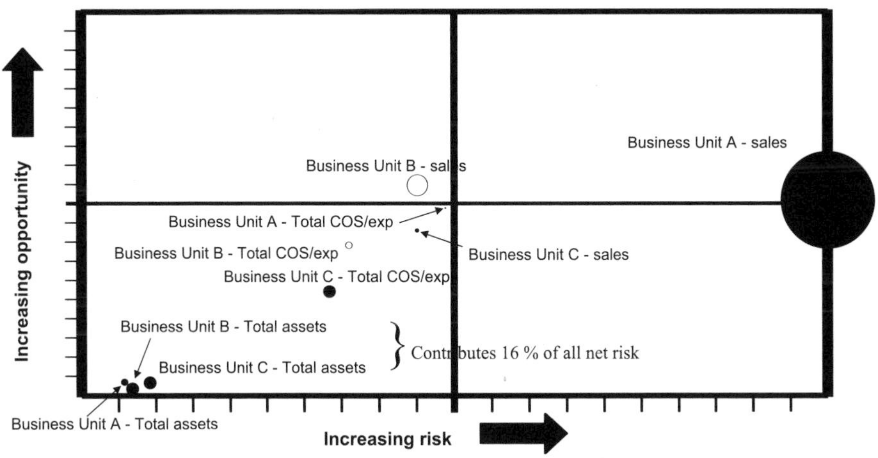

Figure 6.41 Summary of Gamma Utility Performance

(all values in $million except turnover and percentages)

Goal area	2002 actual (Table 6.3)	2004 goal	2004 actual	Probability of achieving 2004 actual (a)	Rating from PTT (b)
Net sales	15,860	23,000	22,503	67%	2.2
Total assets	60,122	53,000	55,470	90%	0.5
Operating profit	2,740	3,500	3,014	59%	2.6
Turnover	0.26	0.43	0.40	89%	0.6
Operating profit (% of sales)	17.28	15.22	13.39	62%	2.4
ROA (%)	4.56	6.60	5.43	63%	2.4

(a) See Figures 6.34 – 6.39   Average rating = 1.78
(b) Refer to Performance Translation Table Figure 6.18

6.7 SOME FINAL THOUGHTS ON THE CASE STUDIES IN THIS CHAPTER

Each of the cases in this chapter highlights the perils of being a CEO in corporate America today. The new CEO at Alpha Paper should know that his days are numbered unless he continues to produce improving results. Likewise for the CEO of Beta Petrochemicals, who was barely able to meet the corporate ROA goal in 2004, but must do better in 2005 if he expects to keep his job. The CEO of Gamma Utility is just another casualty of the corporate quest for improved results. As most readers know, the days of monopoly territories and life-time employment at regulated electric utilities are over as that industry has moved into unregulated markets or has been forced to compete with their peers because of directives from state regulatory commissions. The demand to keep costs down has now clearly reached the electric utility industry. Along with it, there is now a new world order – no sanctuary at the top management level.

Applying Bubble Management Approach to Service Companies

7.1 WHAT THE READER WILL LEARN FROM THIS CHAPTER:

- Suggested goals for service companies
- How to set probability goals for service companies
- Conclusions concerning the appraisal process for service companies

7.2 INTRODUCTION

The principles of Bubble Management are applied in this chapter to three companies in the service sector.

Here we will focus our attention on three major service industries – banking, insurance, and health care. But first, let's have a quick overview of each industry.

7.2.1 Banking

Compared to production companies, banks derive most of their revenues from fees and interest (investment, lending, mortgage, etc), trading gains, credit card income, and securities gains. Key expenses are wages and compensation, occupancy costs, communication expense, professional outside services, marketing, and litigation costs. Banks are in the business of moving money, not products. But, being financial businesses, it is only reasonable to measure bank executives in financial terms – return-on-assets, return-on stockholder equity, asset turnover, trading return, earnings-per-share, etc. Banks generally pay stockholders generous annual dividends.

7.2.2   Insurance Firms

The biggest source of revenue for insurance companies comes from insurance premiums. Like banks, a large share of their revenue comes from commissions, fees, and investment gains. Insurance companies tend to retain more of their earnings than distribute it as dividends to shareholders. Profitability is derived principally from their ability to price and manage uncertainty on insurance products, their ability to attract and retain customer assets, and their ability to control expenses (see Case Study 7-2).

Although insurance companies do not ship durable goods, they have a strong need: 1) to market innovative financial services (e.g., new products) that gain market acceptance, 2) to earn commissions and fees from the distribution and servicing of funds, annuities, and retirement products, and 3) to manage group life, annuity, and disability insurance products. They are market-driven enterprises.

7.2.3   Health Care Firms

Health care firms offer a variety of services to their clients. The firm used in case study 7-3 focuses on pharmacy benefit products and offers sophisticated programs and services to HMOs, insurance carriers, labor unions, and employers. Their main service is offering prescription drug benefits to member enterprises. In most cases they purchase the drugs they dispense on the open market, seeking the best prices available because of their volume of purchases, and pushing generics whenever possible to lower the final price to members. Revenues tend to come mainly from pharmacy products and services to members, sold through company-owned pharmacies or by mail order. Cost of Sales is typically from employee costs, depreciation of facilities, and G&A expense. On the assets side of the balance sheet, goodwill can be high caused by assigning high values to client relationships.

7.3 SUGGESTED GOALS FOR APPRAISING SERVICE EXECUTIVES
7.3.1 Primary Goals

Earlier we discussed primary goals and suggested that they should be focused on metrics that have a significant impact on the financial

Bubble Management Approach to Service Companies

Figure 7.1 Summary of Primary and Secondary Goals for Service Executives

Title	Performance measurement	Primary goal	Suggested secondary goals
Chief Executive Officer (CEO)	Overall corporate financial performance	Earning per share	Net income, stockholder equity, capital expenditures, share price, Return-on - Equity (ROE)
Chief Operating Officer (COO)	Operating income before minority Interest and taxes	Operating income	Revenue growth, cost of operations, total assets, turnover, ROA
Chief Financial Officer (CFO)	Cash flow growth from continuing operations and financial activities	Cash flow growth	Cash flow from operations, cash flow from financial activities, turnover
Chief Admin Officer (CAO)	Overall corporation administrative expenses	G&A expense	Training and administration cost, health care cost control
Business Unit President	Business Unit operating income	Operating income	Revenues growth, BU assets, BU market share, BU turnover
Marketing VP	Net revenues	Revenue growth	Market share, cost of sales, operating profit
Risk VP	Credit and trading risk management	Net trading revenue	Trading loss reduction, credit loss reduction
IT VP	Information system and technology improvement	IT budget control	IT equipment installation cost control
Trading VP	Revenues from trading activities	Net trading revenue	Trading loss reduction

performance of a company, or a business segment of a company. In Figure 7.1, we list some primary goals that we believe are appropriate for measuring performance of selected corporate executives in service companies.

7.3.2   Secondary Goals

Recall that secondary goals are selected to concentrate on areas where the company needs to improve performance if its primary goals are to be achieved. We have listed several secondary goals for measuring performance of the CEO including net income, stockholder equity, return-on-equity, and share price. At least one or two should be included by the board of directors when they set compensation guidelines for the CEO. We have also listed some suggested secondary goals for various executives and managers in Figure 7.1.

7.3.3   Shared Goals

No single manager or executive is usually solely responsible for achieving any goal. Therefore, companies need to consider shared goals. When setting shared goals, it must be recognized that each executive or manager sharing in the goal does not have the same level of

Chapter 7

control over achieving the goal. For that reason, in Figures 7.2 and 7.3 we have chosen to suggest the level of control we think each executive might have over the goal shown. The VBRM analysis will provide a quantitative value to the amount of control. Notice also that we have sorted the shared goals into two categories: 1) those related to core financial factors such as inventory, cash management, and overhead, and 2) those related to calculated financial factors such as turnover, operating profit as a percent of sales, and ROE.

7.3.4 Management Attributes

In Figure 7.4 we have listed about a dozen skill areas we think are good candidates for management attributes. Managers can select the ones they like from our list or add their own.

7.4 EVALUATING GOAL RESULTS USING BUBBLE MANAGEMENT

CASE STUDY 7-1 ALPHA BANKING GROUP
(Managing merger costs)

The Situation: In September, 2004 Alpha Banking completed a merger with a major competitor to increase its asset base by nearly 50 percent. The timing of the merger was right, as Alpha was coming off of a very successful year in 2003 with major improvement in all aspects of its financial statement. Although 2003 performance was much improved, some metrics, such as return-on-assets, still lagged below competitor A (see Figure 7.5).

While seeking to continue the improved performance beyond 2004, the Board of Directors set the following longer-range goals for the CEO: 1) a 5-percent decrease in the combined headcount of the merged company within one year, 2) a $1 billion per year expense reduction during 2005, 2006, and 2007, and 3) a 12-percent reduction in non-performing loans by the end of 2006.

Primary goals for the coming year were: 1) to achieve earnings-per-share (EPS) of $3.18 and 2) to generate a return-on-equity (ROE) of 8.90%. Although the goals were below 2003 pre-merger levels (see Figure7.5), they were considered achievable recognizing that pruning of expenses would take the rest of 2004 and most of 2005, and that 2004 results would be burdened with unneeded costs. Furthermore, recognizing the challenge to merge the two banks, the Board agreed that merger and litigation provisions expected to total

Bubble Management Approach to Service Companies

Figure 7.2 Sharing of Goals Among Service Executives

Core Financial Factors

Factor	Suggested executives sharing the goal	Level of control over goal achievement
Administrative expense	Business Unit President CAO (Chief Admin Officer) Product Line Mgr	Medium High Medium
Operating expenses	Business Unit President Marketing VP COO (Chief Operating Officer)	High High High
Permanent assets	CFO (Chief Financial Officer) Business Unit President CAO	High High Medium
Revenue	Marketing VP Business Unit President COO	High High Medium
Inventories	Business Unit President CFO	High Medium
Accounts receivable	CFO Business Unit President	High High
Cash or cash equivalents	CFO Business Unit President	High High
General expense	CAO Business Unit President COO	High Medium High

Figure 7.3 Sharing of Goals Among Service Executives

Calculated Financial Factors

Factor	Suggested executives sharing the goal	Level of control over goal achievement
Total expenses	Business Unit President Marketing VP CAO	High High High
Current assets	Business Unit President CFO	Medium High
Sales and general expenses (SG&A)	Business Unit President CAO Marketing VP	High Medium High
Total assets	CFO Business Unit President CAO	Medium High Medium
Operating profit	COO Business Unit President CFO	High High Medium

Chapter 7

Figure 7.4 Suggested Management Skills for Rating Service Executives

Management Skill	What to consider
Quality of advice	Is advice sound and well thought out?
Communication	Are oral and written communications clear?
Time management	Is time well managed?
Team-building	Attracts and motivates people?
Problem solving	Manages problems effectively?
Decision making	Generally makes good decisions?
Planning	Shows good planning skills?
Customer relations	Well respected by clients?
Contract negotiations	Is effective in negotiating with others?
Personnel relations	Has good people skills?
Meeting management	Manages meetings well?
Appraising others	Conducts effective appraisals of subordinates?
Delegation	Is not afraid to delegate?

nearly $5 billion for 2004 would be excluded from the financials when appraising performance. The CEO set to work to develop a plan of attack.

The Proposed Solution: Eight task forces were formed to review operations and recommend changes in the following areas: 1) improved products and services, 2) marketing, 3) underwriting, 4) loan risk, 5) trading, 6) technology, 7) credit card management, and 8) branch office consolidation. Simultaneously, each vice-president was given an assignment to identify employees and managers for termination to meet the Board's headcount goal. Reports on task force recommendations were due in five weeks and the first wave of terminations was scheduled for early November, 2004 (4% of the 5% headcount reduction goal was actually achieved in fiscal 2004).

The Numbers: Figure 7.5 shows the financial results for the Alpha Banking Group for 2003 before the merger (results for competitor A are also included) and the financial goals for 2004 (after the merger). Figures 7.6 and 7.7 show the 2004 goals for EPS and ROE in tabular and chart form. Figure 7.8 shows the uncertainty inputs from the team at Alpha Banking with the usual probability estimate and low/high range for each input element.

Bubble Management Approach to Service Companies

Figure 7.5 Financials for Alpha Banking Group

($ million unless shown otherwise)

Goal area	2003 actual before merger	2003 competitor A	2004 goal (after merger)
Total revenue:	44,463	24,517	55,000
Non-interest	20,419	9,181	25,000
Interest	24,044	15,336	30,000
Total expense:	34,435	18,181	44,500
Non-interest	21,716	13,122	30,000
Interest	11,079	4,473	12,500
Credit loss provision	1,540	586	2,000
Merger/ litigation	100	-	-
Income before tax	10,028	6,336	10,500
Income tax	3,309	2,089	1,600
Net income	6,718	4,247	8,900
Common shares	2,009	1,325	2,800
Stockholder equity	46,154	32,135	100,000
Earnings-per-share	$ 3.34	$ 3.21	$ 3.18
Return-on-equity	14.56%	13.22%	8.90%
Total assets	770,912	361,501	1,157,248
Return-on-assets	0.87%	1.17%	0.77%

Figure 7.6 Key Performance Goals for Alpha Banking

Key Performance Boxes (KPBs). KPBs must be calculated values - not inputs.
Input value - not a calculation.

2004   ($ million unless shown otherwise)

Revenues	
Interest	$ 30,000
Non-interest	25,000
Total revenue	$ 55,000

Common shares	2,800
Stockholder equity	100,000

Earnings per share	3.18%

Expenses	
Interest	$ 12,500
Non-interest	30,000
Credit loss	2,000
Merger/litigation	-
Total expenses	$ 44,500

Return on equity	8.90%

Income before tax	$ 10,500

Tax rate	15.24%
Income tax	$ 1,600

Net income	$ 8,900

Chapter 7

Figures 7.9, 7.10, and 7.11 show the probability for the expected (average) value and the goal for earnings per share (EPS) and return-on-equity (actual results are also shown to facilitate comparison). The bubble chart is shown in Figure 7.12 and the uncertainty contributions to EPS are shown in Figure 7.13. Year-end results are shown in Figures 7.14 and 7.15.[J, figures 7.9,

The Conclusion: Both goals (targets) for EPS and ROE were exceeded, as shown in Figures 7.9, 7.10, and 7.11. From the profile charts, we can see that the probability of achieving the EPS actual results came in at 55% and for the ROE at 62%, translating to performance ratings of 2.8 and 2.4 respectively from our Performance Translation Table (see Figure 6.18). The EPS rating would qualify the management for a 5-7% salary increase and a 10-14% bonus using the compensation table (Figure 7.16) developed by the Board compensation committee. The ROE performance would qualify for a lower merit increase and bonus.

Figure 7.7 Alpha Banking 2004 Goals

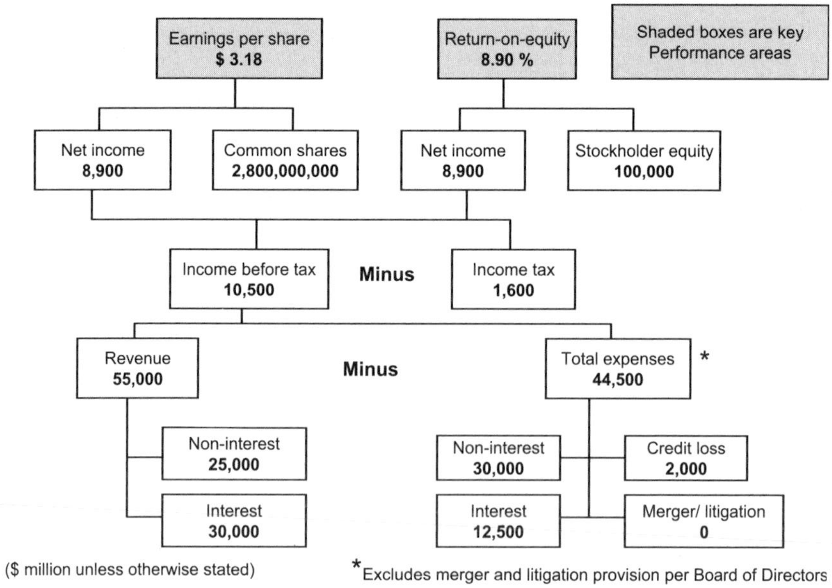

($ million unless otherwise stated)   *Excludes merger and litigation provision per Board of Directors

Bubble Management Approach to Service Companies

Figure 7.8 Alpha Banking Uncertainty Inputs

Input element	Units	Target	Probability*	Low	High
Revenue - interest	$ million	30,000	45	25,000	35,000
Revenue - non-Interest	$ million	25,000	55	23,000	30,000
Expense - interest	$ million	12,500	55	10,000	14,000
Expense - non-Interest	$ million	30,000	50	25,000	32,000
Expense - credit loss	$ million	2,000	60	1,000	3,000
Expense - merger/litigation	$ million	-	-	-	-
Tax rate	$ million	15.24	50	13.00	17.00
Common shares	million	2,800	50	2,700	2,900
Stockholder equity	$ million	100,000	50	97,000	110,000

*Probability of achieving or improving compared to target

Figure 7.9 Probability of Achieving EPS and ROE Goals

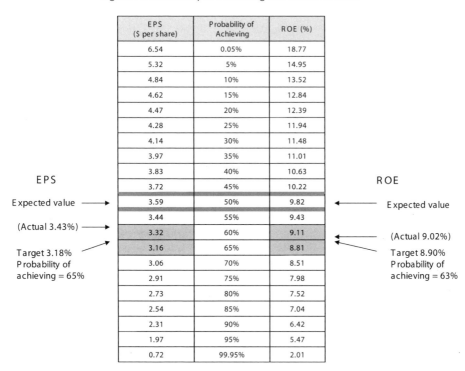

EPS ($ per share)	Probability of Achieving	ROE (%)
6.54	0.05%	18.77
5.32	5%	14.95
4.84	10%	13.52
4.62	15%	12.84
4.47	20%	12.39
4.28	25%	11.94
4.14	30%	11.48
3.97	35%	11.01
3.83	40%	10.63
3.72	45%	10.22
3.59	50%	9.82
3.44	55%	9.43
3.32	60%	9.11
3.16	65%	8.81
3.06	70%	8.51
2.91	75%	7.98
2.73	80%	7.52
2.54	85%	7.04
2.31	90%	6.42
1.97	95%	5.47
0.72	99.95%	2.01

EPS

Expected value →

(Actual 3.43%) →

Target 3.18%
Probability of
achieving = 65%

ROE

← Expected value

← (Actual 9.02%)

← Target 8.90%
Probability of
achieving = 63%

Figure 7.10 Alpha Banking EPS Uncertainty Profile

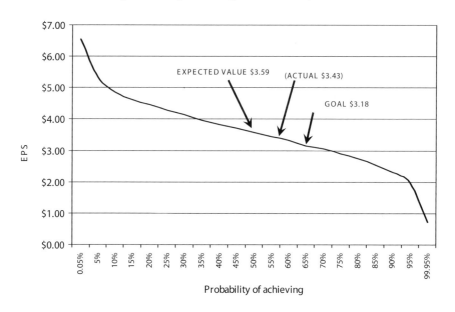

Figure 7.11 Alpha Banking ROE Uncertainty Profile

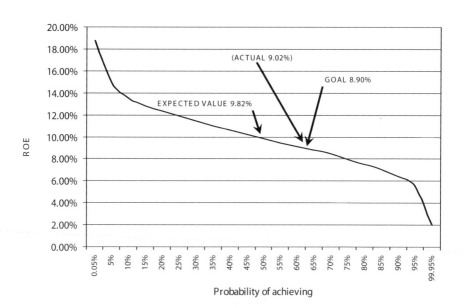

Bubble Management Approach to Service Companies

Figure 7.12 VBRM Bubble Chart

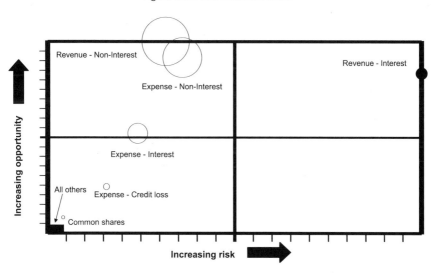

Figure 7.13 Contributions to EPS Uncertainty

Area of uncertainty	Percent contribution to Alpha Banking EPS total uncertainty
Revenue - interest	31.7
Revenue - non-interest	22.8
Expense ..non-Interest	22.1
Expense - interest	13.1
Expense - credit loss	6.9
Common shares	2.1
Tax rate	1.4

Critique of Case Study 7-1: We think the Board was overly generous when it set the table for compensation, especially by awarding a bonus of 5-9% for probabilities over 55%. VBRM analysis confirmed that the EPS and ROE goals were easily obtained, each having a roughly 65% chance. The Board should have set the goals at least to $3.59 for EPS and 9.82% for ROE because these values represent average (50%) per-formance. Notice the slight difference in the probability of achieving the EPS goal (65% on Figure 7.9) and the ROE goal (63%). Even though

Chapter 7

net income is used in each calculation, the EPS probability is affected by the uncertainty in common shares, whereas the ROE probability is affected by the uncertainty in shareholders equity. It is the difference in the common shares uncertainty and shareholders equity uncertainty that is driving the probabilities apart.

Although not part of the goals, the Board of Directors also wanted to know what the impact would be on EPS and ROE if the merger/litigation expenses were included (the belief was that there was a 0 % probability that these expenses would be zero and a maximum of $6 billion could be incurred). Including the merger/litigation expenses would have dropped the chance of achieving the EPS goal of $3.18 from 65% to 30%, and the ROE goal from 63% to 29%. Performance rating at those levels would have been 4.0 and 4.1, respectively.

Let's take a look now at the actual results compared to goal for some of the revenue and expense categories. Management failed to mitigate significant risk and capture opportunity associated with revenue-interest. The actual, although higher than goal, already had roughly a 50% chance of occurring (only average performance). Notice also that this element carried the most net risk on Figure 7.12. Management did capture some opportunity in revenue-non-interest and this resulted in a nice improvement compared to goal.

Figure 7.14 Key Performance Actuals for Alpha Banking

Key Performance Boxes (KPBs). KPBs must be calculated values - not inputs.
Input value - not a calculation.

2004			($ million unless shown otherwise)	
REVENUES				
Interest	$	30,595	Common Shares	2,780
Non-Interest		26,336	Stockholder Equity	105,653
Total Revenue	$	56,931		
			Earnings Per Share	**3.43%**
EXPENSES				
Interest	$	13,834	**Return On Equity**	**9.02%**
Non-Interest		29,294		
Credit Loss		2,544		
Merger/Litigation		0		
Total Expenses	$	45,672		
Income Before Tax	$	11,259		
Tax Rate		15.35%		
Income Tax	$	1,728		
Net Income	$	9,531		

Bubble Management Approach to Service Companies

On the other hand, management failed to control uncertainties in two expense areas (expense-interest and expense-credit loss). Both of these had a better than 50% chance of improving, but even that level of performance was not obtained. This could be a failure in execution or an indication that management needs additional help in understanding the uncertainties in this area of their business. Notice also that management had a problem controlling expense-interest. This could be an indication that this cost element is more volatile and therefore more difficult to control.

CASE STUDY 7-2 BETA INSURANCE
(Improving operating performance)

The Situation: Beta Insurance was coming back from a net income loss of $154 million in 2001 that resulted in a suspension of dividends to shareholders. Performance did improve significantly in 2002 (net $194 million) and again in 2003, as shown in Figure 7.17. The CEO was anxious to continue the improvement into 2004 and set two goals for the Chief Operating Officer (COO): 1) achieve earnings per share of $3.33, and 2) generate a return on equity of

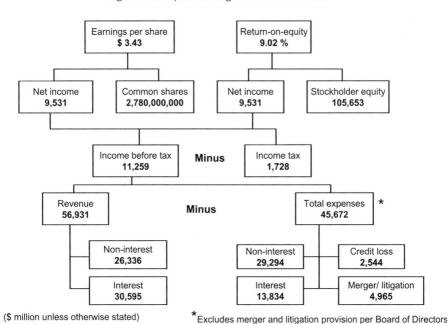

Figure 7.15 Alpha Banking 2004 Actual Results

($ million unless otherwise stated) *Excludes merger and litigation provision per Board of Directors

Chapter 7

Figure 7.16 Conversion Table for Compensation Determination

PTT probability range (%) (a)	Performance rating (Table 6.18)	Salary increase potential (%)	Bonus potential (%)
20 or lower	5.0 - 6.0 (Level 1)	12 - 15	20 - 40
35 - 21	3.8 - 4.9 (Level 2)	8 - 11	15 - 19
55 - 36	2.8 – 3.7 (Level 3)	5 - 7	10 - 14
75 - 56	1.5 – 2.7 (Level 4)	3 - 4	5 - 9
Greater than 75	Under 1.5 (Level 6)	None	None

(a) The lower the probability, the more difficult to achieve the goal

Figure 7.17 Beta Insurance Financials

($ million unless otherwise shown)

Goal area	2003 actual	2004 goal
Revenues:	27,888	28,400
Premiums	13,233	13,000
Policy fee income	2,001	2,200
Investments	8,680	8,900
Commissions	3,704	3,800
Other income	270	500
Expenses:	25,909	25,500
Policyholder benefits	13,424	13,000
Interest to policyholders	1,830	2,100
Dividends to policyholders	2,602	2,500
G&A	7,562	7,400
Casualty losses	491	500
Income before tax	1,979	2,900
Income tax	657	900
Net income	1,322	2,000
Common shares	584	600
Stockholder equity	21,292	22,000
Earnings per share (EPS)	$ 2.26	$ 3.33
Return-on-equity (ROE)	6.21%	9.09%
Total assets	321,274	No goal set
Return-on-assets (ROA)	0.41%	No goal set

9.09%. Meeting both goals would require improving net income significantly over the 2003 performance level of $1.322 billion.

The Proposed Solution: The COO decided to focus revenue growth in two areas – improved policy fee income and gains on investment income. Expense reductions were targeted across-the-board with special emphasis on

Bubble Management Approach to Service Companies

Figure 7.18 Key Performance Goals for Beta Insurance

Key Performance Boxes (KPBs). KPBs must be calculated values - not inputs.		
Input value - not a calculation.		

2004

($ million unless shown otherwise)

Revenues	
Premiums	$ 13,000
Policy fee income	2,200
Investments	8,900
Commissions	3,800
Other income	500
Total sales	$ 28,400

Common shares (million)	600
Stockholder equity	22,000
Earnings per share	**$3.33**
Return on equity	**9.09%**

Expenses	
Benefits	$ 13,000
Interest	2,100
Dividends	2,500
G&A	7,400
Casualty loss	500
Total expense	$ 25,500

Income before tax	2,900
Tax rate	31.034%
Tax	900
Net income	2,000

cutting general and administrative (G&A) expense. The COO knew that the recent increases in interest rates would require the company to post additional interest to policyholder account balances, and he anticipated that some cutback in dividends to policy holders may be necessary in order to grow operating income. He hoped the dividend cut would not be necessary.

The Numbers: Figures 7.17 through 7.20 show the Beta Insurance financials for 2003, goals, and uncertainty inputs for the VBRM analysis. Figures 7.21, 7.22, and 7.23 show the probability profiles for the EPS and ROE goals with the year-end actuals inserted for comparison.

Figure 7.24 shows the VBRM bubble chart which highlights revenues-premiums and expense-interest as the big contributors of net risk, and revenue-policy fee income, expense-benefits, revenue-investments, revenue-other income, and expense-dividends as the majority of net opportunity contributors. Figure 7.25 lists the contributions to uncertainty for the Beta Insurance business plan. Year-end results are shown in Figure 7.26. Figure 7.27 shows the conversion table adopted by the CEO for determining compensation for the COO.

The Conclusion: Both the EPS and ROE goals were met for 2004 (see Figures 7.21 through 7.23). Notice, however, that both goals were set by the CEO at a value that had about a 63% probability of being achieved. This is also reflected by the VBRM bubble chart (Figure 7.24); the combined area of the net opportunities overwhelm the net risks among the uncertainty drivers. There is much more opportunity than risk in this plan. In our opinion, these goals were not very challenging.

Actual results for both goals did come in at a 41% probability of achieving, qualifying the COO for a performance rating of 3.5, equal to only a 1-2% salary increase (Figure 7.27). These amounts may seem a bit unfair at first, but read on below.

Critique of Case Study 7-2: Performance by the COO was above average for the EPS and ROE goals. However, revenues were slightly short of goal. Also, the COO was not able to get revenue–premiums and expense–interest under control as well as had been hoped, both areas failing to meet goal. Further analysis of these two areas, which together contribute 97% of all net risk to the bottom line (Figure 7.24), did not even reach their expected (average) values. The expected value for revenue–premiums was $12.964 billion; actual was $12.580 billion. The expected value for expense–interest was $2.151 billion whereas actual was $2.334 billion. Had the COO achieved these average results, the EPS would have increased from $3.73 to $4.37 (a performance result rating of 5.3), and the ROE would have increased from 10.10 % to 11.84 % (a performance result rating of 5.0). That would have boosted the performance rating for the COO to Level 2 on Figure 7.27, qualifying for a salary increase of 8-11% and a potential bonus of 15-19%.

Does this mean that the COO failed to perform to at least an average level in these two areas? Not necessarily. Suppose previous uncertainty benchmarking and risk grading (refer back to Chapter 4) had uncovered deficiencies in the operating management team's ability to assess reliably the uncertainty in these two areas. Further suppose that the management team had received an uncertainty grade of D regarding these two aspects of business. (Uncertainty grades are mathematical assessments of how well a management team identifies the true risks and opportunities in its business; the mathematical grades are then converted to letter grades similar to those encountered in academia). An uncertainty grade of D would equate to the following description of the management team's ability to identify and quantify uncertainty in these two areas:

BELOW AVERAGE: Team has difficulty identifying and/or considering issues not fully under its control. Over-optimism and/or over-pessimism frequently come into play.

Bubble Management Approach to Service Companies

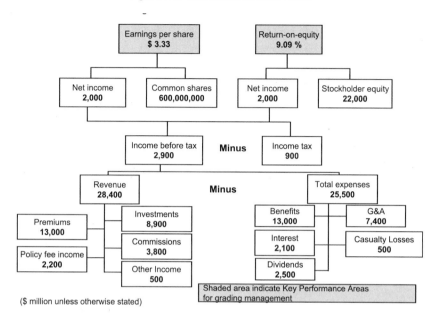

Figure 7.19 Beta Insurance 2004 Goals

($ million unless otherwise stated)

Figure 7.20 Beta Insurance Uncertainty Inputs

Input element	Units	Target	Probability*	Low	High
Revenue - premiums	$ million	13,000	40	12,000	13,500
Revenue - policy fee income	$ million	2,200	75	2,000	2,800
Revenue - investments	$ million	8,900	60	8,500	9,500
Revenue - commissions	$ million	3,800	35	3,500	4,500
Revenue - other income	$ million	500	65	400	850
Expense - benefits	$ million	13,000	65	12,250	13,500
Expense - interest	$ million	2,100	30	1,800	2,700
Expense - dividends	$ million	2,500	55	2,000	2,800
Expense - G&A	$ million	7,400	45	7,000	7,600
Expense - casualty loss	$ million	500	50	-	1,000
Tax rate	%	31.03	50	30.00	32.00
Common shares	million	600	50	550	650
Stockholder equity	$ million	22,000	40	21,000	23,000

* Probability of achieving or improving compared to target

Chapter 7

Figure 7.21 Probability of Achieving EPS and ROE Goals

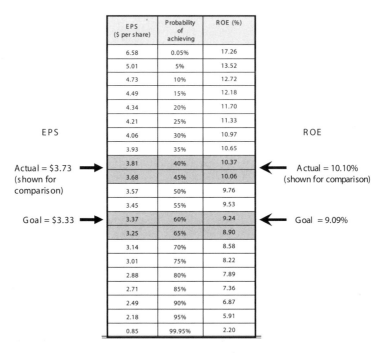

EPS ($ per share)	Probability of achieving	ROE (%)
6.58	0.05%	17.26
5.01	5%	13.52
4.73	10%	12.72
4.49	15%	12.18
4.34	20%	11.70
4.21	25%	11.33
4.06	30%	10.97
3.93	35%	10.65
3.81	40%	10.37
3.68	45%	10.06
3.57	50%	9.76
3.45	55%	9.53
3.37	60%	9.24
3.25	65%	8.90
3.14	70%	8.58
3.01	75%	8.22
2.88	80%	7.89
2.71	85%	7.36
2.49	90%	6.87
2.18	95%	5.91
0.85	99.95%	2.20

EPS

ROE

Actual = $3.73 (shown for comparison)

Actual = 10.10% (shown for comparison)

Goal = $3.33

Goal = 9.09%

Figure 7.22 Beta Insurance EPS Profile

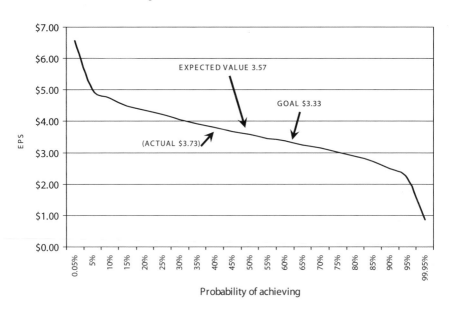

EXPECTED VALUE 3.57

GOAL $3.33

(ACTUAL $3.73)

EPS

Probability of achieving

Bubble Management Approach to Service Companies

Figure 7.23 Beta Insurance ROE Profile

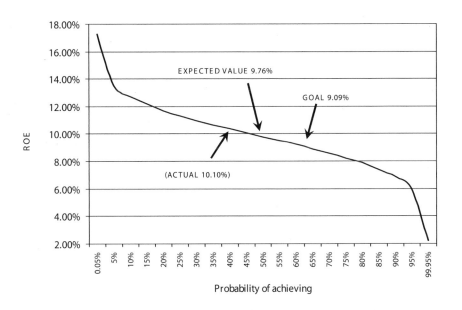

Figure 7.24 VBRM Bubble Chart

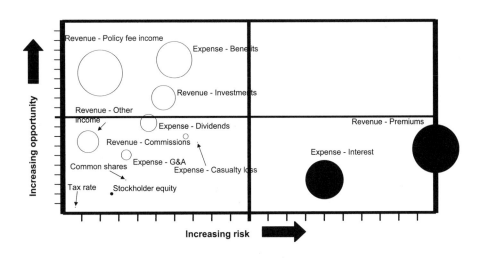

Chapter 7

Figure 7.25 Contributions to Beta Insurance Uncertainty

Area of uncertainty	Percent contribution to Beta Insurance total uncertainty
Revenue - premiums	15.3
Expense - benefits	12.6
Expense - interest	10.0
Revenue -investments	10.0
Revenue - policy fee income	9.6
Expense - casualty loss	8.4
Revenue - commissions	8.4
Expense - dividends	8.0
Expense - G&A	5.4
Revenue - other income	5.0
Common shares	3.8
Stockholder equity	2.7
Tax rate	0.8
Revenue - premiums	15.3
Expense - benefits	12.6
Expense - interest	10.0
Revenue - investments	10.0

Figure 7.26 Key Performance Actuals for Beta Insurance

Key Performance Boxes (KPBs). KPBs must be calculated values - not inputs.
Input value - not a calculation.

2004

REVENUES		($ million unless shown otherwise)	
Premiums	$ 12,580	Common Shares	605
Policy Fee Income	$ 2,317	Stockholder Equity	$ 22,344
Investments	$ 9,079		
Commissions	3,646	**Earnings Per Share**	$ 3.73
Other Income	726		
Total Sales	$ 28,348	**Return On Equity**	10.10%

EXPENSES	
Benefits	$ 12,896
Interest	2,334
Dividends	2,485
G&A	7,346
Casualty Loss	0
Total Expense	$ 25,061

Income Before Tax	$ 3,287
Tax Rate	31.366%
Tax	1,031
Net Income	2,256

Bubble Management Approach to Service Companies

Figure 7.27 Conversion Table for Compensation Determination

PTT probability range (%) (a)	Performance rating (Table 6.18)	Salary increase potential (%)	Bonus potential (%)
11 or lower	5.5 - 6.0 (Level 1)	12 - 15	20 - 40
21 - 12	4.9 – 5.4 (Level 2)	8 - 11	15 - 19
28 - 22	4.2 – 4.8 (Level 3)	5 - 7	10 - 14
39 - 29	3.6 – 4.1 (Level 4)	3 - 4	5 - 9
51 - 40	3.0 – 3.5 (Level 5)	1 - 2	None
Greater than 51	Under 3.0 (Level 6)	None	None

(a) The lower the probability, the more difficult to achieve the goal

Figure 7.28 Gamma Healthcare Financials

($ million unless otherwise shown)

Goal area	2003 actual	2004 goal
Revenues:	34,264	35,000
Product	33,913	34,600
Services	351	400
Cost of operations:	33,536	34,180
Cost of products	32,553	33,100
Cost of services	190	150
Sales, G&A	686	680
Amortization	94	200
Interest	13	50
Income before tax	729	820
Income tax	303	320
Net income	426	500
Common shares (million)	270	270
Stockholder equity	5,080	5,600
Earnings per share (EPS)	$ 1.57	$ 1.85
Return-on-equity (ROE)	8.39%	8.93%
Total assets	10,263	10,400
Return-on-assets (ROA)	4.15%	4.81%

If this scenario proved to be true, the VBRM process would have tracked and documented this issue so that it could be corrected in future analyses of performance. In one actual case, VBRM identified a contractor's consistent level of optimism, allowing new forecasts from

Chapter 7

Figure 7.29 Key Performance Goals for Gamma Healthcare

Key Performance Boxes (KPBs). KPBs must be calculated values - not inputs.
Input value - not a calculation.

($ million unless shown otherwise)

Revenues	
Product revenue	$ 34,600
Service revenue	400
Total sales	$ 35,000

Common shares (millions)	270
Stockholder equity	5,600
Total assets	10,400

Cost of operations	
Product cost	$ 33,100
Service cost	150
Sales - G&A	680
Amortization	200
Interest	50
Total cost of operations	$ 34,180

Earnings per share   **$ 1.85**

Return on equity   **8.93%**

Return on assets   **4.81%**

Income before tax   820

Tax rate   39.024%
Income tax   320

Net income   500

Figure 7.30 Gamma Healthcare 2004 Goals

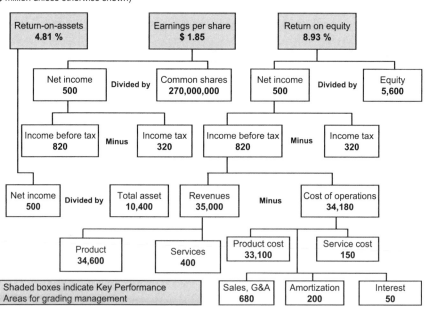

($ million unless otherwise shown)

Bubble Management Approach to Service Companies

the contractor to be adjusted to an acceptable level of confidence in attaining goal while simultaneously releasing contingency funds to other investment opportunities.

CASE STUDY 7-3 GAMMA HEALTHCARE
(Accumulating cash for acquisitions)

The Situation: As a drug prescription company, Gamma Healthcare operates in a competitive market where clients seek to control the growth in prescription drug costs which have risen sharply over the last few years due to inflation in brand-named drugs, escalation of pre-scriptions utilized, and new products from pharmaceutical manufactur-ers (drug cost increases are called "drug trend" in the industry). In its efforts to hold drug costs down for its clients, Gamma has pushed generic drugs to increase market penetration. This effort can be a two-edged sword because the company must maintain a strong relationship with the brand-name manufacturers.

For 2004, the Board of Directors set a primary goal for the CEO to grow net income and EPS by 17% over 2003 results. They also set sec-ondary goals to improve ROE and ROA, and to accumulate cash in anticipation of making another acquisition in 2005. The goal for cash was set to double cash from the 2003 level of $639 million. Other goals were set for operations as shown in Figures 7.28, 7.29, and 7.30.

Figure 7.31 Gamma Healthcare Uncertainty Inputs

Input element	Units	Target	Probability*	Low	High
Revenue - products	$ million	34,600	45	33,500	35,500
Revenue - services	$ million	400	35	300	425
Cost - products	$ million	33,100	40	32,750	33,500
Cost - services	$ million	150	45	125	200
Cost - sales-G&A	$ million	680	55	660	700
Cost - amortization	$ million	200	25	100	225
Cost - interest	$ million	50	60	20	80
Tax rate	%	39.024	40	39.000	40.500
Common shares	million	270	45	265	280
Shareholder equity	$ million	5,600	40	5,500	5,800
Total assets	$ million	10,400	45	10,000	11,500

* Probability of achieving or improving compared to target

Chapter 7

Figure 7.32 Probabilities of Achieving EPS, ROE and ROA Goals

Probability of achieving	EPS	ROE	ROA
0.05%	4.41	21.38	11.83
5%	3.39	16.33	8.66
10%	3.05	14.70	7.77
15%	2.72	13.02	6.94
20%	2.48	11.94	6.37
25%	2.22	10.75	5.72
30%	2.07	9.98	5.32
35%	1.93	9.35	5.01
40%	1.82	8.74	4.67
45%	1.72	8.30	4.42
50%	1.60	7.70	4.15
55%	1.48	7.17	3.81
60%	1.38	6.56	3.48
65%	1.21	5.85	3.12
70%	1.06	5.11	2.71
75%	0.88	4.29	2.25
80%	0.65	3.11	1.65
85%	0.33	1.59	0.83
90%	0.02	0.10	0.05
95%	-0.34	-1.68	-0.92
99.95%	-1.43	-6.74	-3.82

Target goals:

EPS = 1.85
ROE = 8.93
ROA = 4.81

Actual results:
(shown for comparison)

EPS = 1.76
ROE = 8.41
ROA = 4.56

Figure 7.33 Gamma Healthcare EPS Profile

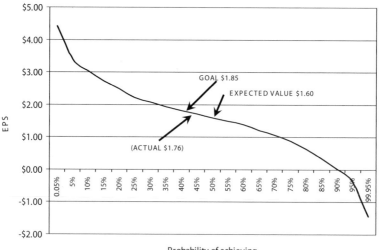

GOAL $1.85

EXPECTED VALUE $1.60

(ACTUAL $1.76)

EPS

Probability of achieving

Bubble Management Approach to Service Companies

Figure 7.34 Gamma Healthcare ROE Profile

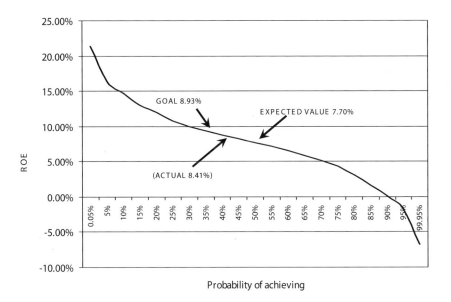

Figure 7.35 Gamma Healthcare ROA Profile

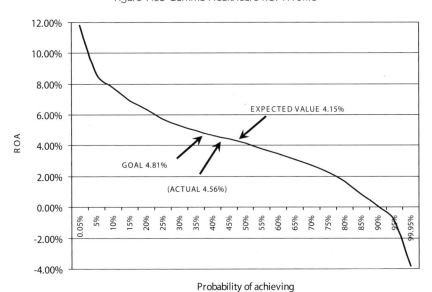

Chapter 7

The Proposed Solution: The CEO's strategy for improving revenues centered on increasing revenues-products. Cash accumulation was to be achieved by increasing net income and reducing cash drain from financing activities. Accounts receivables were expected to offset as sales volume increased.

Figure 7.36 VBRM Bubble Chart

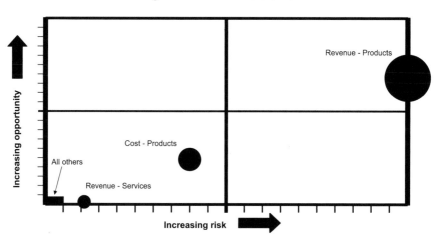

Figure 7.37 Contributions to Gamma Healthcare Goal Uncertainty

Area of uncertainty	Percent contribution to EPS uncertainty	Percent contribution to ROE uncertainty	Percent contribution to ROA uncertainty
Common shares	1.4	0.0	0.0
Cost - amortization	2.7	2.7	2.7
Cost - interest	1.8	1.8	1.8
Cost - products	23.3	23.3	22.8
Cost - sales-G&A	1.2	1.2	1.2
Cost -services	2.4	2.4	2.3
Revenue - products	61.9	61.9	60.6
Revenue - services	4.5	4.5	4.4
Shareholder equity	0.0	1.4	0.0
Tax rate	0.7	0.7	0.7
Total assets	0.0	0.0	3.6

Bubble Management Approach to Service Companies

The Numbers: Similar to previous case studies, Figures 7.28 through 7.41 show the typical tables and charts for Gamma Healthcare.

The Conclusion: Figure 7.40 summarizes the 2004 goals, actual results, and ratings for the CEO and the Gamma management. Notice also that none of the primary or secondary goals were fully achieved, falling about 5 to 6 % short in each case. The Board compensation committee had set up Figure 7.41 as the conversion table for compensation determination (the cash accumulation goal was not included in the rating). Using the table, the management rated 3.4 on each goal, qualifying for a 3-4% salary increase and a 5-9% bonus potential. Even a 1% improvement in the performance rating would have qualified the management for double that compensation (see the critique below).

Critique of Case Study 7-3: The probabilities and uncertainties identified by management indicate that the 2004 goals were slightly optimistic (EPS, ROE, and ROA each had roughly a 35 to 40 % chance of being achieved). Revenue from products contributed, by far, the most significant risk of under-achievement as well as the most likely place to improve performance (see Figure 7.36). Management will need to remain focused on this area to increase the probability of achieving its goals in the coming year. Second to product-revenue in risk contribu-

Figure 7.38 Key Performance Actuals for Gamma Healthcare

Key Performance Boxes (KPBs). KPBs must be calculated values - not inputs.		
Input value - not a calculation.		

2004		($ million unless shown otherwise)	
Revenues			
Product revenue	$ 35,024	Common shares (million)	274
Service revenue	328	Stockholder equity	5,719
Total sales	$ 35,352	Total assets	10,542

Cost of operations			
Product cost	$ 33,497	**Earnings per share**	**$1.76**
Service cost	133	**Return on equity**	**8.41%**
Sales - G&A	676		
Amortization	180	**Return on assets**	**4.56%**
Interest	60		
Total cost of operations	$ 34,546		

Income before tax	806

Tax rate	40.323%
Income tax	325

Net income	481

Chapter 7

Figure 7.39 Actual Results for Gamma Healthcare

($ million unless otherwise shown)

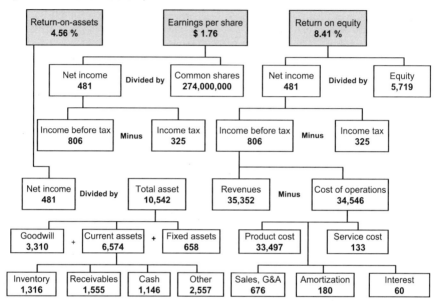

Figure 7.40 Summary of Management Rating for Gamma Healthcare

Goal area	2004 goal	2004 actual	Probability of achieving actual	Performance Rating (Fig 6.18)
Earnings per share	$ 1.85	$ 1.76	43%	3.4
Return on equity	8.93%	8.41%	42%	3.4
Return on assets	4.81%	4.56%	42%	3.4

tion and opportunity was product cost. Along with product revenue, product cost contributed more than 85% of all uncertainty associated with Gamma's business plan (Figure 7.37). Unless management stays focused on these issues, it is unlikely that actual results will improve significantly in the future.

Let's look a bit closer. First, management did succeed in addressing the uncertainty associated with product revenues – beating the goal by

Bubble Management Approach to Service Companies

Figure 7.41 Conversion Table for Compensation Determination

PTT probability range (%) (a)	Performance rating (Table 6.18)	Salary increase potential (%)	Bonus potential (%)
20 or lower	5.0 - 6.0 (Level 1)	12 - 15	20 - 40
31 - 21	4.0 - 4.9 (Level 2)	8 - 11	15 - 19
41 - 32	3.5 – 3.9 (Level 3)	5 - 7	10 - 14
50 - 42	3.0 – 3.4 (Level 4)	3 - 4	5 - 9
Greater than 51	Under 3.0 (Level 6)	None	None

(a) The lower the probability, the more difficult to achieve the goal

$0.424 billion. However, it failed to mitigate the risks or capture the opportunities in product cost, which overran the goal by 0.397 billion. Had management been able to achieve both of these goals, EPS would have been $2.57, ROE would have been 12.31%, and ROA would have been 6.68%. These values would have probabilities of achieving of 17 to 19 %, bringing the performance rating up from 3.4 to 5.1-5.2 and raising management's compensation to Level 1 on Figure 7.41. Clearly, future focus on these cost elements will substantially improve corporate performance and compensation to the executives.

7.5 SOME FINAL THOUGHTS ON THE CASE STUDIES IN THIS CHAPTER

Service industries' financial results tend to be more volatile than the results of production companies, which can curtail a shift or shutter a plant temporarily during economic downturns. That's not as easy to do for service companies. Banking customers expect to get access to their deposit boxes and to tellers to make deposits or withdrawals in good times as well as bad. Once a branch or service office is closed, it tends to stay closed with a risk of permanently losing customers in that area. Insurance companies, because of their large asset portfolio and international makeup, must deal with the volatility of currency fluctuations, derivative changes, and other issues that can significantly impact income if they take actions that turn out to be unfavorable. As the United States moves more toward a service economy and away from a manufacturing economy, the unfavorable risk of service company financial decisions will continue to grow.

Applying Bubble Management Approach to Not-For-Profit Organizations

8.1 WHAT THE READER WILL LEARN FROM THIS CHAPTER:

- Suggested goals for appraising not-for-profit organizations
- How to set probability goals using VBRM for not-for-profit organizations
- Conclusions concerning the appraisal process for not-for-profits

INTRODUCTION

In this chapter, we will apply Bubble Management to not-for-profit entities. Foundations, charities, and other not-for-profit (NFP) organizations are tax-exempt from federal income taxes under Section 501(c)(3) of the IRS code. Although income tax exempt, they have to pay federal excise tax.

In this chapter, we will focus on case studies for a foundation, a major charity, and a service organization to illustrate goal setting using the Bubble Management approach to appraise key managers in these enterprises. A brief overview of each type of enterprise follows.

8.2.1 Foundations

Foundations derive most of their income from investments – dividends, interest, and appreciation of investments. Their major expense is philanthropic grants and expenses for offering loans at below-market rates.

Chapter 8

Although income tax exempt, they may pay federal excise tax, although usually at very low rates.

8.2.2   Charities

Charities, like foundations, are tax-exempt under IRS code 501(c)(3). Charities tend to raise revenues in a variety of ways including: 1) contributions, 2) bequests, 3) fees for services, 4) investments, 5) grants, and 6) contracts with government agencies. Fund raising is a major expense, frequently exceeding 20 percent for some charities. We will show a case study later that has fund raising exceeding goal.

8.2.3   Service Organizations

Service organizations have missions to provide humanitarian service, build goodwill through international understanding, and promote ethics, among others. They are usually guided through a Board of Directors, and may operate through local and/or regional branches. Members are expected to make financial contributions to the organization to help promote and cover the expenses of various programs. Contributions and investment income tend to be the largest sources of revenue; expenses are for program spending, humanitarian grants, and educational programs. Operating expenses typically are modest and tend to be mostly travel-related expenses, informational costs, and fund raising.

8.3 SUGGESTED GOALS FOR APPRAISING NOT-FOR-PROFIT EXCUTIVES

8.3.1   Primary Goals

In Chapter 2 we discussed primary goals and suggested that they should be focused on metrics that have a significant impact on the financial performance of a company, or business entity. In Figure 8.1 we list some primary goals that we believe are appropriate for measuring performance of certain executives in not-for-profit enterprises; these goals include net revenues, cost and expense control, operating gain, and cash flow.

Management Approach to Not-For-Profit Organizations

Figure 8.1 Summary of Primary and Secondary Goals for NFP Executives

Title	Performance measurement	Primary goal	Suggested secondary goals
President	Overall enterprise financial performance	Return-on-assets (ROA)	Income gain, capital expenditures
Chief Operating Officer (COO)	Net operating income	Operating income gain,	Expense control, revenue growth, ROA, cost of operations, program cost control
Chief Financial Officer (CFO)	Cash flow growth from continuing operations and financial activities	Cash flow growth	Grant management, G&A expense, investment gain, excise tax control
Chief Admin Officer (CAO)	Overall corporation administrative expenses	G&A expense	Training administration, health care cost control
Marketing VP	Income (revenues)	Income growth	Contribution gain, grant gain, fund raising
Investment VP	Investment gain	Investment rate-of-return	Investment loss reduction

Figure 8.2 Sharing of Goals Among NFP Executives

Core financial factors

Factor	Suggested executives sharing the goal	Level of control over goal achievement
G&A expense	COO	High
	CAO (chief Administrative officer)	High
Operating expenses	COO (Chief Operating Officer)	High
Permanent assets	CFO (Chief Financial Officer)	High
	COO	High
	CAO	Medium
Revenue	Marketing VP	High
	COO	Medium
Inventories	CFO	High
Depreciation	CFO	High
Cash or cash equivalents	CFO	High
	COO	High
General expense	CAO	High
	CFO	High
	COO	High

8.3.2 Secondary Goals

We have listed several secondary goals in Figure 8.1 for measuring performance of not-for-profit executives, including program and grant control, investment risk management, and marketing/promotion activities.

Figure 8.3 Sharing of Goals Among NFP Executives

Calculated financial factors

Factor	Suggested executives sharing the goal	Level of control over goal achievement
Total expenses	COO Marketing VP CAO	High High High
Current assets	COO CFO	High High
Sales and general expenses (SG&A)	COO CAO Marketing VP	High Medium High
Total assets	CFO COO CAO	High High Medium
Operating profit	COO CAO CFO	High High Medium

Figure 8.4 Suggested Management Skills for Rating NFP Executives

Management skill	What to consider
Quality of advice	Is advice sound and well thought out?
Communication	Are oral and written communications clear?
Time management	Is time well managed?
Team-building	Attracts and motivates people?
Problem solving	Manages problems effectively?
Decision making	Generally makes good decisions?
Planning	Shows good planning skills?
Customer relations	Well respected by clients?
Contract negotiations	Is effective in negotiating with others?
Personnel relations	Has good people skills?
Meeting management	Manages meetings well?
Appraising others	Conducts effective appraisals of subordinates?
Delegation	Is not afraid to delegate?

8.3.3 Shared Goals

As we have noted in earlier chapters, no single manager or executive is usually solely responsible for achieving any goal. When setting
shared goals, it must be recognized that each executive or manager
sharing in the goal does not have the same level of control over achiev-

ing the goal. For that reason, in Figures 8.2 and 8.3, we have chosen to rank the level of control we think each executive might have over the goal shown, and have also split the goals into core and calculated financial factors.

8.3.4 Management Attributes

In Figure 8.4 we have listed about a dozen skill areas we think management might want to consider in the appraisal process.

8.4 EVALUATING GOALS RESULTS USING BUBBLE MANAGEMENT

CASE STUDY 8-1 ALPHA FOUNDATION
(Managing investment income)

The Situation: Like most investors during the recent recession, Alpha Foundation saw its investment rate of return fall in 2003 to 7.72 percent (Figure 8.5). Because the foundation's charter mandated a 5 percent payout of its investment portfolio each year, its investment objective was to generate an inflation-adjusted return in excess of the mandated payout. Acting on the advice of the foundation president, the Board of Trustee approved the hiring of a new investment vice-president. Her goal for 2004 was to raise the return on market investments to 15 percent. She was requested to present her near-term strategy to the Trustees at their next meeting.

This foundation had a fair market investment portfolio of $10.492 billion in 2004. Their mandatory payout at 5% would require them to issue grants equal to $525 million, which was close to what they paid out ($514 million). The foundation in 2004 did cut grants by $35 million and other operating expenses by $6 million from 2003 to cover the payout. Because their investment gain in 2004 was 13.7%, the fair market value of their investment portfolio grow substantially (by $674 million) from 2003 to 2004.

The Proposed Solution: Having come from an investment banking firm, the new investment VP had wide experience in the equity market. Currently equities constituted 55 percent of the foundation's portfolio, and although the VP did not plan to change that ratio significantly, she did plan extensive changes to the mix within the portfolio; in addition,

Chapter 8

Figure 8.5 Alpha Foundation Financials

($ 1000 unless otherwise stated)

Goal area	2003 actual	2004 goal
Income (revenue):	1,238,964	1,300,000
Dividends	104,071	120,000
Interest	156,761	150,000
Appreciation of investments	978,132	1,030,000
Expenditures:	630,064	600,000
Grants	488,962	460,000
Charitable activities	16,082	15,000
Program support	52,032	50,000
Loss provision	(394)	-
G&A	53,071	50,000
Depreciation	8,851	10,000
Provision for excise tax	11,460	15,000
Gain in net assets	608,900	700,000
Investment base (at market)	9,818,946	10,492,960
Investment rate of return *	7.72%	15.00%

* Gain in fair market value over cost of investments

she also planned to change the mix of fixed investments.

The Numbers: Figure 8.5 through 8.13 show the input values, VBRM analysis results, and actuals for Alpha Foundation.

The Conclusion: Under the guidance of the new investment VP, the net gain on Alpha's investment base increased to 13.70% in 2004, up significantly over 2003 but 1.3% short of goal. Asset gain for 2004 exceeded goal by $28.933 million, 4.13%. Actual gain came in at a 42% probability of achievement (Figure 8.10), yielding a 3.4 results rating (see Figure 6.18) and a level 3 performance compensation for the president and senior staff (Figure 8.14).

Critique of Case Study 8-1: Management's focus on revenue–appreciation risks and opportunities paid off by increasing the outcome by nearly $22 million over goal (Figure 8.13). As expected, expense–loss provision was much greater than the $0 forecast. If management wanted to supply a more realistic forecast, $1.250 million would represent the mean between the low ($0) and the high ($2.500 million), assuming a normally distributed expense (Figure 8.8). However, the normal

Management Approach to Not-For-Profit Organizations

Figure 8.6 Key Performance Goals for Alpha Foundation

Key Performance Boxes (KPBs). KPBs must be calculated values - not inputs.		
Input value - not a calculation.		

2004

REVENUES			($1000)
Dividends	$	120,000	
Interest		150,000	
Appreciation		1,030,000	
Total Sales	**$**	**1,300,000**	

EXPENSES		
G&A	$	50,000
Depreciation		10,000
Excise Tax		15,000
Grants		460,000
Charitable Activities		15,000
Programs		50,000
Loss Provision		0
Total Cost of Sales/Expense	**$**	**600,000**

Gain in Assets   **$ 700,000**

Figure 8.7 Alpha Foundation 2004 Goals

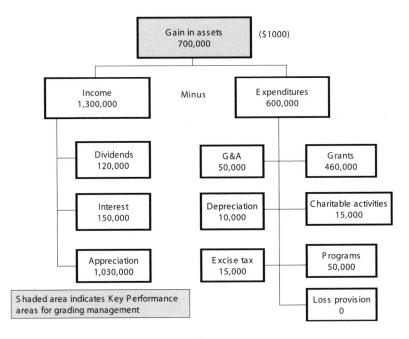

217

Chapter 8

Figure 8.8 Alpha Foundation Uncertainty Inputs

Input element	Units	Target	Probability*	Low	High
Revenue - dividends	$1000	120,000	40	90,000	155,000
Revenue - interest	$1000	150,000	50	125,000	180,000
Revenue - appreciation	$1000	1,030,000	35	900,000	1,150,000
Expense - G&A	$1000	50,000	50	40,000	60,000
Expense - depreciation	$1000	10,000	-	-	-
Expense - excise tax	$1000	15,000	-	-	-
Expense - grants	$1000	460,000	65	420,000	500,000
Expense - charitable activities	$1000	15,000	-	-	-
Expense - programs	$1000	50,000	50	40,000	62,000
Expense - loss provision	$1000	-	-	0	2,500

* Probability of achieving or improving compared to target

Figure 8.9 Probability of Achieving Asset Gain

Gain ($1000)	Probability of achieving
874,205	0.05%
817,237	5%
799,457	10%
786,918	15%
773,511	20%
762,633	25%
753,237	30%
742,736	35%
734,531	40%
727,547	45%
721,353	50%
714,408	55%
706,933	60%
700,178	65%
690,345	70%
680,640	75%
668,942	80%
654,235	85%
633,656	90%
602,653	95%
532,338	99.95%

(Actual = $728,933)
Shown here for comparison

Gain expected value is $721,353

Gain goal = $700,000

Management Approach to Not-For-Profit Organizations

Figure 8.10 Alpha Foundation Gain Profile

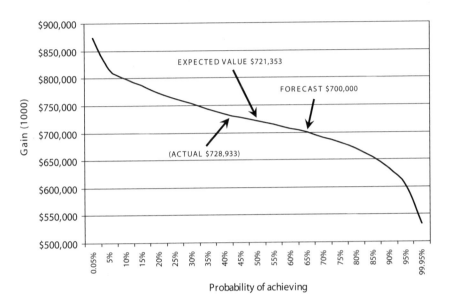

Figure 8.11 VBRM Bubble Chart

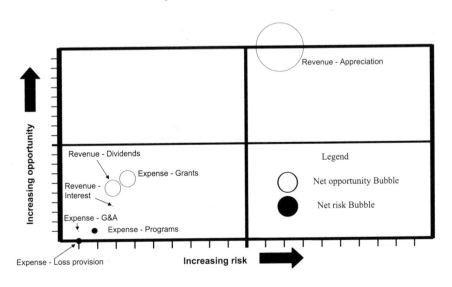

Chapter 8

curve does not typically apply to revenues and expenses as they tend to be skewed in the real world. (Many students of elementary statistics come away with the impression that most uncertainty inputs follow a normal distribution; the opposite is true in business forecasting!) Management had more success with its actions for expense programs, except for expense-G&A, as it was able to control these costs to roughly 7% lower than forecast.

Notice that some inputs in Figure 8.8 were not assigned a probability or range. That's because these particular inputs do not contribute the minimum required amount of uncertainty in order to justify analysis of their variability. To include them increases the odds that iatrogenic (self-induced or understated) risk will be introduced into the analysis and generate a flawed set of results. Revenue–appreciation is the largest contributor (50.7%) of net opportunity to be captured (see Figure 8.12).

As a general point of information, opportunities can frequently be lost early in the planning stages of a business plan because many depend on how the plan is executed. Once the decision is made to implement a plan in a certain manner, some opportunities may well be lost. Management should focus on revenue–appreciation, first by trying to protect the available opportunities and second by mitigating the risks; revenue–appreciation is the largest of the net opportunities and net risks. It contains the largest portion of total risk because it appears as the furthest driver to the right of the origin. However, it has a large net opportunity (unfilled bubble) because the amount of opportunity here far exceeds the amount of risk. Expense–grants and revenue–dividends should next be addressed because they are large contributors of net opportunity.

Figure 8.12 Contributions to Gain Uncertainty

Area of uncertainty	Percent contribution to Alpha Foundation gain uncertainty
Revenue - appreciation	50.7
Expense - grants	15.9
Revenue - dividends	13.0
Revenue - interest	11.6
Expense - programs	4.3
Expense - G&A	2.9
Expense - loss provision	1.4

Management Approach to Not-For-Profit Organizations

Figure 8.13 Key Performance Actuals for Alpha Foundation

Key Performance Boxes (KPBs). KPBs must be calculated values - not inputs. Input value - not a calculation.		

2004 Revenues		($1000)
Dividends	$ 119,946	
Interest	146,655	
Appreciation	1,051,889	
Total sales	$ 1,318,490	

Expenses	
G&A	$ 55,901
Depreciation	7,845
Excise tax	11,512
Grants	453,632
Charitable activities	12,216
Programs	46,489
Loss provision	1,962
Total cost of sales/expense	$ 589,557

Gain in assets $ 728,933

Investment rate of return 13.70%

Figure 8.14 Conversion Table for Compensation Determination

PTT probability range (%) (a)	Performance rating (*Figure* 6.18)	Salary increase potential (%)	Bonus potential (%)
20 or lower	5.0 - 6.0 (Level 1)	12 - 15	20 - 40
35 - 21	3.8 - 4.9 (Level 2)	8 - 11	15 - 19
55 - 36	2.8 – 3.7 (Level 3)	5 - 7	10 - 14
75 - 56	1.5 – 2.7 (Level 4)	3 - 4	5 - 9
Greater than 75	Under 1.5 (Level 6)	None	None

(a) The lower the probability, the more difficult to achieve the goal

Finally, expense–loss provision and expense–program are the biggest, and equal, contributors to Net Risk (Figure 8.11). Unlike revenue–appreciation, which has the biggest opportunity and biggest risk to the bottom line (asset gain), these two areas represent the largest Net Risk, meaning that they are substantially more likely to reduce bottom line gain than to improve it. This can also mean that they are more difficult to control toward a favorable outcome. However, because their total contribution of risk and opportunity is small (they appear at the bottom of the lower left quadrant in Figure 8.11), management would be ill-advised to focus on these two areas before attending to the elements previously mentioned.

CASE STUDY 8-2 BETA CHARITY
(Improving operating income)

The Situation: Even though Beta Charity is a not-for-profit enterprise, its long-term objective has always been to generate positive operating income (gain) each year (expenses less than revenues). A look at Figure 8.15 shows that objective was not met in 2003. The Board of Trustees was sufficiently concerned that they set a goal for the CEO to turn operating gain at least breakeven in 2004. The CEO and the COO, along with the CFO, were directed to present their action plan at the next Board meeting in three weeks.

The Proposed Solution: Because the need for Beta's charitable services was always greater than its resources, the plan was to break even by: 1) increasing public support by corporate and public giving, grants, and bequests, 2) reduce G&A expenses by appealing for volunteers to take over certain current employee functions, and 3) reducing program

Figure 8.15 Beta Charity Financials

($ 1000 unless otherwise shown)

Goal Area	2003 Actual	2004 Goal
Income (revenues):	3,033,775	3,175,000
Public support	692,417	735,000
Products and services	2,165,460	2,260,000
Contracts	59,970	60,000
Investments	69,485	70,000
Other income	46,443	50,000
Operating expenses:	3,369,653	3,175,000
Program services	3,070,627	2,900,000
Fund raising	122,946	110,000
G&A	176,080	165,000
Operating gain	(335,878)	Gain = breakeven
Investment base (at market)	1,315,820	1,385,820
Investment rate of return	5.28%	5.32%

service expenses as much as prudent (Figure 8.16). Several sources of income over the next year were expected to decrease and make the job more difficult; these sources included investment income, government contract revenue, and the marketing of informational materials.

Figure 8.16 Beta Charity Action Plan for Improving Operating Income

(Selected sources of income and expense)

($ 1000)

Activity	2003 actual	2004 target	
Corporate and individual giving	285,880	330,000	
Bequests	93,780	110,000	
Grants	75,100	100,000	
Actual/projected revenue	454,760	540,000	Improvement 85,240
G&A expense	176,100	165,000	
Program services	3,070,600	2,830,000	
Actual/projected expenses	3,246,700	2,995,000	Improvement 251,700
Target operating income improvement	-	336,940	

Figure 8.17 Key Performance Goals for Beta Charity

Key Performance Boxes (KPBs). KPBs must be calculated values - not inputs.
Input value - not a calculation.

2004

REVENUES		($1000)
Public Support	$ 735,000	
Products & Services	2,260,000	
Contracts	60,000	
Investments	70,000	
Other Income	50,000	
Total Revenue	$ 3,175,000	

EXPENSES	
Program Services	$ 2,900,000
Fund Raising	110,000
G&A	165,000
Total Expenses	$ 3,175,000

Operating Gain	$ 0

Chapter 8

Figure 8.18 Beta Charity 2004 Goals

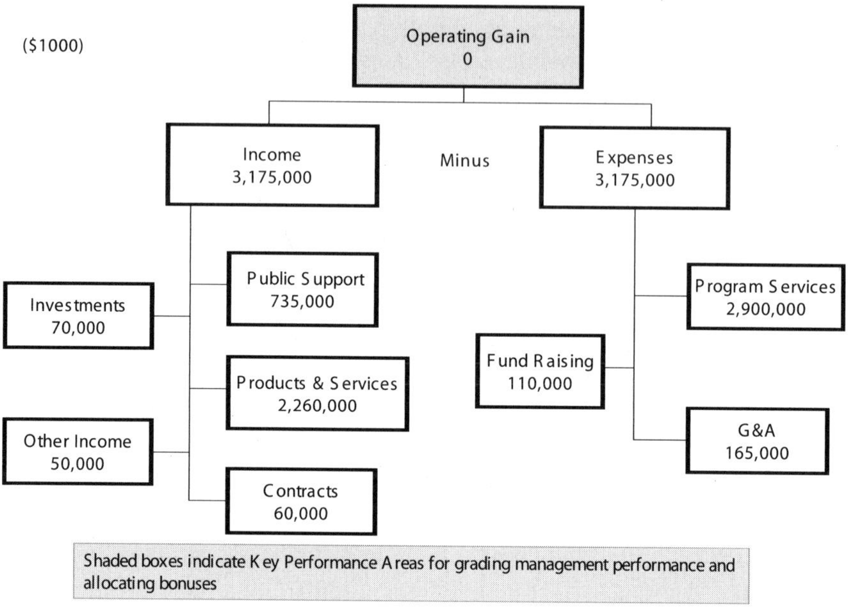

($1000)

Operating Gain
0

Income
3,175,000

Minus

Expenses
3,175,000

Investments
70,000

Public Support
735,000

Products & Services
2,260,000

Other Income
50,000

Contracts
60,000

Fund Raising
110,000

Program Services
2,900,000

G&A
165,000

Shaded boxes indicate Key Performance Areas for grading management performance and allocating bonuses

The Board of Trustee compensation committee had designated a total bonus pool for the three executives of $100,000, to be awarded in accordance to specific guidelines, one of which was that no bonus would be awarded if the probability of achieving the operating gain goal was higher than 50%. The committee also set salary increase guidelines that were based on the CEO and COO having a 70% results/30% contribution split; and the CFO a 50%/50% split (see Figure 8.27 later).

The Numbers: Figure 8.15 shows the 2003 actuals and the 2004 goals for Beta Charity. Figure 8.16 shows the action plan for improving operating gain which focuses on certain elements of income and expense. Figure 8.17 through 8.25 show the usual figures for goals, uncertainty inputs, probability profiles, VBRM bubble chart, operating gain uncertainty, and actual results. Figure 8.26 is a new chart showing a variance analysis for the 2004 results.

The Conclusion: Performance against goal for 2004 was an improvement over 2003, but fell short of meeting goal by about $106 million

Management Approach to Not-For-Profit Organizations

Figure 8.19 Beta Charity Uncertainty Inputs

Input element	Units	Target	Probability*	Low	High
Revenue - public support	$1000	735,000	30	650,000	750,000
Revenue - products & services	$1000	2,260,000	50	2,100,000	2,400,000
Revenue - contracts	$1000	60,000	35	40,000	70,000
Revenue - investments	$1000	70,000	45	55,000	80,000
Revenue - other income	$1000	50,000	40	40,000	55,000
Expense - program services	$1000	2,900,000	40	2,750,000	3,150,000
Expense - fund raising	$1000	110,000	50	100,000	120,000
Expense - G&A	$1000	165,000	35	155,000	180,000

* Probability of achieving or improving compared to target

Figure 8.20 Beta Charity Operating Gain Profile

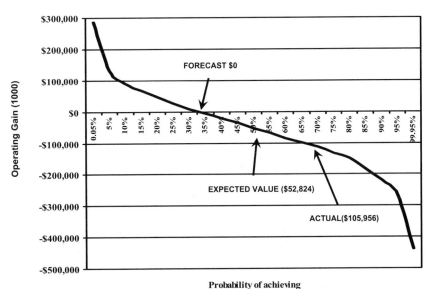

(Figure 8.24). A closer look at Figure 8.26 shows that only one element of income or expense (products and services income) beat goal.

Even the rate of return on the charity's investments failed to meet goal (4.47% versus the goal of 5.32%), coming in below actual results for

225

Figure 8.21 Probability of Achieving Operating Gain

Gain ($1000)	Probability of Achieving
286,121	0.05%
130,819	5%
90,037	10%
67,031	15%
46,844	20%
25,937	25%
8,618	30%
-6,299	35%
-21,978	40%
-35,026	45%
-52,824	50%
-67,254	55%
-85,496	60%
-98,373	65%
-112,580	70%
-133,190	75%
-149,698	80%
-182,527	85%
-219,352	90%
-266,553	95%
-437,901	99.95%

→ Gain target = $0

→ Gain expected value is ($52,824)

→ Actual = ($105,956) Shown here for comparison

2003. Look at Figure 8.20 and you can see that the probability of meeting the operating gain actual of negative $105 million came in at 68%, disqualifying the three top executives for any bonus. Figure 8.23 shows that program services expenses make up the largest contribution (risk and opportunity) to operating gain uncertainty (43.5%), and although services were cut from 2003, the goal for 2004 was not met. The variance analysis (Figure 8.26) shows that lack of revenue from public support was the biggest contributor for failing to meet the operating gain goal for 2004. Although no bonus was awarded, performance was adequate to qualify each of the three executives for a merit salary increase (Figure 8.27).

Critique of Case Study 8-2: Expense – program services contributed the highest amount of Net Risk (risk minus opportunity), indicating that the potential negative effect it has on the bottom line will need to be addressed aggressively (Figure 8.22). Although management should be able to contain this expense (simply spend less on program services), failure to do so will likely result in further drawdown of assets in the future. This area must be the first that management addresses, and, if

Management Approach to Not-For-Profit Organizations

Figure 8.22 VBRM Bubble Chart

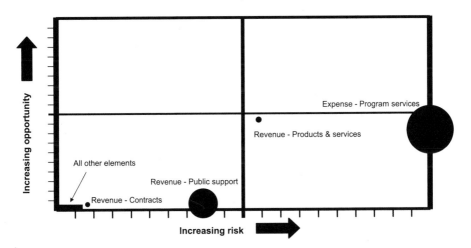

Figure 8.23 Contribution to Operating Gain Uncertainty

Area of uncertainty	Percent contribution to Beta Charity gain uncertainty
Expense - program services	43.5
Revenue - products & services	31.4
Revenue - public support	13.0
Revenue - contracts	3.3
Expense - G&A	2.9
Revenue - investments	2.5
Revenue - other income	1.7
Expense - fund raising	1.7

handled well, could lead to significant improvement in operating gain in the future. Revenue – products & services is another area that requires management attention to ensure that opportunities available in this area are captured as much as possible.

Revenue – public support is a problem. The management team determined that there was only a 30% chance of attaining this goal ($735 mil-

Chapter 8

lion). The reasons for their lack of confidence were documented during the VBRM input session. Unfortunately, except for improved public education regarding Beta Charity's efforts, little can be done because the level of contributions strongly correlates to the overall economy and availability of donor discretionary monies. An improved education plan is being developed. However, its impact will be minimal for the immediate future of this operating cycle.

Finally, revenue–contracts contributed more risk of falling short of goal than opportunity for exceeding goal. Overall, the operating gain goal was optimistic, having only a 33% chance of success (Figure 8.20).

CASE STUDY 8-3 GAMMA SERVICE ENTERPRISES (Improving asset gain)

The Situation: Gamma Services Enterprises (GSE) net assets declined significantly in 2002 because of market losses on their investments. Although improvement occurred in 2003, net assets were still over $40 million below pre-recession levels. The Board of Trustees instructed the president to take the following actions to prop-up assets: 1) hold pro-

Figure 8.24 Performance Actuals for Beta Charity

Key Performance Boxes (KPBs). KPBs must be calculated values - not inputs.	
Input value - not a calculation.	

2004		
Revenues		($1000)
Public support	$ 668,763	
Products & services	2,264,358	
Contracts	48,826	
Investments	62,345	
Other Income	49,204	
Total revenue	$ 3,093,496	

Expenses	
Program services	$ 2,914,756
Fund raising	111,178
G&A	173,518
Total expenses	$ 3,199,452

Operating gain	$ (105,956)

Management Approach to Not-For-Profit Organizations

Figure 8.25 Beta Charity 2004 Actuals

($1000)

Shaded boxes indicate Key Performance Areas for grading management performance and allocating bonuses

Figure 8.26 Variance Analysis for Beta Charity

Actuals		Forecasts		Variance
	2004 ($1000)			
REVENUES		**REVENUES**		
Public Support	$ 668,763	Public Support	$ 735,000	$ (66,237)
Products & Services	2,264,358	Products & Services	2,260,000	4,358
Contracts	48,826	Contracts	60,000	(11,174)
Investments	62,345	Investments	70,000	(7,655)
Other Income	49,204	Other Income	50,000	(796)
Total Revenue	$ 3,093,496	*Total Revenue*	$ 3,175,000	$ (81,504)
EXPENSES		**EXPENSES**		
Program Services	$ 2,914,756	Program Services	$ 2,900,000	$ 14,756
Fund Raising	111,178	Fund Raising	110,000	1,178
G&A	173,518	G&A	165,000	8,518
Total Expenses	$ 3,199,452	*Total Expenses*	$ 3,175,000	$ 24,452
Operating Gain	$ (105,956)	*Operating Gain*	$ 0	$ (105,956)

Variances – Predicted by VBRM Process

Expense – program services was a known key area of uncertainty (more risk as opposed to opportunity). Management was able to keep this expense from becoming the overwhelming problem it could have been. However, the forecast was still exceeded as predicted (i.e., it had a better chance of being overrun than being contained).

Management was able to capture some of the opportunity provided by Revenue – products & services. This helped mitigate risk issues in other areas which were less controllable.

Revenue – public support was also a known key risk with much of the risk uncontrollable. The negative variance between the actual and forecasted values represented over 80% of the revenue reductions compared to its Net Risk contribution of 86%. Management was forewarned that this area would be a problem and that there was little which could be done in this operating cycle to correct it.

Finally, Revenue – contracts contributed roughly 13% of revenue reductions compared to its Net Risk contribution of 8%.

Chapter 8

Figure 8.27 Conversion Table for Compensation Determination

PTT probability range (%) (a)	Performance rating	Salary increase potential (%)	Bonus potential (%)
20 or lower	5.0 - 6.0 (Level 1)	12 - 15	16 - 25
35 - 21	3.8 - 4.9 (Level 2)	8 - 11	11 - 15
51 - 36	3.0 ...3.7 (Level 3)	5 - 7	5 - 10
65 - 52	2.3 ...2.9 (Level 4)	2 - 4	None
Greater than 65	Under 2.3 (Level 6)	None	None

(a) The lower the probability the more difficult to achieve the goal

Executive	Results/contribution split	Results rating (b)	Contribution rating (c)	Overall rating
CEO	70%/30%	2.1	3.0	2.4
COO	70%/30%	2.1	3.0	2.4
CFO	50%/50%	2.1	4.0	3.1

(b) From Figure 6.18 based on 68% probability of achieving operating gain goal
(c) Rating determined by Board of Trustees compensation committee based on
    evaluation of individual contribution to achieving the goal

Figure 8.28 Gamma Services Enterprises Financials

($ 1000 unless otherwise shown)

Goal area	2003 Actual	2004 Goal
Income (revenues):	138,400	160,000
Contributions	133,000	130,000
Investments	5,400	30,000
Operating expenses:	110,200	103,000
Grants	28,400	27,000
Education programs	26,900	28,000
G&A	4,600	4,500
Other	50,300	43,500
Operating gain	28,200	57,000
Investment rate of return	1.04%	7.00%

gram and operating expenses flat for 2004, and 2) decrease certain program awards and expenses, diverting the savings into the investment account (currently over 70 percent in U.S. and foreign stocks) in anticipation of the continuing run-up in the market value of equities.

Management Approach to Not-For-Profit Organizations

Figure 8.29 Gamma Services Enterprises 2004 Goals

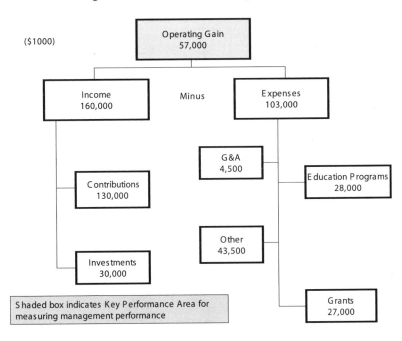

Figure 8.30 Key Performance Goals for Gamma Services Enterprises

2004 ($1000)

Revenues	
Contributions	$ 130,000
Investments	30,000
Total revenue	$ 160,000

Expenses	
Education programs	$ 28,000
Grants	27,000
G&A	4,500
Other	43,500
Total cost of sales/expense	$ 103,000

Operating gain	$ 57,000

231

Chapter 8

Figure 8.31 Gamma Services Enterprises Uncertainty Inputs

(Before VBRM Mitigation)

Input element	Units	Target	Probability*	Low	High
Revenue -contributions	$1000	130,000	15	80,000	145,000
Revenue -investments	$1000	30,000	40	0	60,000
Expense -grants	$1000	27,000	50	25,000	30,000
Expense -education programs	$1000	28,000	30	27,000	30,000
Expense -G&A	$1000	4,500	50	4,000	5,000
Expense -other	$1000	43,500	35	41,000	52,000

* Probability of achieving or improving compared to target

Figure 8.32 Probability of Achieving Operating Gain

Probability of Achieving	Gain ($1000)
0.05%	98,242
5%	73,139
10%	65,519
15%	61,739
20%	57,327
25%	54,050
30%	51,911
35%	49,536
40%	47,183
45%	44,396
50%	41,457
55%	38,233
60%	35,428
65%	32,297
70%	29,233
75%	25,727
80%	22,353
85%	17,371
90%	11,407
95%	3,981
99.95%	-28,452

Shading indicates location of single-point forecast (target)

Expected results ...value has 50% chance of being improved

The Proposed Solution: The president had recently seen the yield figures on the enterprises' investment portfolio for 2003 and they were not very good (a gain of about 1 percent). He met with their outside investment management firm and agreed to restructure the portfolio to move more assets into higher yielding stocks and bonds. The only stipulation by the president was that only investment-grade securities would be considered, no junk bonds or non-investment-grade equities were to be bought.

Management Approach to Not-For-Profit Organizations

Figure 8.33 Gamma Services Enterprises Operating Gain Profile (Before VBRM Mitigation)

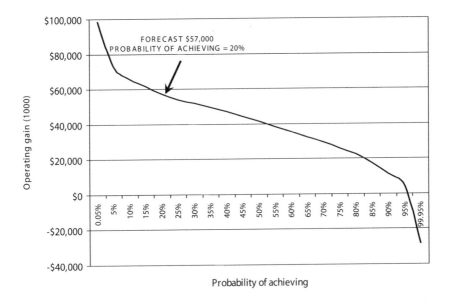

Figure 8.34 VBRM Bubble Chart Before VBRM Mitigation

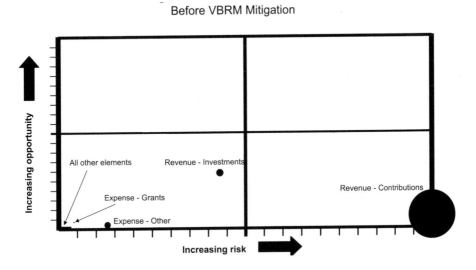

Figure 8.35 Gamma Services Enterprises (GSE) Uncertainty Inputs
(After VBRM Mitigation)

Input element	Units	Target	Probability*	Low	High
Revenue - contributions	$1000	130,000	40	80,000	145,000
Revenue - investments	$1000	30,000	65	0	90,000
Expense - grants	$1000	27,000	50	25,000	30,000
Expense - education programs	$1000	28,000	70	25,000	30,000
Expense - G&A	$1000	4,500	50	4,000	5,000
Other	$1000	43,500	60	40,000	45,000

Shading indicates a value which was impacted by one or more revisions to GSE's plan. GSE did not change original goals. However, the new plan does impact the probabilities and ranges associated with areas affected by the revised plan.

*Probability of achieving or improving compared to target

Figure 8.36 Probability of Achieving Operating Gain (After VBRM Mitigation)

Probability of Achieving	Gain ($1000)
0.05%	132,231
5%	106,606
10%	96,218
15%	89,301
20%	82,955
25%	76,549
30%	73,002
35%	68,299
40%	65,733
45%	62,362
50%	59,700
55%	56,704
60%	54,001
65%	51,040
70%	47,211
75%	43,252
80%	39,079
85%	32,921
90%	26,042
95%	16,409
99.95%	-19,896

Shading indicates location of single-point forecast (target)

With the revised plan, GSE has improved its chance of achieving its goal from 20% to nearly 55%

Expected results ... value has 50% chance of being improved

Management Approach to Not-For-Profit Organizations

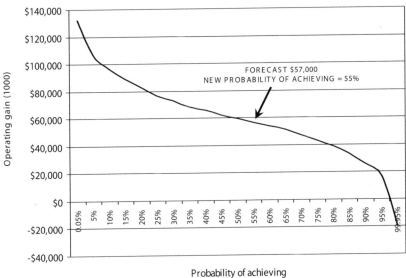

Figure 8.37 Gamma Services Enterprises Operating Gain Profile
(After VBRM Mitigation)

The Numbers: Figures 8.28 through 8.34 show the original inputs, goals, and operating gain achievement probabilities for Gamma Service Enterprises. When the president saw that the probability of meeting the goal of a $57 million operating gain was only 20% (Figures 8.32 and 8.33), he decided to use the VBRM bubble chart (Figure 8.34) to alter the execution plan for 2004, focusing on ideas and plans to capture the available opportunities and to mitigate the existing risks as much as possible.

Once these plans were developed, management re-evaluated its chance of success based on the revised plan (Figure 8.35). The new actions did not alter the target forecast numbers; however, they did impact the probability of achieving the goal and the potential range of outcomes possible. Figures 8.36 and 8.37 show that, with the re-focused plan, the chance of achieving the original goal now increased to 55%.

Figure 8.38 shows the original and new plans side-by-side on the operating gain probability profile. Comparing the VBRM bubble charts before and after mitigation (Figures 8.34 and 8.39) shows that much of the net risk from investments, grants, and other expenses were significantly reduced, leaving revenue from contributions as the key net risk element. In fact, investments has now become a major net opportunity. Figures 8.40 through 8.43 show the final results for 2004. Figure 8.44 shows the performance rating of the president, COO, and CFO.

The Conclusion: GSE's management was very concerned that it had only a 20% chance of achieving its bottom line goal of $57 million operating gain. One option was to set a new, more attainable goal, like reducing the goal from $57 million to $41.5 million, which would have had a 50% chance of achievement. However, GSE had previous experience with the VBRM process. They knew that the initial analysis of any plan should only be used as a guide for improvement (i.e., the first analysis should not be considered to be the only analysis, but rather just the starting point). Therefore, they decided to re-focus their actions. GSE also knew that it had to attack the largest net risk bubble first: revenue-contributions (Figure 8.34).

GSE had identified a new approach to contributor education and marketing, one that had been successfully used by similar organizations, although not by GSE. After careful considering the overall impact this new method would introduce, GSE decided to apply the new marketing and education approach on a trial-basis to a portion of its contributions. GSE determined that the new approach would not

Figure 8.38 Gamma Services Enterprises Operating Gain Profile

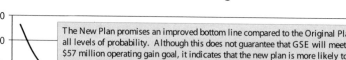

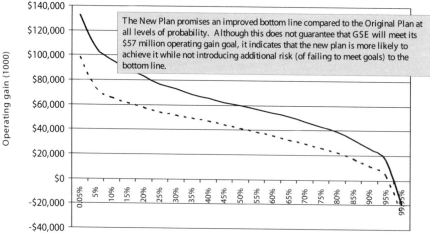

Probability of achieving

Management Approach to Not-For-Profit Organizations

impact the total variability of this revenue (i.e., it would not impact the potential range of contributions revenue). However, it would improve the probability of attaining the contributions goal in the future.

Next, GSE addressed revenue-investments. Although this driver was within the lower left quadrant of the chart, GSE knew that trying to

Figure 8.39 VBRM Bubble Chart After VBRM Mitigation

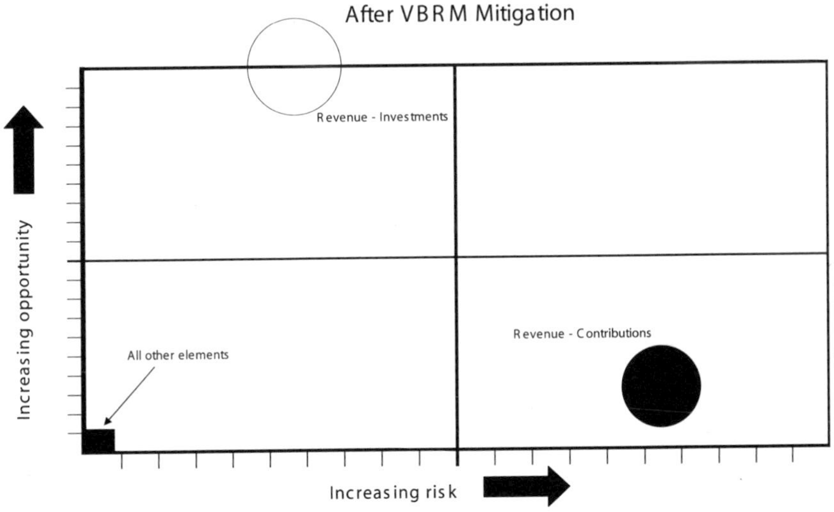

Figure 8.40 Key Performance Actuals for Gamma Services Enterprises

Key Performance Boxes (KPBs). KPBs must be calculated values - not inputs.
Input value - not a calculation.

2004 ($1000)

Revenues	
Contributions	$ 106,000
Investments	73,600
Total revenue	$ 179,600

Expenses	
Education programs	$ 27,900
Grants	27,200
G&A	4,900
Other	43,200
Total cost of sales/expense	$ 103,200

| Operating profit | $ 76,400 |

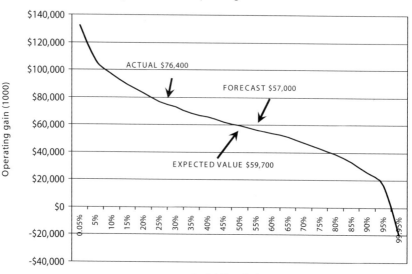

Figure 8.41 GSE Operating Gain Profile

move all of the drivers toward the origin would further improve the plan. During the initial VBRM session (called "Provoke-To-Evoke®" by DSC), GSE uncovered a potential investment which, although carrying a higher risk than originally planned, promised a substantial upside potential. GSE also discussed to shift more resources away from expense – education programs, in addition to what was already anticipated.

The impact of these actions was not, and should not have been, included in the initial analysis because it would have represented a fundamental change to the plan. Addressing the two investments area opportunities captured virtually all opportunity available in the plan. Finally, GSE decided that it could implement some cost reduction plans in the other expenses area of the business without substantial impact to the bottom line.

GSE now had a new plan that included: 1) a change to a slightly higher risk investment strategy, 2) deeper cuts in education programs to add additional fuel to investments, 3) the addition of a new marketing plan for contributions, and 4) additional cuts in other expenses.

GSE then applied VBRM to re-analyze the feasibility of the revised plan. As can be seen from Figure 8.39, GSE has managed to alter the plan so that the amount of net opportunity (the area of any unfilled

Management Approach to Not-For-Profit Organizations

Figure 8.42 Probability of Achieving Operating Gain (After VBRM Mitigation)

Gain ($1000)	Probability of Achieving
132,231	0.05%
106,606	5%
96,218	10%
89,301	15%
82,955	20%
76,549	25%
73,002	30%
68,299	35%
65,733	40%
62,362	45%
59,700	50%
56,704	55%
54,001	60%
51,040	65%
47,211	70%
43,252	75%
39,079	80%
32,921	85%
26,042	90%
16,409	95%
-19,896	99.95%

Under the revised plan, GSE achieved a gain of $76,400,000 ..a result which had less than 5% chance of occurring under the original plan!

Actual = $76,400

Gain expected value is $59,700

Gain target = $57,000

bubbles) outweighs the amount of net risk (solid bubbles) The risk and opportunity scales of the bubble chart are adjusted so that at least one uncertainty driver (bubble) appears at the maximum risk or opportunity level (i.e., along the top or right-hand margin). The size of the bubbles are also adjusted so that the largest net risk or net opportunity has a large bubble associated with it – even if the amount of net risk or net opportunity is relatively small. These adjustments help management focus first on the most critically uncertain elements within the plan and, through successive analysis, fine tune it until no more alternatives or options are available.

Critique of Case Study 8-3: GSE's revised plan was a marked improvement over the original plan. Clearly, GSE's revised plan captured much of the available investment opportunity, exceeding goal by $43.4 million and also reducing the amount of contribution Net Risk. Even so, contributions continued to be the biggest risk to bottom line performance (contributions originally had only a 15% chance of being met). Although the revised plan improved that chance to 40%, no

Figure 8.43 Contribution to Operating Gain Uncertainty

Area of uncertainty	Percent contribution to Gamma Services Enterprises operating gain total uncertainty
Revenue - investments	52.5
Revenue - contributions	38.2
Expense - other	3.0
Expense - education programs	3.0
Expense - grants	2.8
Expense - G&A	0.5

other controllable aspects were available in this area to further improve its probability of success, leading to the weak performance in 2004.

Even with the poor contributions results, GSE managed to improve itsbottom line potential significantly by letting Bubble Management guide it to areas to focus attention. It also profiled the impact of those actions before making its commitment to the Board of Trustees. Finally, the VBRM analysis of the revised plan exposed the fact that GSE's actions would achieve the expected results without introducing additional risk to the bottom line. (In most cases, VBRM motivates management to implement changes to plans that improve their chances of a successful outcome). The decision to re-focus paid off for the president and his top management, as seen in their Level 1 performance awards (Figure 8.44).

8.5 SOME FINAL THOUGHTS ON THE CASE STUDIES IN THIS CHAPTER

We happen to think that the job of being a top executive in a not-for-profit enterprise is easier than being an executive in a manufacturing corporation. Here's why we think so. An NFP executive doesn't have to deal with any of the following issues: 1) managing large fixed assets in production plants, 2) dealing with stockholders or security analysts, 3) worrying about product obsolescence through technology and 4) foreign competition (the diversion of contributions to tsunami

Management Approach to Not-For-Profit Organizations

Figure 8.44 Conversion Table for Compensation Determination

PTT probability range (%) (a)	Performance rating	Salary increase potential (%)	Bonus potential (%)
25 or lower	4.5 - 6.0 (Level 1)	12 - 15	16 - 25
35 - 26	3.8 - 4.4 (Level 2)	8 - 11	11 - 15
51 - 36	3.0 ...3.7 (Level 3)	5 - 7	5 - 10
65 - 52	2.3 ...2.9 (Level 4)	2 - 4	None
Greater than 65	Under 2.3 (Level 6)	None	None

(a) The lower the probability the more difficult to achieve the goal

Executive	Results/contribution split	Results rating (b)	Contribution rating (c)	Overall rating
President	80%/20%	4.5	5.2	4.64
COO	80%/20%	4.5	5.0	4.60
CFO	60%/40%	4.5	5.0	4.70

(b) From Figure 6.18 based on 25% probability of achieving operating gain goal
(c) Rating determined by Board of Trustees compensation committee based on evaluation of individual contribution to achieving the goal

relief is one recent exception to the lack of foreign competition to charities).

They do have some issues in common with executives in other sectors such as: 1) the quest for sales (revenue) growth, 2) the constant need to control expenses, 3) worry about government encroachment and 4) concern for their public image. Public image for an NFP enterprise can be a real problem. If the public believes the enterprise is too bureaucratic and top-heavy with administration it can seriously impact contributions. Likewise, if the public perceives that the top management is overpaid for the service they provide, it can seriously impact image, as shown in several situations recently.

In this chapter we introduced for the first time a case study where the management discarded their original financial plan and reworked it to improve their chance of success. It's a simple process involving

Chapter 8

only three steps:
- Performing an initial VBRM analysis to determine the probability of achieving the goals
- Re-evaluating the uncertainty inputs and revising the financial plan if the original plan appears to be unobtainable, and
- Adopting a revised plan that improves the probability of success

In many cases, even one rework of the plan may not be enough.

Getting Your Organization Goals–Oriented

9

9.1 WHAT THE READER WILL LEARN FROM THIS CHAPTER:

- Constraints imposed on all managers
- A concept called the "Unit President"
- Organization structure that promote "goals-orientation"
- Ways to improve performance
- Tips on building a goals-oriented team

9.2 INTRODUCTION

This chapter, although not a long one, is important as we approach the conclusion of this book. Setting goals seems like a simple task. You and your boss sit down and knock-out a few goals which, if met, makes him happy and his boss happy, perhaps both of them willing to award you a salary increase, or maybe even a bonus. Up to now we've talked a lot about setting goals, monitoring goals, and appraising performance against goals. What we haven't talked about very much is the difficulty of actually achieving goals. As we know, other people have a way of making that job more difficult.

Take a look at Figure 9.1. The chart shows just a few of the constraints imposed on all managers as they try to achieve their goals. Let's talk about a few of them.

9.2.1 Government Constraints

Government laws, especially at the Federal level, have been around forever it seems, trying to regulate business. Although most are justified, they can impose significant reporting and oversight burden on industry. There are anti-trust laws, corrupt practice laws, anti-collu-

Chapter 9

Figure 9.1 Typical Constraints on Managers

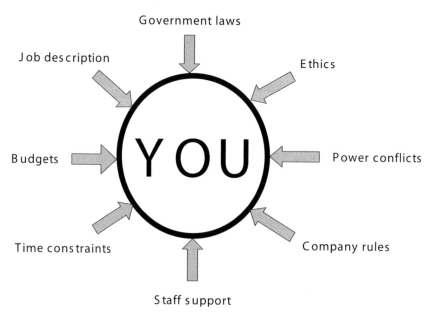

Government laws

Job description

Ethics

Budgets

YOU

Power conflicts

Time constraints

Company rules

Staff support

sion laws, and more recently corporate laws like Sarbanes-Oxley to prevent fraud. For these, we can thank unethical executives. There are labor relations laws, SEC reporting laws, and insider-trading laws, just to name a few more. Most managers don't have to deal with all of these laws on a daily basis, but they can have an adverse impact on your future.

Consider this situation. You represent your company on a trade association board of directors. At a meeting, someone suggests discussing what everybody is doing to generate more business during the current recession. Should you participate, or leave the meeting? Could participating be considered a violation of anti-collusion laws?

Suppose you inadvertently overhear a senior manager of your company mention a pending merger with XYZ Company. Would it be inside-trading to buy XYZ stock? Probably. The point is there are government constraints at work that can make your job not only more difficult, but even cause you to lose it if you operate on the wrong side of the law.

A New Approach

9.2.2 Your Job Description

Your job description and your budget are probably the two best defined of all the constraints listed on the chart. At least they should be.

Unfortunately, job descriptions can be a two-edged sword. When written properly, they spell out both the responsibility and authority of the job. When poorly written, they do neither. First time managers are often given the task of developing or re-writing the job description for their position. Depending on how much control the boss demands, any listing of authority can be redacted quickly. As a rule, managers should have the latitude and authority to manage freely as long as they perform within budget and company rules (that's the theme of the "Unit President" concept which we will discuss shortly).

9.2.3 Company Rules

Company rules generally are meant to control the work environment within an organization, providing guidance in areas such as work hours, expense account reporting rules, and anti-discrimination policy. For the most part, they don't interfere with manager performance.

9.2.4 Power Conflicts

This constraint can be one of the most sinister when it comes to meeting performance against goal. Power struggles go on all the time in businesses, at all levels of the organizational structure. They can really get bloody at the upper echelons of management. As we mentioned earlier in this book, most goals require some support from other persons or departments in the organization (the "shared goals" concept). The other party is just as interested as you are to perform well, even if that means "taking a little credit" from others for achieving the shared goal. Other than having a fair-minded boss, about the only thing any manager can do to offset the back-stabber is to be predictable and credible, as we will discuss later.

9.3 THE UNIT PRESIDENT CONCEPT

About thirty years ago, the American Management Association offered a management training program where the focus of the workshop was a concept called the "Unit President." The concept was simple. Managers should be aware of the constraints on their authority (such as those shown in Figure 9.1), but relatively free to manage otherwise. Some examples of company constraints are:

- A decision to hire a new employee, or terminate an existing employee, requires the approval of the next two higher levels of management.
- Business unit presidents can approve capital expenditures up to $50,000.
- The Corporate Communications manager must be present during all interviews with the media.
- Only computer codes inspected and approved by the IT department can be used on company computers or networks.
- Expenditures expected to overrun budget by 10% require senior management approval.

All of these constraints seem reasonable in the overall scheme of things, like the budget constraint if planned expenditures are expected to cause a budget overrun of 10% or more. This constraint still gives managers ample opportunity to manage their unit's budget without getting second-guessed at every turn. That's the principle behind the Unit President concept. It can do a lot to promote a sense of autonomy and create a goal-oriented attitude in the organization. If most of the constraints indicated on Figure 9.1 were clearly understood, the job of management would be a lot easier.

9.4 ORGANIZATIONAL STRUCTURES THAT PROMOTE GOAL-ORIENTATION

There are many ways to organize the resources of a company. They include: 1) the traditional functional structure which can include units like marketing, engineering, and manufacturing, 2) divisional or business unit structures that may have a functional alignment within them, 3) matrix structures that can have both functional and product line managers overlapping, and 4) lateral structures with a lot of dotted-line reporting. Regardless of the structure used, all have certain advantages and disadvantages regarding the division of labor, chain of command, assignment of authority and responsibility, and degree of control. We think some structures are more conducive to creating a goals-oriented environment than others.

Getting Your Organization Goals-Oriented

We happen to think highly of matrix organization structures like the one shown in Figure 5.1. It may not be as perfect as Mendeleyev's Periodic Table of the Elements, but it's pretty good*. It provides both clarity and functionality for managing the business. It has the advantages of the functional structure (reducing duplication of effort and concentrating technical expertise) while, at the some time, adding an element of coordination below the business unit manager. The product line mangers are essentially "mini general managers," overseeing the entire product line P&L from marketing and sales through engineering and manufacturing.

This structure provides a great way to train up-and-coming managers to become senior managers, and to do it at a level where a few mistakes here and there won't break the corporate bank account. The product line managers are the glue who hold the whole structure together. They manage the conflicts that typically arise between engineering, manufacturing, project management, and the controller. If you're the business unit vice president, product line managers shield you from having a long line of managers outside your office each day wanting you to settle their conflicts or disagreements. However, the price you may have to pay to get this extra quiet time is to spend some of it ensuring that goals for the organization have been set (especially the shared goals) and are being monitored regularly.

9.5 WAYS TO IMPROVE PERFORMANCE

Being a manager in business usually means directing and controlling some assets of the business. Although it seldom appears on the balance sheet, probably the most important asset of any organization is its people. In that sense, all managers should primarily be managers of people. Who else is going to do the work? (Don't say the computer; after all, people had to program it first.)

If you are going to manage people you need to have a management style. We all tend to have a natural style which feels comfortable to us in dealing with people. But our natural style may not produce the right sort of motivation for the organization we control; this mismatch can lead to poor performance. The hard realities of the business world fre-

---

* Robert E. Krebs in From the History and Use of Our Earth's Chemical Elements, Greenwood Press (1999) states "without a doubt, the Periodic Table of the elements is the most elegant organization chart ever devised."

quently dictate that we adjust our natural style to achieve an acceptable balance between what we like personally and what the business needs. Usually, this adjustment means getting more goal-oriented. We will cover nine points for helping you get there.

9.5.1 Learn to Size up Your Boss

Throughout your career, you will have a boss; even being your own boss, you will always have someone to report to – your clients. If you are successful enough, your boss may be the Board of Directors. If you become a member of the board, your boss will be the shareholders. Carl Jung, the Swiss psychologist, divided people (managers) into four categories: 1) feelers, 2) thinkers, 3) intuitors, and 4) sensors. Drake-Beam and Associates, a management consulting firm in the 1970s, built an effective communications training program around Jung's concept.

The concept is simple. Basically, by observing how people act, dress, furnish their office, etc., you can place them into one of Jung's four categories. Once you've done that, you know basically what makes that person tick. For example, a "feeler" is a people-oriented person. If your boss is a feeler, performance on any assignment he gives you will be judged more effective if you consider the impact of your recommendations on people (employees, customers, others). A "thinker," on the other hand, places high value on logic and ideas, and seeks alternatives. Your recommendation to a thinker is doomed to failure if you don't consider and evaluate alternative approaches for solving the problem.

An "intuitor" absorbs information in complex ways. They sometimes seem to be able to see around corners. If the boss is an intuitor, you have to learn to think outside the box. Finally, the "sensor" is a person good at looking and listening to grasp the situation, relying on perception rather than judgment of information. Satisfying a sensor can be difficult.

9.5.2 Learn to Control Your Time

Probably two-thirds of your time at work is entirely within your control to schedule or allocate; the rest is controlled by the whims of your boss, or his boss, and so on up the line. Learn to size up the job and determine how much time you want to spend on each part of the assignment. Maintain a log of how you spend your time for a week or so. It can reveal places where time is wasted or ineffectively applied. It's also good to set an allocation mix for your time: How much of your time is spent on activities internal to your organization vs. how much on external activities such as dealing with upper management, customers, or legislative or community affairs?

9.5.3 Look Good on Your First Assignment

If you're new to management, your boss, his boss, and your peers will all have their eyes on you during your first assignment. Understand the ground rules for the assignment. Above all, deliver a quality and concise report.

9.5.4 Develop Self-Discipline

Set up solid work practices. Don't be afraid to come in early and get the benefit of the extra quiet time. Because your boss might be the kind who likes to come in late and stay late, you may have to come in early and also stay late. Set reasonable schedules for yourself, and practice staying on schedule. Set aside a little buffer time in your schedule to handle unexpected events. If you call a 30-minute meeting with your staff, end it in 30 minutes. Learn to develop orderly and logical approaches to problem solving. Commit important things to writing. Document key decisions, but don't fall into the trap of contributing trivia or "C.Y.A." memos. Avoid interoffice memos, even though e-mail makes it easier. If the person you are communicating with sits in the next cubicle or office, try just walking over there to talk. If you're the boss, it might just be the highlight of their day.

9.5.5 Watch Your Appearance

If you don't have a part in setting it, then size up the dress code in your company or at the client's facility. At most production plants, neckties are seldom worn; therefore, it can be okay to arrive without one. IBM used to be famous for its dress code – dark suit and white shirt with conservative tie. They tell a story about an IBM executive riding down in an elevator with an executive from a bank. Onto the elevator steps a young guy dressed in blue-jeans and a sweat shirt. After he gets off, the IBM man says, "you guys sure have lowered your dress code here at the bank." "Not so," says the bank executive, "that guy works for IBM." Remember, what happens at the home office doesn't always happen in the field.

9.5.6 Learn to Listen

You don't learn anything when you're doing the talking!

9.5.7 Innovate

Innovation doesn't just mean patents and inventions. It's also ideas, concepts, and new procedures for doing something at a lower cost or at a higher rate of return. Is it just a perception, or has rewarding employees for cost-reduction ideas fallen out of practice?

9.5.8 Learn to Be Predictable

Most people dislike surprises, except possibly on Christmas or their birthday. Top management abhors surprises. Start now to develop a "no surprise" concept of management. Do this through your personal actions and by using foresight to seek out business trends. Look for clues of impending change. A clue is a non-statistical, non-verifiable, early-warning indicator that something is about to change. A clue must first be detected, then analyzed, and then monitored to see if it develops. If it does, it could have profound impact on achieving your goals.

9.5.9 Build Credibility

Nobody can be right all the time, unless you do nothing! But you need a good batting average in business; the higher, the better. There was a documentary on TV some years ago where a reporter was interviewing a securities expert in his office. On one wall of the office was a huge display with all the latest prices and volumes of stock sales changing constantly. At one point during the interview, the expert picked up the telephone and said "buy 20,000 shares of XYZ" and hung up. Where upon the interviewer asked, "doesn't it worry you that you may have just made a mistake buying that stock?" "Not at all" said the expert. "I only have to be right about 70% of the time; if I'm only right 50% of the time I lose clients, at 60% I do okay, and at 70% or higher I make a lot of money!"

Start now to give good advice. You will probably remember that back in previous chapters we considered Quality of Advice to be one of most important management attributes.

Getting Your Organization Goals–Oriented

9.6 SOME TIPS ON BUILDING A GOALS-ORIENTED TEAM

If you're going to develop a goals-oriented team (your direct reports), you have to communicate with them regularly. Schedule (yes, in advance) at least one hour every two weeks to meet and discusses issues that can affect performance. Check to see if things are on schedule against tactical plans. Talk about the results to date. Discuss ways to mitigate goals that are under-performing.

But don't forget about the rest of the organization. It's a good practice to have a general meeting with all employees, including hourly employees, at least twice a year. Stress where the organization stands against goals: 1) show the sales figures, good as well as bad, 2) discuss areas where productivity has increased or dropped, and 3) don't be afraid to show bottom-line results, even if you have to disguise them (like showing "% of goal" rather than actual numbers). Above all, be sure to allow some time to answer questions. When you talk to hourly employees, very often the first question you will get is "are we going to have any layoffs?" If the answer is possibly "yes," say so or your credibility will be shot later when it happens.

Don't forget the importance of preparing for the performance appraisal. Notice we didn't say "annual" performance appraisal. During your routine meetings with your staff, the status of performance against goals should always be on the table. If it is, there should never be any surprises when formal appraisal time comes around. Trust us on that one. Remember, the performance appraisal process is an excellent way to develop your people. If your employees perceive that you are goals-oriented, they will become goals-oriented. Really trust us on that one.

Appendix
Glossary of Financial Terms

Terms used in this glossary are excerpted from Campbell R. Harvey's Hypertextual Financial Glossary, courtesy of Campbell R. Harvey, Professor of International Business, Duke University Fuqua School of Business (with permission).

Accounts payable: Money owed to suppliers.

Accounts receivable: Money owed by customers.

Amortization: The repayment of a loan by installments.

Budget: A detailed pro forma schedule of financial activity, such as an advertising budget, a sales budget, or a capital budget.

Cash: The value of assets that can be converted into cash immediately, as reported by a company. Usually includes bank accounts and marketable securities, such as government bonds and banker's acceptances. Cash equivalents on balance sheets include securities that mature within 90 days (e.g., notes).

Cash flow: In investments, cash flow represents earnings before depreciation, amortization, and non-cash charges. Sometimes called cash earnings. Cash flow from operations (called funds from operations by real estate and other investment trusts) is important because it indicates the ability to pay dividends.

Consignment: Transfer of goods to a seller while title to the merchandise is retained by the owner.

Constant dollar: Condition in which inflation or escalation is not applicable. Prices and costs are de-escalated or re-escalated to a single point in time.

Appendix

Contingency: An additional amount or percentage added to any cash flow item. Care is needed to ensure it is either to be spent or to remain as a cushion.

Cost of goods sold: The total cost of buying raw materials, and paying for all the factors that go into producing finished goods.

Current assets: Value of cash, accounts receivable, inventories, marketable securities, and other assets that could be converted to cash in less than 1 year.

Days in receivables: Average collection period.

Debt: Money borrowed.

Depreciation: A non-cash expense (also known as non-cash charge) that provides a source of free cash flow. Amount allocated during the period to amortize the cost of acquiring long-term assets over the useful life of the assets. To be clear, this is an accounting expense, not a real expense that demands cash. The sum of depreciation expenses of prior years leads to the balance sheet item Accumulated Depreciation.

Earnings: Net income for the company during a period.

Earnings before interest and taxes (EBIT): A financial measure defined as revenues less cost of goods sold and selling, general, and administrative expenses. In other words, operating and non-operating profit before the deduction of interest and income taxes.

Earnings per share (EPS): A company's profit divided by its number of common outstanding shares. If a company earning $2 million in one year had 2 million common shares of stock outstanding, its EPS would be $1 per share. In calculating EPS, the company often uses a weighted average of shares outstanding over the reporting term. The one-year (historical or trailing) EPS growth rate is calculated as the percentage change in earnings per share. The prospective EPS growth rate is calculated as the percentage change in this year's earnings and the consensus forecast earnings for next year.

Equity: Ownership interest in a firm. Also, the residual dollar value of a futures trading account, assuming its liquidation is at the going trade price. In real estate, dollar difference between what a property could be sold for and debts claimed against it. In a brokerage account, equity equals the value of the account's securities minus any debit balance in a margin account. Equity is also shorthand for stock market investments.

Fixed asset: Long-lived property owned by a firm that is used by a firm in the production of its income. Tangible fixed assets include real estate, plant, and equipment. Intangible fixed assets include patents, trademarks, and customer recognition.

Goodwill: Excess of purchase price over fair market value of net assets acquired under the purchase method of accounting.

Intangible asset: A legal claim to some future benefit, typically a claim to future cash. Goodwill, intellectual property, patents, copyrights, and trademarks are examples of intangible assets.

Inventory: For companies: Raw materials, items available for sale or in the process of being made ready for sale. They can be individually valued by several different means, including cost or current market value, and collectively by FIFO (First in, first out), LIFO (Last in, first out) or other techniques. The lower value of alternatives is usually used to preclude overstating earnings and assets. For securities firms: Securities bought and held by a broker or dealer for resale.

Long-term debt/capitalization: Indicator of financial leverage. Shows long-term debt as a proportion of the capital available. Determined by dividing long-term debt by the sum of long-term debt, preferred stock and common stockholder's equity.

Market share: The percentage of total industry sales that a particular company controls.

Net assets: The difference between total assets on the one hand and current liabilities and non-capitalized long-term liabilities on the other hand.

Net income: The company's total earnings, reflecting revenues adjusted for costs of doing business, depreciation, interest, taxes, and other expenses.

Net sales: Gross sales less returns and allowances, freight out, and cash discounts allowed.

Not-for-profit: An organization established for charitable, humanitarian, or educational purposes that is exempt from some taxes and in which no one has profits or losses.

Appendix

Operating Assets: Another term for working capital.

Operating cash flow: Earnings before depreciation minus taxes. Measures the cash generated from operations, not counting capital spending or working capital requirements.

Operating profit (or loss): Revenue from a firm's regular activities less costs and expenses and before income deductions.

Operating profit margin: The ratio of operating profit to net sales.

Outstanding shares: Shares that are currently owned by investors

Overhead: The expenses of a business that are not attributable directly to the production or sale of goods.

Permanent Current Assets: The minimum level of current assets that a firm needs to continue operation. Because some level is always maintained, they are called permanent current assets.

Present value: The amount of cash today that is equivalent in value to a payment, or to a stream of payments, to be received in the future. To determine the present value, each future cash flow is multiplied by a present value factor. For example, if the opportunity cost of funds is 10%, the present value of $100 to be received in one year is $100 x [1/(1 + 0.10)] = $91.

Pro forma financial statements: A firm's financial statements as adjusted to reflect a projected or planned transaction. "What-if" analysis.

Probability: The relative likelihood of a particular outcome among all possible outcomes.

Probability density function: The function that describes the change of certain realizations for a continuous random variable.

Probability distribution: A function that describes all the values a random variable can take and the probability associated with each. Also called a probability function.

Production Cost Advantage: A source of competitive advantage that depends on producing some product or service at the lowest

Profit: Revenue minus cost. The amount one makes on a transaction.

Appendix

Profit center: A division of an organization held responsible for producing its own profits.

Purchase order: A written order to buy specified goods at a stipulated price.

Receivables turnover ratio: Total operating revenues divided by average receivables. Used to measure how effectively a firm is managing its accounts receivable.

Return on equity (ROE): Indicator of profitability. Determined by dividing net income for the past 12 months by common stockholder equity (adjusted for stock splits). Result is shown as a percentage. Investors use ROE as a measure of how a company is using its money. ROE may be decomposed into return on assets (ROA) by multiplying by financial leverage (total assets/total equity).

Return on investment (ROI): Generally, book income as a proportion of net book value.

Return on sales: A measurement of operational efficiency equaling net pre-tax profits divided by net sales expressed as a percentage.

Return on total assets: The ratio of earnings available to common stockholders to total assets.

Risk: Often defined as the standard deviation of the return on total investment. Degree of uncertainty of return on an asset. In context of asset pricing theory.

Sale: An agreement between a buyer and a seller on the price to be paid for a security, followed by delivery.

Selling, general, and administrative (SG&A) expenses: Expenses such as salespersons' salaries and commissions, advertising and promotion, travel and entertainment, office payroll and expenses, and executives' salaries.

Severance: A settlement received after being released from a corporation. In the context of corporate governance, an agreement that assures high-level executives of their positions or some compensation and are not contingent upon a change in control.

Short-term debt: Debt obligations, recorded as current liabilities, requiring payment within the year.

Appendix

Total asset turnover: The ratio of net sales to total assets.

Total capitalization: The total long-term debt and all types of equity of a company that constitutes its capital structure.

Total revenue: Total sales and other revenue for the period shown. Known as "turnover" in the U.K.

Turnover: For mutual funds, a measure of trading activity during the previous year, expressed as a percentage of the average total assets of the fund. A turnover rate of 25% means that the value of trades represented one-fourth of the assets of the fund. For finance, the number of times a given asset, such as inventory, is replaced during the accounting period, usually a year. For corporate finance, the ratio of annual sales to net worth, representing the extent to which a company can grow without outside capital. For markets, the volume of shares traded as a percent of total shares listed during a specified period, usually a day or a year. For Great Britain, total revenue. Percentage of the total number of shares outstanding of an issue that trades during any given period.

Working capital: Defined as the difference between current assets and current liabilities. There are some variations in how working capital is calculated. Variations include the treatment of short-term debt. In addition, current assets may or may not include cash and cash equivalents, depending on the company.

Write-off: Charging an asset amount to expense or loss, such as through the use of depreciation and amortization of assets.

10-K: Annual report required by the SEC each year. Provides a comprehensive overview of a company's state of business. Must be filed within 90 days after fiscal year-end. A 10-Q report is filed quarterly.

10-Q: Quarterly report required by the SEC each quarter. Provides a comprehensive overview of a company's state of business.

Index

INDEX

INDEX